The First Year
Of Life

Psychological and Medical Implications of Early Experience

Edited by
David Shaffer
Psychiatric Institute, New York State

and

Judy Dunn
MRC Unit, Cambridge

JOHN WILEY & SONS
Chichester · New York · Brisbane · Toronto

Copyright © 1979 by John Wiley & Sons, Ltd.

Reprinted October 1980

Library of Congress Cataloging in Publication Data:
Main entry under title:

The first year of life.

   Includes bibliographical references and index.
   1. Infant psychology. 2. Mother and child.
3. Developmental psychology. 4. Infants—
Diseases—Psychological aspects. I. Shaffer,
David. II. Dunn, Judy. [DNLM: 1. Evaluation
studies—Child psychology. 2. Child development—
Infant. WS105.5.E8 F527]
BF723. 16F524   155.4′22   78–11237

ISBN 0 471 99734 X

Photosetting by Thomson Press (India) Limited, New Delhi and
printed in Great Britain by The Pitman Press, Bath

The First Year
Of Life

Contributors

ARNON BENTOVIM
Department of Psychological Medicine, Hospital for Sick Children, Great Ormond Street, London WC1N 3JH.

NICHOLAS BLURTON JONES
Institute of Child Health, Guilford Street, London WC1N 1EH.

ANNE M. CLARKE
Department of Psychology, University of Hull, Hull HU6 7RX.

ALAN D. B. CLARKE
Department of Psychology, University of Hull, Hull HU6 7RX.

JAMES S. CHISHOLM
Institute of Child Health, Guilford Street, London WC1N 1EH.

JUDY DUNN
M.R.C. Unit, Sub-Department of Animal Behaviour, University of Cambridge, Madingley, Cambridge CB3 8AA.

FAE HALL
Family Research Unit, London Hospital Medical College, 16 Walden Street, London E1.

OLWEN H. M. JONES
Leon Gillis Unit, St. Mary's Hospital Roehampton, London SW15 5PN.

ALEX F. KALVEBOER
Laboratory for Experimental Clinical Psychology, State University, Groningen, The Netherlands.

JOHN NEWSON
Child Development Research Unit, University of Nottingham, Nottingham.

MARTIN PACKER
Pediatric Research Unit, St. Mary's Hospital, Praed Street, London W2.

SUSAN J. PAWLBY — *Family Research Unit, London Hospital Medical College, 16 Walden Street, London E1.*

MARTIN P. M. RICHARDS — *Medical Psychology Unit, University of Cambridge, Free School Lane, Cambridge CB2 3RF.*

DEBORAH ROSENBLATT — *Pediatric Research Unit, St. Mary's Hospital, Praed Street, London W2.*

BARBARA TIZARD — *Thomas Coram Research Unit, 41 Brunswick Square, London WC1N 1AZ.*

STEPHEN WOLKIND — *Family Research Unit, 16 Walden Street, London E1.*

ROBERT H. WOODSON — *Institute of Child Health, Guilford Street, London WC1N 1EH.*

Series Preface

During recent years there has been a tremendous growth of research in both child development and child psychiatry. Research findings are beginning to modify clinical practice but to a considerable extent the fields of child development and of child psychiatry have remained surprisingly separate, with regrettably little cross fertilization. Much developmental research has not concerned itself with clinical issues, and studies of clinical syndromes have all too often been made within the narrow confines of a pathological condition approach with scant regard to developmental matters. The situation is rapidly changing but the results of clinical-developmental studies are often reported only by means of scattered papers in scientific journals. This series aims to bridge the gap between child development and clinical psychiatry by presenting reports of new findings, new ideas and new approaches in a book form which may be available to a wider readership.

The series includes reviews of specific topics, multi-authored volumes on a common theme, and accounts of specific pieces of research. However, in all cases the aim is to provide a clear, readable and interesting account of scientific findings in a way which makes explicit their relevance to clinical practice or social policy. It is hoped that the series will be of interest to both clinicians and researchers in the fields of child psychiatry, child psychology, psychiatric social work, social paediatrics and education—in short all concerned with the growing child and his problems.

Preface to First Volume

THE FIRST YEAR OF LIFE

This first volume in the series focuses on issues arising in the first year of life. The approach is a fresh one in focusing on the *two-way* interaction between parent and child and on the changing factors in the process of developing relationships. Very few infants are referred to clinicians in the first year because of emotional or behavioural problems but, as the studies reported in this volume make clear, experiences during that early phase of development do have important implications for what happens later. It is not that it constitutes a circumscribed critical period, and certainly not that early stresses inevitably damage future development. In fact, the process of development is a remarkably fluid one, children are surprisingly resilient in the face of adversity, and the continuities between infancy and the later years are quite limited. Yet, the first year still has a particular importance—because it comes first and because it sets in motion the train of events and the course of development to follow. Clinicians concerned with the problems of older children will find much of interest and of relevance to them in these accounts of happenings in the first year of life.

MICHAEL RUTTER

Contents

Introduction

David Shaffer and Judy Dunn

This book comprises a series of papers prepared by a group of developmental researchers for a clinical group of child psychiatrists and psychologists. The authors were asked to document their own research or to prepare a critical review summarizing knowledge on a particular aspect of early childhood experience and its significance for later social development.

Clinicians who are concerned about development, whether they be paediatricians, psychiatrists or child psychologists, have historically regarded the first year of life as being a period when environmental disturbances—both biological and interpersonal—are critically important in influencing later development. For example, it is widely believed that complicated pregnancy or traumatic delivery is causally related to later disturbances of learning ability, attention and cognitive skills. Equally, environmental perturbations such as those which result in parent–child separation are thought to have an enduring effect on later social development, and psychoanalysts have long held notions that intrapsychic experiences in infancy are influential in shaping later personality.

It has, therefore, been an unsettling experience for clinicians to see so many of these tenets fall, unsubstantiated by sound empirically based research. Perhaps the best examples of a failure to document a link between early events and later outcome are derived from research into the sequelae of perinatal morbidity. At least three major prospective studies (Graham and coworkers, 1962; Corah and coworkers, 1965; Werner and coworkers, 1971; Broman, Nichols and Kennedy, 1975) have taken as their starting point clearly and reliably measured morbid events. In their subsequent analysis they have utilized sophisticated multivariate statistical techniques to take account of such factors as social economic status and maternal education. None has demonstrated an enduring association between early morbidity and later psychological dysfunction.

However, we would be unwise to accept such evidence as conclusive. It may well be, as is eloquently argued in the paper in this book by the Clarkes, that the human organism is sufficiently adaptable and that later behaviour is determined by so many different variables that we should expect recovery from transient biological and environmental adversity. Alternatively, our failure to demonstrate continuity may simply be a consequence of a variety of measurement problems, both at birth and at the time of follow-up. To stay with the example of perinatal events: factors such as low birth weight, antepartum haemorrhage, and neonatal asphyxia are often assumed to be markers of neurological damage. However, any sample of low birth weight or asphyxiated infants, or infants born after a complicated pregnancy, will include both those with and without brain damage. Our ability to reduce the 'noise' generated within such samples will depend on our having adequate techniques for measuring early neurological dysfunction. There are also problems in measuring outcome variables. Most commonly, these have been either I.Q. or a global measure of psychiatric maladjustment. However, these are gross and complicated variables and although they may include elements which are sensitive to early experience, it is probably naive to expect these to show themselves with any strength. This volume contains two papers which shed light on such measurement problems. On the one hand Alex Kalverboer's paper looks for relationships—not between perinatal morbidity, but between early neurological state and behavioural outcome. It is unusual in being one of the few studies in the literature to start with a clear definition of type and severity of neurological dysfunction in infancy. The results are inconclusive. This may be because mild deviations in the newborn neurological examination are responses to transient rather than enduring dysfunction, or because the analysis presented by Kalverboer is essentially a simple linear one that fails to take account of social environmental variables, or because the outcome measure is too narrow. The second paper which deals with measurement issues is that by Barbara Tizard which examines the social functioning in middle childhood, of a group of children who endured multiple caretaking experiences during early life. While there were no differences in gross maladjustment levels it does seem as if Dr. Tizard has identified persisting differences in social behaviour of a subtle but readily recognizable kind.

An alternative explantion for our failure to demonstrate links between early experience and later behaviour may be that we have relied upon inappropriate developmental models. By and large developmental research has used linear rather than interactive or transactional models. There is much to suggest that complex outcome variables such as social behaviour are modified both by factors within the family and the wider environment and by the child's own 'temperament'. The complex interactions between parents, medical intervention and infant temperament are dealt with in a number of the chapters in this book. The chapter by Martin Richards and that by Martin Packer and Deborah Rosenblatt both demonstrate how parent variables may not only influence medical intervention in the newborn period but may also be influenced by them. The study by Fae Hall, Sue Pawlby and Stephen Wolkind sets out to define parent variables, to examine the influence of experiences in the mother's own childhood on these variables, and to describe how these parent variables shape and are shaped by the individual differences between infants that are frequently referred to as temperamental characteristics. Judy Dunn's review discusses the difficulties of making inferences about infant temperament, and in particular the problem of knowing whether the persistence or lack of persistence of a trait can be inferred, when superficially similar items of behaviour possess quite different meanings at different stages of development.

Repeated reference is made in this book to studies which examine the interaction between mother and infant. John Newson's chapter highlights the ways in which infant behaviour both initiates and maintains interactive sequences; Olwen Jones demonstrates how disturbance in the infant in the case of the developmental delay of Down's syndrome interferes with the process. John Newson directs attention to the importance of the context of interactive sequences between mother and infant for the development of intentional communication behaviour. This discussion, together with an awareness of the richness of the infant's early perceptive capabilities, may redirect clinicians to certain psychodynamic theories of child development. These have been discredited in the past, in part because of their reliance on what seemed to be improbable levels of infant competence. In a chapter which deals with this issue Arnon Bentovim attempts to integrate newly acquired knowledge from empirical research with psychodynamic theory. A crucial challenge is now presentted to psychodynamic theorists to identify the elements of their theory which can be confirmed or refuted by available techniques.

This volume amply documents the increasing awareness of perceptual and cognitive processes in the infant, and a greater sophistication among researchers in classifying both early behaviour and the environmental circumstances which impinge on the infant. Of course advances of this kind offer no assurance that the phenomena which can now be measured and classified necessarily have long term significance. The Clarkes persuasively argue the common sense proposition that it is *enduring* influences which make an enduring impression, whereas 'recovery' is the rule after transient disturbances or deviations. This argument deserves respect, and has yet to be refuted. However, it is important that we should not be led into believing that there are no enduring effects simply because we are not yet good enough at measuring them.

REFERENCES

Broman, S. A., Nichols, P. L., Kennedy, W. A. (1975). *Preschool I. Q.: Prenatal and early developmental correlates*, Laurence Erlbaum Assoc., Publishers, Hillsdale New Jersey.

Corah, N. L., Anthony, E. J., Painter, P., Stern J. A. and Thurston, D. L. (1965). 'The effect of perinatal anoxia after seven years', *Psychological Monographs*, **79**, 3 (Whole Number 596).

Graham, F. K., Ernhard, C. B., Thurston, C. B., and Craft, M. (1962). 'Development 3 years after perinatal anoxia and other damaging newborn experiences', *Psychological Monographs*, **76**, 1–53.

Werner, E. E., Bierman, J. M., and French, F. E. (1971), *The children of Kauai*, Honolulu, University of Hawaii Press.

Werner E. E., and Smith, R. S. (1977), *Kauai's children come of age*, Honolulu, The University Press of Hawaii.

Section I

Infancy and Later Development

Chapter 1

Issues in the Study of Social Behaviour in the First Week of Life

Martin Packer and Deborah Rosenblatt

INTRODUCTION

The issue of whether social behaviour is determined in part by events early in life is of interest to a number of disciplines. Members of the 'caring' professions—psychiatrists, psychologists, and paediatricians—hope that correct diagnosis of developmental problems and the ability to prevent long-term consequences of early events will result from research on this topic. But at a research level the problem becomes one of disentangling relationships of cause and effect—of deciding whether a particular event will give rise in time to a predictable outcome, and whether, in reverse, a given outcome is related to one or another candidates as a possible cause (Sameroff, 1975). Questions of this nature cannot be tackled adequately without a proper understanding of the processes through which the causal link is established. A model involving relatively complex and detailed hypotheses is essential when relationships are multiple and extended over long periods of time.

In studying the growth of social relations, psychologists commonly examine the effects of specific factors on the behaviour between a mother and her infant (Moss, 1967; Lewis, 1972). Two distinct approaches have now focussed on the postpartum period as an important source of the origins of particular styles of interaction between the two partners. On the one hand there are empirical studies suggesting that events such as separation of mother and baby can have deleterious effects (Klaus and Kennell, 1970; Richards, Chapter 2, this volume), and that characteristics of the mother's handling (Sander, 1969), or the baby's temperament and behaviour (Osofsky and Danzger, 1974), partly determine subsequent interaction. In contrast, microanalytic studies of the behaviour between mothers and slightly older infants have revealed that the infant himself contributes a great deal to the 'dialogue' with his mother (Stern, 1971; Trevarthen, 1975), and that similar attention to an earlier period of development would be of value.

There has been a tendency, however, to ignore some of the complexities of the postpartum period by compartmentalizing features into 'independent' and 'dependent' variables. It seems more profitable to view this period as being affected by a host of complex—and often inseparable—factors. This chapter will highlight some of what is known about the setting of birth in our culture today, the abilities and skills that mother and baby bring to the emerging social relationship, and some of the attendant methodological problems involved in studying social behaviour and interaction in the first week. To illustrate these points data will be presented on 145 mother–infant pairs collected during a study carried out in a London teaching hospital on the effects of obstetric medication on the neonate. Discussion will be limited to characteristics of the sample as a whole because analysis is in a preliminary phase, and it would be premature to specify significant labour or drug effects. The intention is to emphasize the diversity of experiences and attitudes of mothers, and the range of differences between infants, which shape early social relations and thus make the study of this period so difficult and inexact.

NEWBORN CAPABILITIES

Recent work on social behaviour now recognizes the greater role played by the infant (cf. Schaffer, 1977a), and it is appropriate to begin with a description of the neonate's capabilities. The myth that babies neither see nor hear in the first six weeks has been dispelled by systematic experiments on perception, although unfortunately mothers do continue to be given such outdated information in many maternity units. Most empirical work has concentrated on perception and learning, but the experience of the neonate (and to some extent, the older infant), is strongly social in character, for all contact with the world of material objects and natural events is mediated by the actions of his caregivers.

The infant's readiness to participate in social interaction depends on at least two developments: his perceptual abilities in orienting and maintaining attention to social stimuli, and his capacity for sustaining an alert and responsive state. To a lesser degree his motoric control (holding his head in the midline, and sitting at an angle without flopping), and his autonomic maturity (not startling or becoming tremulous in response to changes in light, noise, and temperature) also play a part. Mothers may well take account of the infant's individual characteristics—willingness to smile, 'cuddliness', physical appearance, and propensity to be soothed by her voice—in initiating and sustaining interaction.

State

The infant's ability to modify his wakefulness and alertness to suit the circumstances contributes to his status as a partner, rather than just a recipient, in social interaction. The concept of behavioural 'state' has proved very valuable in infant research (Gregg, Haffner and Korner, 1976). Most of the work on state treats it as a descriptive evaluation defined by observable behaviour (Escalona, 1962; Brazelton, 1973), though reference to physiological measurements such as EEG has clarified some of the parameters (Prechtl and coworkers, 1968; Stern and coworkers, 1969). Six states are generally utilized in infancy work: (1) deep sleep, where breathing is regular and movement absent; (2) light sleep, with irregular breathing, occasional restlessness and rapid eye movements; (3) drowsy awakeness; (4) alert awakeness; (5) a fussing, high activity state; and (6) crying.

State must be taken into account in research for a number of reasons:

1. The type and quality of response that the infant makes to stimuli is strongly related to the state which he is in at the time (Korner, 1969; Thoman, 1975). For example, it is easiest to obtain consistent orienting responses in an alert state (Prechtl, 1965; Brazelton, 1973).
2. Both internal and external events determine state. Important factors such as time since last feed, amount of sleep, noise, light, and temperature levels can be modified to bring an infant into an appropriate state for testing. If such variables are not taken into account in observational and experimental work spurious or misleading conclusions may be drawn (Beintema, 1968).
3. The infant shows a tendency to change to, and remain in, a state that is appropriate for the situation. Stimulation will wake him, and usually he will become alert. If he is overwhelmed by stimulation he will fuss, and finally cry. But he is able, usually, to quiet himself again and return either to an alert state or to sleep. The particular pattern of the state changes will depend on the demands of the situation, on the baby's resources, and on the particular baby (Thoman, Leiderman and Olson, 1972).

The infant's ability to maintain his own state is influenced by the efforts of those caring for him to manipulate his state. The stimuli most likely to bring him in a controlled way from sleep to alertness are human stimuli, and several studies have documented the way in which human sounds become more effective at stopping his crying over the first few weeks (Wolff, 1969; Korner and Grobstein, 1966). Opinions differ on the extent to which the neonate's behaviour can be called intentional; we must recognize the problems of defining such an intangible and elusive aspect of human action. Nothing we have said here about control of state goes beyond the degree of sophistication of a simple homeostatic mechanism, but clearly the infant does *become* intentional in his actions as he develops. It may be that the most important contributor to this is the degree to which a mother will inevitably *treat* behaviour as deliberate and conscious. A mother devotes a great deal of time to shaping the infant's state. Thus she will attempt to wake him to ensure stronger suckling, or reduce his heightened state of activity and crying by soothing him to sleep. As Thoman (1975) puts it, 'state acts as a prelude, a mediator, and an elicitor, as well as the context for any interaction that occurs between the infant and his mother'.

Perceptual abilities and state: the first hour

Numerous studies have documented the infant's perceptual skills during the early weeks. It is well established, for example, that the infant can discriminate visual patterns of relatively fine detail, and tends to prefer areas of high contrast or movement (Fantz, Ordy and Udelf, 1962; Brennan, Ames and Moore, 1966). Extensive work has been devoted to the topic of an innate preference for social stimuli, particularly 'facedness' as reported by Fantz (1961). Hershenson (1965) and Wilcox (1969), however, both failed to confirm a preference for faces in infants under 16 weeks. Comprehensive reviews of perceptual behaviour in the neonatal period are contained in Bronson (1974), Cohen and Salapatek (1975), and McGurk(1974).

Few have described these skills in the period immediately after delivery, although the manner in which the mother makes use of such skills in the first interactions is discussed by many (Klaus and Kennell, 1970; MacFarlane, 1977). Of the 145 infants in the study of obstetric analgesia, detailed observations and assessments are available on 116 of the infants at delivery, beginning from the moment that the head was delivered.

There was great variation in the interval after birth before the baby first opened his eyes, and in the total length of time for which the eyes were open during the first 20 minutes. Although one-quarter of the sample had opened their eyes within the first 15 seconds, and a third within the first minute, more than one-third had not opened their eyes by 10 minutes, including seven infants who had not opened their eyes by the end of the observation period. Slightly less than half of the sample kept their eyes open for more than 10 minutes, including eight babies whose eyes were almost always open. However, it was rather more difficult to specify how well they were seeing things during this time, as there was often nothing near enough to the infant for him to focus on while unattended in the cot. Three-quarters of the infants exhibited scanning behaviour during that period, and half of them focussed during at least one 15-second time interval. However, although almost half of the infants showed scanning for 3 minutes, fewer than 10% focussed for as long. A summary is presented in Table 1.1.

The first 20 minutes were also characterized by frequent state changes with only brief periods of alertness. The typical infant gave a short 'birth cry', and then settled into a quiet, semi-alert state, interspersed with an occasional alert episode of less than a minute. Only half of the infants cried for more than 3 minutes, although many of them fussed a great deal. Conversely few of them slept; 75% never went into State 1 or 2, and those who did so tended to have had minor respiratory depression. More than one-third of the infants never

Table 1.1 Spontaneous visual behaviour in the 20 minutes immediately following birth: % infants

	Latency to open eyes	Total time eyes open	Time scanning	Time focusing
Never	7	9	33	50
0–15 sec	25	2	1	9
15 sec–1 min	9	5	6	13
1–13 min	15	15	17	19
3–5 min	11	11	13	5
5–10 min	17	21	22	2
10–15 min	12	25	6	1
15–20 min	4	12	2	1
	100	100	100	100

reached a spontaneous alert state, and fewer than 20% stayed alert for more than 10 minutes.

The infants at delivery were far more labile than they would be 24 hours later during a full neonatal assessment. Again, the 'typical' infant shifted into a new state about every 90 seconds. Only a third changed state fewer than 5 times, and 4% changed more than 30 times. Some of this lability was undoubtedly due to the propensity for medical staff to intervene in these early minutes with caretaking tasks—weighing, measuring, and so on. Nearly one-quarter of the infant's time was spent being handled by medical staff, and 4 of these 5 minutes were coded as 'aversive' procedures. Not surprisingly, the typical response was to cry. About half of the infants always cried to such handling; only 10% never cried in these situations.

At the end of the observation period 88% of the infants could be coaxed into a quiet and alert state in which visual and auditory skills could be assessed using selected items from the Brazelton Neonatal Assessment Scale (1973). Of these the majority showed evidence of response to sound, and of the ability to follow briefly a bright object or human face as shown in Figure 1.1.

It is striking that more babies tracked the examiner's face at delivery better than they did a string of bright beads, and were more likely to turn if the examiner talked at the same time. There was no difference in their responses to a rattle versus a voice, but it is possible that the rattle was slightly louder.

The infant's perceptual abilities at birth are likely to help the mother to consider her infant as a real person. Klaus and Kennell (1970) noted that nearly three-quarters of the mothers in their sample 'asked' the infant to open his eyes, and spent increasing periods of time adjusting the infant so that they were in an *en face* position. Like Robson and Moss (1970) they also mention that mothers often commented on feeling closer to the baby after he had looked at them.

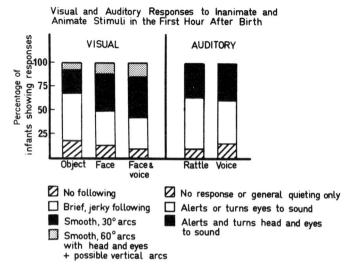

Figure 1.1 Visual and auditory responses to inanimate and animate
stimuli in the first hour after birth

Developmental changes

Over the next few days and weeks the infants in the study came to spend more
time in an awake state, and to be quite capable of responding to maternal
solicitations. Infants were awake for 7 hours on the first day, despite the fact
that they received fewer feeds than on subsequent days. This accords well with
physiological studies of the first few days (Theorell and coworkers, 1973),
and suggestions that the first 24 hours are an optimal time for social interaction
(Hales and coworkers, 1977). By day 2, time asleep had increased, and feeds
occupied most of the awake periods; only on day 7 did the awake periods reach
the level they had been on the first day.

During administration of the Brazelton Neonatal Assessment from day 1
(24 hrs) onwards, three-quarters of infants were in a predominantly quiet and
alert state, thus maximizing the possibility of interaction with the tester.
When disturbed by stimuli in the test, half of the infants quieted spontaneously
or were easily calmed by the examiner's face and voice alone. When this was not
effective a variety of additional procedures were tried. As generations of parents
have discovered, the most consistently successful method of soothing was to
hold the baby and rock him. On day 1, 95% could be quieted in this way, but
subsequently infants polarized into two groups: those who quieted very easily,
and an increasing number (12–15%) who became extremely difficult to soothe
by any means. This core of 'irritable' babies were in the first week less likely
to maintain a stable alert state unless held tightly, swaddled, or given a dummy
to suck, but they were as competent as the more amenable infants on orientation
tasks when such conditions were met.

Visual skills developed rapidly in the first week, particularly tracking in-animate objects as can be seen in Table 1.2. Though the concern here is with the first week, it is interesting to note that very little change took place between week 1 and week 3 in the sample, but that at 6 weeks almost all the infants demonstrat-ed reliable visual tracking. In the auditory sphere the number of babies who, at the least, alerted to sound increased steadily. However, although the behaviour of individuals was very consistent over the weeks, the mean of the group fluctuated from session to session. From the observations of the infants in the testing situation their early response to sounds often seemed to be an automatic orienting response of reflex type.

The inconsistent progress of the group over the first six weeks therefore, might reflect the changing nature of this response as it gradually approximates to true visual localization under voluntary control that occurs around 3 months (Uzgiris and Hunt, 1975). In interactions with the infants at 6 weeks, it seemed that their visual behaviour also was *qualitatively* different; they were interested not only in the immediate stimulus object, but in scanning the entire room and then fixating on items or people of particular interest. Experimental studies

Table 1.2 The development of orienting skills over the first six weeks: %of infants demons-trating behaviour at, or better than, this level

	Birth	Day 1	Day 3	Day 7	Day 21	Day 42
Visual Following:						
Object						
a. Brief, jerky	83	95	92	95	98	100
b. Smooth, $\geq 30°$ arcs	50	57	67	75	79	95
Visual: Face						
a. Brief, jerky	86	97	97	98	100	100
b. Smooth, $\geq 30°$ arcs	50	71	74	81	74	97
Visual and Auditory:						
Face + Voice						
a. Brief, jerky	89	95	95	98	99	100
b. Smooth, $\geq 30°$ arcs	58	74	80	85	87	97
Auditory: Rattle						
a. Alert to, or eyes						
turn	89	90	98	97	98	100
b. Turn head and eyes	36	61	70	63	60	70
Auditory: Voice						
a. Alert to, or eyes						
turn	84	90	95	94	94	98
b. Turn head and eyes	38	54	59	61	54	69
Number of infants						
tested	89	120	125	121	131	126

suggest that this is the age at which one would expect smooth object tracking (White, Castle and Held, 1964; Dayton and Jones, 1964), accommodation to various distances, and the ability to maintain a 'steady fixation on small centrally located stimulus elements' (Bronson, 1974).

Although 12% of the infants could not maintain an alert state long enough to orient to stimuli immediately after birth, this proportion had dropped to 6% by the seventh day, and to less than 1% at 3 and 6 weeks. With three-quarters of the sample reliably attentive to a human face and voice, by the third day there was obviously much scope for social interaction between these mother–infant dyads in the first week.

TECHNIQUES OF INVESTIGATING NEONATAL BEHAVIOUR

Infant tests

It is only recently that neonatal observation has moved from single-variable studies of the infant's capacities towards a more global, multidimensional concept appropriate to the study of social behaviour (Yang and coworkers, 1976). Even for the assessment of the effect of medical interventions on the neonate much reliance has been placed on the Apgar score (Apgar, 1953), which is an observation of five vital signs made at 1, 5, and sometimes 10 minutes. It is inadequate for reflecting subtle or sophisticated behaviours (Scanlon, 1973; 1974), or for interpreting delayed birth effects which are common even in the normal neonate (Brazelton, 1970; Escardo and De Coriat, 1960). However, medical researchers have frequently concluded that various obstetric pratices, including medication, had no effect on the neonate simply because the Apgar scores do not differentiate the experimental and control groups (Noble and coworkers, 1971; Wingate, 1974; Thalme, Belfrage and Raabe, 1974). The poor predictive value of such assessments may be because later socioeconomic circumstances are of greater importance (Sameroff, 1975), or that single obstetric events thus measured are of only transient importance (Parmelee and Haber, 1973). But it could also be because the 'trauma' is only evident in more complex behaviours which are not easily observable in the neonatal period (Parmelee and coworkers, 1975).

During the same period, however, developmental psychologists and paedi-atricians have developed a variety of 'neurobehavioural' tests (Rosenblith, 1961; Scanlon and coworkers, 1974; Brazelton, 1973). Brazelton's test, in published form (1973), is probably the most comprehensive and widely used of these. It also offers an explicit focus on social behaviour, aiming to measure those characteristics of the infant which are most likely to promote appropriate caretaking and interaction from the mother. Special attention is paid, therefore, to visual and auditory responsiveness (see previous section), and the infant's ability to control his state and respond in a systematic and appropriate manner to both stimuli and tester. Higher neurological functions are also assumed to be reflected in the test items which require the infant to habituate to, or 'tune out' repeated presentations of an 'irrelevant' stimulus. Motor tone, power, and activity are observed, as well as tremulousness and startles. A selection of reflexes drawn from the more comprehensive neurological examinations of Prechtl and his colleagues (Prechtl and Beintema, 1964) are also included.

Unlike tests for older infants (Bayley, 1969; Griffiths, 1954), the Brazelton assessment is designed to elicit and rate the best performance from an infant rather than his average, and is therefore more sensitive to the neonate whose skills may only be evident for transient periods between a sleeping and a crying state. The test has been used to compare the normal, full term neonate with those who are of low birthweight (Als and coworkers, 1976), malnourished (Brazelton and coworkers, 1977), or suffering the effects of maternal obstetric medication (Aleksandrowicz, Cayne and Aleksandrowicz, 1974; Tronick and coworkers, 1976). It has also proved sensitive to cultural characteristics of non-Western populations: the Zinacanteco Indians (Brazelton, Robey and Collier, 1969); Chinese, Malay, and Tamil infants (Woodson and Woodson, 1977); Chinese–American infants (Freedman, 1969); Navajo Indians (Chisholm, 1977); and Zambian infants (Tronick, Koslowski and Brazelton, 1973).

Despite its popularity this type of investigation is not flawless. As with other infant tests the Brazelton assessment assumes that the infant's behaviour is systematic and quantifiable, and can be classified into neat categories. Although quite easy to obtain high reliability between observers (Horowitz and coworkers, 1971), it is a test in which each clinician seems to elicit behaviour in a slightly different manner; for instance, simply by holding the infant closer or talking in a softer voice the tester may unconsciously encourage a better performance from a given infant. Scanlon (1974) indicates some of the problems inherent in behavioural observation of this sort as being: 'observer subjectivity or bias, the quantification of measurement criteria, difficulties in controlling extraneous variables during testing, and inherent biases in population selection.' This last problem applies to any observations or experiments that depend on the infant's initial state conforming to set criteria; the selection of 'alert' babies as subjects, for example, introduces a bias towards higher scores. Estimates of an infant's appearance and 'cuddliness' as included in the Brazelton assessment are difficult to make, and are highly subjective and difficult to justify to medical clinicians. Despite these problems the Brazelton Neonatal Assessment remains at present one of the most useful tools in the investigation of neonatal behaviour.

Experimental methods

Laboratory studies have been more commonly employed in the study of perceptual development and learning, but such techniques occasionally have been used to assess aspects of social skills under controlled conditions. For instance, early studies of perception suggested that the eyes are salient features when neonates scan faces and face-like stimuli (Fantz, 1961; Ahrens, 1954). Carpenter (1974) utilized a 'preference' technique in which she measured the amount of looking to each of two visual stimuli, and found that 2-week old infants preferred mother's face to a stranger's, and that some infants even showed gaze aversion to the stranger's face. Three-week old infants can learn to suck significantly longer when the mother's voice follows the sucking than when a stranger's voice rewards their performance (Mills and Melhuish, 1974). MacFarlane (1975) has demonstrated the development of olfactory discrimination and preference for mother over stranger. By presenting mother's vs. stranger's breast pad on either side of the infant's cheeks he found that at 2 days the babies turned equally frequently to both, whereas by 5, and more clearly at 10 days, they turned towards the pad of the mother rather than that of the stranger. These early abilities in discriminating the mother from other caregivers are considered to be an important base for later 'attachment' behaviours (Schaffer and Emerson, 1964; Ainsworth, 1967; Blehar, Lieberman and Ainsworth, 1977).

Many conditioning experiments also have implications for social behaviour. For example, extensive research has documented the differences between non-nutritive and nutritive sucking patterns (Dubignon and coworkers, 1969; Wolff, 1968), and specified those variables which reinforce particular aspects of sucking. In experimental situations nutritive sucking rates can be altered by the amount of fluid delivered with each suck (Crook, 1976), the frequency with which the sucks are reinforced (Bosack, 1973), the characteristics of the nipple (Christensen, Dubignon and Campbell, 1976), the taste of the fluid (Crook and Lipsitt, 1976; Crook, 1977), and exteroceptive stimuli (Crook, Burke and Kittner, 1977).

Obvious comparisons can be drawn with components of the mother's behaviour and the feeding situation in the early weeks. The neonate's well-organized sucking behaviour therefore can be modulated by the mother's selection of certain formulas, bottles, and probably by the manner in which she interrupts the regular burst–pause pattern of his sucking, or reinforces his sucks by faster milk delivery. It is possible that subtle shifts in, say, the speed of administering milk, or teats which vary in hole-dimension from feed to feed, coupled with an infant whose sucking is rather irregular, may lead to disynchronies in interaction which present as feeding problems in the early weeks and months.

One must use caution, however, in generalizing from the laboratory to the real life situation for a number of reasons. The experimental situation is usually highly artificial, with the infant restrained in a chair, attached to wires, electrodes, and feeding tubes, and in a silent, and temperature-controlled room.

White (1971) has suggested that a situation in which reinforcements are delivered at a constant rate, is quite unlike the natural situation, where the relationship between the stimuli and responses is more erratic. Such an experimental situation may then not be representative of the way young infants really learn. Because of the rigorous demands on the infant inherent in experimental modification of behaviour there is some degree of selection and bias introduced. To be included in a learning experiment infants usually must reach either a criterion number of sucks in the baseline minute, or a criterion amplitude, in order to activate equipment which delivers the reinforcement (Crook, 1976; Swoboda, 1976). Those infants whose sucking is strong and regular may well be developmentally more mature, or suffering less from the effects of birth trauma, thus yielding a less-than-representative group. Lewis and Johnson (1971) have commented that those babies who do not complete an experiment initially, but are subsequently retested do, in fact, perform differently, so that their elimination results in significant bias.

In order to validate experimental findings it is necessary then to discover whether the mother, and other caregivers, predictably reinforce infant behaviour, and whether the infant regularly responds.

In early observational work, Gunther (1955, 1961) described how aversive or avoidance conditioning takes place naturally when the infant's nostrils are occluded by the mother's breast while he is sucking so that he turns his head, struggles, and becomes agitated. Lipsitt (1970) suggests that some infants then develop a conditioned aversion to the mother which is a result of the simultaneous elicitation of strong approach and avoidance responses in the feeding situation. His research group has gone on to demonstrate that classical aversive conditioning can occur in the early weeks (Little, 1970). Kaye (1977) has investigated the social implications of the modification of feeding responses by observing the mother's stimulation of her infant when he pauses between sucking bursts; these findings are discussed in the later section on feeding. His study provides a useful corollary to the experimental investigations of Crook, Burke and Kittner (1977) into the way in which auditory stimuli may disrupt nutritive sucking, and its implications for strategies of encouraging sucking through external stimulation.

Indirect assessment

Direct observation and infant testing have often been supplemented by 'second-hand' data on the infant given by the mother. Richards and Bernal (1972), for example, asked mothers to keep diaries of the infants' daily cycle of feeding, sleeping, and crying. These records produced valuable information on feeding; breast fed babies tended to cry more after feeds, and their mothers responded quickly to their crying (Bernal, 1972). These diaries also made it clear that babies who were regular night wakers at 14 months had been more irritable and wakeful during the first 10 days of life, and continued to have consistently shorter sleep bouts in the intervening months (Bernal, 1973). Carey has also investigated factors relating to night-waking (1974) and 'difficult' behaviour (1972) in infancy by means of a maternal self-administered questionnaire based on Thomas and associates' (Thomas and coworkers, 1963; 1969) interview concerning infant temperament. Sleep disturbance between 6–12 months showed a significant correlation with low sensory threshold (Carey, 1974), while 'difficult' babies were more apt to have colic, as well as to have more lacerations requiring suture in the second year (Carey, 1972). In a follow-up of the Richards and Bernal cohort at 3 years, Barnes (1975) found an association between lacerations and 'poor birth status'; another attribute of the 'poor birth status' group was sleep disturbance at both 14 months and 3 years.

The Carey Infant Temperament Scale has only recently been modified for use in the neonatal period (Sostek and Thomas, 1977). In their small study of 18 infants, 'distractible' infants showed *better* social and motoric interaction and state control in a previously administered Brazelton Neonatal Assessment, and 'intense' infants had better motoric interactive scores. Distractibility and intensity also predicted better Bayley test scores at 10 weeks.

Diaries and temperament scales have also been used in the present research, but their predictive value and interrelationships have not yet been established. They contribute another valuable dimension to evaluating infant behaviour and, in particular, allow a global assessment covering traits, or time periods where direct observation is impractical. Nonetheless they may be methodologically less sound than other forms of measurment. Bernal (1972) notes that diaries are 'crude and can be unreliable' because mothers vary in the accuracy of their remembering and recording, or there may be a bias toward, say, multiparae being too busy to notice or record accurately. This point is, in the authors' experience, particularly important in hospital where night records are possibly less accurate because the mother herself is asleep, and nursing staff may infrequently check on, and record, the state of the infant. Carey discusses some of the methodological problems of his scale (1970), such as the discrepancies between the mother's impression of her infant's temperament and the actual behaviour which she describes. Thus mothers minimized the difficulties of their infants, possibly because of their wish to make the infant seem more socially desirable; in the long term follow-up of the drug study cohort there was a tendency for the mother to rate her infant as 'easy' or 'average' even though she may have indicated elsewhere that her infant wakes at night, refuses food, and does not settle easily into a routine.

STUDIES OF THE MOTHER AND INFANT

In the previous section the extent of the neonate's abilities, and some aspects of the way his behaviour is constrained, regular, and modifiable, were discussed;

in this section the social relations of mother and child in the first week of life are examined. There are two particular topics of interest for many researchers: the delivery room and the feeding situation. Both are of theoretical importance and provide opportunities for detailed investigation of some aspects of the baby, or of the mother–child relationship. Many authors, however, have argued that even while in utero the infant is influenced by factors in the mother or her environment, so that it is important to consider potential prenatal determinants of neonatal and maternal behaviours first.

Pre-natal influences

An attempt to relate maternal factors and subsequent infant behaviour was made as early as the 1940s when Sontag looked at the role of anxiety in pregnancy (Sontag, 1941). His findings were responsible for a surge of interest into the effect of the emotional status of the mother on her attitude to the baby, as well as the conduct of the labour and delivery (Turner, 1956; Ottinger and Simmons, 1964; Abramson, Singh and Mbambo, 1969). The problems here are typical of this work in general: that of developing an adequate model of the delayed or long-term consequences of interacting events, or selecting properly controlled sample groups, and of designing robust and reliable assessments. In reviewing the literature on the role of emotional factors in obstetric outcome, McDonnald (1968) concluded that anxiety is the major agent; 'anxiety and extremes in its duration and intensity are postulated as necessary and sufficient conditions, respectively, for the development of psychogenic obstetric complication'. But he points out that the findings of such studies are often marred by small samples, inadequate or absent control groups, and retrospective data. These points are re-emphasized by Copans (1974) who adds to this list the lack of 'non-blind' testing and the failure to distinguish between environmental and intrapersonal variables.

In the drug study there are significant correlations between anxiety and depression in pregnancy, and the mother's initial behaviour and attitude toward her infant at birth, but these emotional states are also dependent on her parity and social class, as well as being confounded with the type of drug she received for pain relief. Emotional status did not determine her length of labour, or the amount of medication administered to her. This is in contrast to several other studies (Yang and coworkers, 1976; Brown and coworkers, 1975; Zuckerman and coworkers, 1963) which do report a relationship between poor adaptation to pregnancy and analgesic administration. Yang stresses that 'such a maternal disposition may be enduring', so that the mother's need for more drugs may be a part of a particular personality which also determines her interactive style. The absence of such effects in the present study may be attributable in part to the more normative sample, or the smaller drug dosage.

These points are extremely important; any study of the neonate that attempts to link his characteristics to the behaviour or emotions of his mother some months beforehand must take great pains to exclude any possible effects due to the mother's handling and caring for her child. Yet psychologists have often shown minimal appreciation of the adaptability of the newborn. Neonates have been tested at any of a variety of times during the first week, and on occasion no attempt has been made to control for feeding differences (i.e. breast versus bottle; e.g. Ourth and Brown, 1961). Even Copans' suggested solution to this problem seems to underestimate the reactivity of the neonate; he argues for 'making the necessary assumption that postnatal influences are at a minimum on day 3 since the predominant environment is the hospital nursery'. Admittedly, mother–child contact is very much less in America in the first days after delivery than it is in Britain (cf. Barnet and coworkers, 1970), but even so it could be argued that the neonate will already have made many adjustments to his environment and the people caring for him (Sander and coworkers, 1970).

And, equally important, these caregivers will have made adjustments to him. There is a failure, when looking for prenatal effects, to recognize that the baby exerts a powerful influence on his mother as well. Psychologists have begun to proffer more complex models of this transaction—such as Sameroff's 'mutual modification' (1975)—but these models lend themselves poorly to operationalization and testing. If, for instance, one wanted to examine the likelihood of behaviour disturbance after mild respiratory difficulties, and accepted that particular factors in the mother (such as schizophrenia) might modify or exacerbate individual characteristics of the infant (excessive irritability), it would be necessary to observe a great number of mother–infant dyads to test adequately all combinations of mother and child characteristics. Furthermore, only intervention studies can determine whether detrimental consequences of a prenatal or perinatal event are inevitable, or merely a reflection of the lack of resources, or knowledge for appropriate management or treatment. The fixed belief that premature infants were likely to have later handicaps or do poorly in school was challenged when new techniques and equipment were developed to cope with respiratory distress and feeding problems which frequently accompanied prematurity. Now that these hazards can be controlled the gestational age of the infant is of less prognostic importance than the complications he may develop after delivery. The consequences of adverse events during pregnancy may well have to be evaluated in a similar fashion.

Studies of the delivery room and first contact

The most recent statistics for the UK (DHSS, 1974) indicate that 90% of all births take place in hospital. Thus in most cases the experience of a hospital delivery will stand at the beginning of the relationship of a women with her child. It is important to know if any aspects of birth in a hospital can affect this relationship, or the development of the child in the long term. The events of the delivery room have also attracted attention for other reasons—first, because the delivery room provides the first opportunity for a detailed examination of the neonate's abilities, and second, because the mother's responses to her child at their first meeting, are presumed to be of much significance.

A hospital's policy on the use of such techniques as induction and acceleration of labour, forceps extraction, caesarean section, and analgesia, may impose certain general characteristics on the infant population in that hospital. Some infants will show the effects of drowsiness or minimal depression resulting from maternal medication (Tronick and coworkers, 1976), bruising caused by forceps delivery (Vulliamy, 1972), or slight prematurity associated with induction (Calder and coworkers, 1974). The stress may be compounded by the interrelations of these factors; primiparous women tend to have longer, more painful labours, and in the present study more often received epidural anaesthesia and an instrumental delivery. Kitzinger (1975) suggests that induced labour tends to be more intense and painful, and thus also may result in epidural administration. Paediatricians cite the use of forceps as a factor in the occurrence of neonatal jaundice (Friedman and Sachtleben, 1976), and some have implicated the use of induction agents such as oxytocin as well (Jeffares, 1977). The jaundiced infant suffers from an increased demand upon the liver detoxification systems, and so is less well able to metabolise the drugs that cross the placenta during labour (Burt, 1971). These medical interventions may result in particular responses from the mother which are more attributable to the condition of the infant than to any 'natural' behaviours.

Labour and delivery experiences may also be determined by sociological parameters. For example, decisions about the choice of pain-killing drugs will depend on such objective indications as parity, and cervical dilation, but also on the woman's preconceptions about the degree of pain to expect, her attitude about the extent to which pain 'ought' to be endured, the support she receives from the nursing and medical staff, and the way that the latter interpret her signs of discomfort as indications for the use of analgesia (O'Driscoll, 1975).

The experiences of mother and of baby will vary from one situation to another partly because they will involve those aspects of hospital policy that relate to ways of dealing with the labouring woman, the mother she becomes, and the baby. The mother who delivers in hospital, for example, is less likely to handle her baby in the first hour than one who has a home confinement (Garrow and Smith, 1976). The baby may be given to the mother at times which suit the convenience of the medical attendants, but are not necessarily the most appropriate for the mother's comfort or for the baby's state of alertness. In the present study the two periods when contact is most likely are immediately after the cord is clamped, for a brief cuddle, and after the infant is cleaned up;

at both these times the baby is often crying as a result of the stressful handling he has just received, and may not give the mother much positive feedback.

Having said that there are a complex of factors—social, psychological, and physiological—at work at the time of delivery, how are we to interpret studies of early maternal handling and the effects of separation? These studies are based on the concept of 'attachment', or 'bonding', and this in turn owes much to the ethologists' observations of 'imprinting'. The findings are striking, but it is hard to take seriously the explanations that are given for the importance of early contact. Several authors have now discounted the notion that parturition brings about particular hormonal changes that constitute a critical or sensitive period for mothering (Wortis 1971; Schaffer, 1977).

Just what is important about early contact remains to be discovered; is it physical contact per se, or the attitude changes that may accompany it? What is 'early'—the first hour, the first eighteen hours (Hales and coworkers, 1977), or the first week? Do the infant's characteristics play no part? The careful work of Robson and Moss (1970) goes some way toward extending our insights into the process of 'attachment'. Defining attachment as 'the extent to which a mother feels that her infant occupies an essential position in her life', 54 primiparae were interviewed during the three months following the birth. The researchers noted a typical pattern of response by the mothers; at delivery they were preoccupied with finishing the task as quickly and painlessly as possible, and on first seeing their infant interest was in appearance only. Strong feelings of attachment in the mother were not present until the third month.

By this stage the infant's particular responses to the mother apparently contributed in an important way to the feelings of maternal attachment; in contrast 34% felt that their first contact with the child had elicited no feelings at all. Robson and Moss argue that there is an important difference between the mothers' emotional responses, and the attachment observable in animal species; the latter is triggered by species-specific infant behaviour, and involves attendance to physical needs, while the onset of positive feelings in the human mothers seemed to reflect the 'infant's capacity to exhibit behaviours that characterize adult forms of social communication'.

Barnet and coworkers (1970), again on the basis of interview data, consider that separation—routinely after delivery, or that experienced by the mothers of premature babies—may produce differences in at least three areas: the sense of commitment or attachment to the infant; the development of confidence in mothering abilities; and the ability to establish an efficient caretaking routine. They point out that each of these will be affected in addition by such factors as parity, desire to have the child, birthweight, and the infant's prognosis. The two cases of negative reactions to the baby in their study were associated with an initially poor prognosis for the very premature baby— cases, in effect, of 'anticipatory mourning'.

In a random allocation of mothers of premature babies to contact or no-contact groups, however, Leifer and coworkers (1972) failed to demonstrate any consistent caretaking differences between their groups. Leiderman and Seashore (Seashore and coworkers, 1973) found that mothers separated from their premature infants held, caressed, and smiled less at the infants after discharge from hospital, but that by one year this difference had nearly disappeared. Separation seemed to lower the confidence of mothers of first born infants, and there was a higher divorce rate in the twenty-two families where the mothers of prematures had not had contact. These findings implicate stress as creating problems within the family unit rather than just between mother and infant, and draw attention once more to the interplay of factors in the mother's previous experience, personality, family support, and her expectations and trust in the medical institution.

The authors' observations in the delivery room suggest that the *first* contact between mother and infant is not a very long or satisfying one. Most mothers were given the infant within a few minutes of delivery, but 6% did not interact with the infant, and half of the sample interacted at this time for less than 5 minutes. Many mothers held the baby without actually interacting with him; that is, they 'discussed' the infant with their husband, with occasional glances at the infant as if to maintain him as the object of reference. Thus 18% never looked at their infant in the first 20 minutes, and fewer than 20% sustained visual contact for more than half the observation period. Talking was infrequent, nearly half of the mothers not talking to their infant at all.

The tactile exploration seen by Klaus and Kennell (1970) was very rare in this group of mothers; half of them never touched the infant or stroked him during this period, and only a very few stroked the hands or feet in the manner described by Klaus and Kennell. It is, of course, possible that mothers would have shown greater interaction if circumstances had been more favourable. For example, the infants were nearly always swaddled in this early period, and warnings about 'cold' were frequent enough to discourage mothers from unwrapping or undressing the infants while staff were present. It is also common in the unit studied to encourage the mothers to hold their infant while being sutured after routine episiotomy, in order to give them a distraction from the discomfort. In a semi-recumbent position, and with their legs in stirrups it is not surprising that mothers found it extremely difficult to devote their full attention to the baby.

After a further period of interaction with the baby the mother's behaviour was rated, albeit crudely, on the amount of holding and contact and its quality. By this criterion 62% had a rating of 'good' while 31% showed 'indifferent' behaviour, marked by few interactions, although they may have talked quite positively about the baby with their husband; 7% of the mothers were rated 'negative', in that they refused to hold the baby at all. The mothers who were less positive toward their infant had indicated greater depression and anxiety during pregnancy, but their infants also were in marginally poorer condition at birth. Infants of these mothers performed no worse on the behavioural tests, but they did smile less to the examiner at 6 weeks of age. It was intriguing to find that in a postal follow-up of these infants later on in the first year (where 80% of the study mothers replied overall, 6 out of the 7 'negative' mothers did not return the questionnaire. This might indicate that they were finding child-rearing a less satisfying experience, or simply unwilling to share such experiences with someone connected with the hospital.

Fathers too were involved in the delivery room, three-quarters of them being present for the birth of their infant. Of those not attending, 11% chose not to see the birth while the rest were generally absent due to circumstances such as work obligations or insufficient warning. Of those attending, half were rated as having a 'good' attitude to the infant, and half 'indifferent', again in the sense of not actively talking and interacting with the baby. Unlike the mothers none of the fathers observed actually ignored their infant or refused to hold him when encouraged to do so. It seemed, in fact, that more fathers would have interacted with the infant had they been encouraged to actually hold him, rather than just gaze at him from afar; therefore the fewer 'good' scores may have been an artifact of the coding system, which specified 'holding and talking' to the baby. No importance can yet be attached to the father's attendance at the delivery and his early attitude to the baby. Richards, Dunn, and Antonis (1977) noted a correlation between presence at birth and later participation in caretaking activities in their longitudinal study of 80 infants. However, they emphasize that this is not necessarily a causal relationship, particularly as Greenberg and Morris (1974) found that attendance or non-attendance at the birth did not have later effects on paternal attitude. This does not mean, of course, that further efforts should not be directed toward making fathers feel welcome at the birth of their infant. Most of the fathers spoken to in this study were delighted to have had a part in the experience, and the mothers generally felt that their husband's support during labour had been rewarded by his being able to see the moment of birth.

Observations of mothers and infants during feeding

Quite apart from any theoretical arguments about the importance of feeding for the psychological development of the infant, an observer on the postnatal ward will notice that the feeding of her child provides a mother with almost her only meaningful contact with him. In addition it has the advantage for the psychologists that it is an often repeated activity, it usually involves mother and infant alone, and it is a goal-directed operation that has, furthermore, an apparently well-defined and unambiguous goal. It has therefore been studied more often and in greater detail than any other maternal caretaking activity.

However, on closer examination the purpose of this work has usually not been to tell us much about the *process of feeding* itself. Rather, the existence of a common activity has been used to provide a basis for comparisons of various groups. Research has documented differences between primiparae and multi-parae (Thoman and coworkers, 1972), breast with bottle-feeders (Dunn, 1975; Bell, 1968), high with low-maternal contact groups (De Chateau and Wiberg, 1976), schizophrenic and normal mothers (Schacter and coworkers, 1977), and greater versus lesser quantities of analgesic medication (Brown and coworkers, 1975; Parke, O'Leary and West, 1972). The study by Schacter, in fact, completely excluded coding of offering and accepting of food during the feed as they were interested only in extra-nutritive behaviour. A variety of measures have been produced to facilitate these comparisons, e.g. looking at baby, time *en face*, amount of affectionate contact, and so on, but we end up in the paradoxical position of knowing that groups of mothers may differ in their behaviours toward their infants, while knowing nothing about why these differences appear, how they relate to the process of feeding, and whether they are likely to have any significance for the child's later development.

In a sample of black low-income mothers who bottle-fed their infants, Brown (Brown and coworkers, 1975) observed that the 'feeding' session actually turned out to consist of a series of brief feeding episodes which only lasted a total of 11 minutes out of the observed 30. They engaged in caretaking tasks about 10% of the time, while 21% of their time was spent in rubbing, kissing, rocking, and other affectionate behaviour. The fact that the infants kept their eyes open for 43% of the time, and that the infants were more likely to have their eyes open when the mother was presenting the bottle emphasizes the potential for turning the feed into a social occasion. Although light and heavy infants responded similarly to stimulation, mothers were more likely to stimulate the heavier baby by talking to him, and male infants were more likely to elicit affectionate behaviours. Brown suggests that in their particular population large male infants are most valued, whereas in Thoman's (Thoman and coworkers, 1972) sample of breast-feeding infants, mothers talked to and smiled at their female infants more often than the males.

By examining the sequences of talking and looking in greater detail, Dunn and Richards (1977) demonstrated that these activities did occur when the baby was on the nipple, but when he was not sucking, and that the probability of looking away and not talking while he was actually sucking increased over the days. The feeds became more coordinated and 'successful' over time as well, as measured by an increase in the time spent sucking, and a corresponding decrease in the number of times the nipple came out of the infant's mouth, and in the mother's attempts to stimulate sucking or change the infant's position. It was found that despite previous suggestions (Levy, 1958), the mother's 'affectionate' behaviours were not closely related to each other or with their response to crying; rather, 'affectionate' talking was significantly associated with the infant's sucking rate. The breast-feeding infant was more likely to determine the pacing of his mother's behaviour than the bottle-feeder, particularly in terminating sucking bouts and affecting his mother's talking and touching.

In several of their papers, Dunn and Richards have drawn attention to some of the methodological problems inherent in the study of mother–infant interaction. Firstly (Dunn and Richards, 1977), a finer analysis may be necessary to elucidate elements in the interaction; the use of time-sampling, for example, in such a fast-paced situation, makes it impossible to attend to subtle changes in the direction of gaze or postural adjustment. For this reason video-taping of the situation improves the available depth and breadth of focus and has been the choice in recent studies of face-to-face interaction in an *en face* play situation (Brazelton and coworkers, 1975) and during feeding (Kaye, 1977). Another problem in the interpretation of mother–infant studies is that neither maternal nor infant measures can be assumed to be independent of previous interactions between the two (Dunn, 1975). Their work has been invaluable in demonstrating the need to take related variables into account even when one is dealing with a fairly homogeneous obstetrically normal population. The measure of 'affectionate' talking, for instance, was related consistently to suck rate in the early feeds which were influenced by labour and delivery events; the relative smoothness of the feed, and the incidence of difficulties in feeding were not useful predictors of later interactive behaviours.

More serious theoretical issues about methodology have been raised by Rosenthal (1973) who begins by stating that '"Interaction" has been one of the most evasive and misused concepts in the literature of Developmental Psychology'. Most psychologists, she argues, have really been engaged in examining the impact that one member of the pair has on the other, i.e. the 'unidirectional arrow' whereas interaction involves 'the changing pattern of the mutual perceptions and behaviours of both infant and caretaker vis-a-vis each other as a result of their respective previous mutual perceptions and behaviour via-a-vis each other'. The use of a variable such as 'dyadic gazing' (Robson, Pederson and Moss, 1969) or the charting of variables such as simultaneous smiling, looking, and talking (Lewis, 1972) goes some way toward elucidating frequency of interaction, types of behaviours, and the context in which interaction takes place. Rosenthal also cautions that even when an adequate design and observation framework has been developed there are problems in finding an adequate statistical model to deal with such an analysis. The usefulness of contingency tables with statements of conditional probabilities has been reported by Gewirtz and Gewirtz (1969) and Freedle and Lewis (1971): correlation coefficients between aspects of the infant's behaviour and of the mother's behaviour are not a sufficient indication of interaction between the two partners.

The microanalytic studies provide clearer descriptions of the 'meshing' of feeding behaviours that can really be termed interaction. Kaye's (1977) approach regards feeding as an example of the development of 'dialogue', and he cites two distinct themes as giving impetus to his own theoretical position. The first of these is 'turn-taking', which involves the use of fairly standardized signals by both partners, whether they be adults (Kendon, 1967; Duncan, 1972) or mother–infant dyads (Robson, 1967; Jaffe, Stern and Peery, 1973), and the implication that these 'rules' for turn-taking might be learned in early infancy. The other concerns such early dialogue as a precursor to language proper, particularly as it contributes to what Bruner (1975) terms the alternation-of-comments-upon-a-common-topic.

In a study of 30 newborn infants observed during a feed, Kaye concentrated attention on two superficially simple phenomena, the infant's sucking and pausing, and the mother's attempts to alter the tempo by jiggling the infant or the bottle. And yet the pattern of jiggling and sucking brings together aspects of a mother's need to find regularity in the interaction with her infant, as well as the increasing ability of the infant to accommodate his own actions to the demands of the situation. Thus, initially, mothers interpret the infant's pausing as 'signs of flagging' and stimulate him by jiggling. The infant, however, responds instead to the end of jiggling by a resumption of sucking, so that the mothers change their response to 'jiggle-stop', which leads at two weeks of age to a shorter duration of jiggling and pausing. She utilizes his immaturity, with its guarantee of 'salient regularity, rhythmicity, predictability ... she can predict the temporal structure of her infant's behaviour ... to build, through mutual differentiation of responses, a basic pattern of interaction which will *not* depend upon biological clocks, but upon mutual monitoring and feedback'.

Kaye considers that later interactions will reiterate the phenomenon found in feeding during the newborn period: a first phase in which the mother accommodates to the infant's autonomous patterns of behaviour, then the next phase in which the actions form a 'mutual contingency' or 'game'. He also suggests that the social interaction between mother and baby will show continuity and consistency across other tasks, events, and ages. For example, the mutual regulation between the partners should predict (to some extent), the mother's postpartum recovery and sense of role satisfaction; smoothness and self-regulation in the baby's behaviour during a Brazelton Neonatal Assessment should predict the success of the mother's anticipation of her infant's sucking and pausing pattern. There is some evidence that this may be the case. Osofsky (1976) found that the behaviour of both mother and infant was consistent between a feeding session and the mother's 'stimulation' of her own infant using selected Brazelton items. In particular the mother's attentiveness to the infant, and the infant's predominant state, eye contact with the mother, and responsiveness were consistent across situations. The finding that infant responsiveness during a feed correlated strongly with maternal attentiveness and sensitivity to the infant gives credence to Kaye's predictions, even though

Osofsky was not directly concerned with food intake and sucking regulation.

CONCLUSIONS

Safe delivery of an infant marks the climax of nine months of hopes and expectations, and often anxieties and irrational fears about his well-being. When the mother leaves hospital at the end of the first week with her infant she will have mastered, or re-established, the rudiments of caretaking, and made a start at understanding the rhythms of his behaviour and at predicting his immediate needs. During this long period she will have depended on the professional skills of a great many hospital staff, and absorbed new information through her contact with friends, relations, and fellow patients. She will use all of this experience in developing an individual and idiosyncratic style of interacting with her equally individual and idiosyncratic infant. She knows this new baby of hers is unique, regardless of the inevitable policies and procedures designed for the 'average' baby which constrain her activities.

And yet, the assumptions in studying this period have often been limited to a search for group differences or effects of specific events which might predict later behaviour. It is too early to make long term predictions from the small data base, imprecise methods of measurement, and great number of uncontrolled variables which distinguish many studies in this area. Indeed Dunn (1975) emphasizes that the mother adapts to her first infant so rapidly over the first 10 days that predictions made from the first few feeds could be misleading. If anything, insight into the postnatal period is more important for pinpointing the complexities and methodological problems in evaluating and interpreting social relations, *even* when the behavioural repertoire of the infant and the contingent responses of his mother are fairly narrow and predictable. The findings now appearing on the nature of the neonate's abilities and the relationship with his mother have a *practical* significance, in so far as they provide an informed basis for decisions on the organization of obstetric and paediatric care, in order to provide not only a safe delivery and puerperium for the mother and her infant, but also a relaxed and supportive environment in which they can develop patterns of interaction. The findings also have a value for *theoretical* issues, providing evidence that supports a certain type of view of the nature of a child's development. They can contribute to our understanding of the *processes* of the child's development, and the initiation of these processes in the early experience of mother and child together. From this point of view the outcome of development is effectively certain; the vast majority of infants grow to become competent adults acting efficiently in a social world, and our interest is focused on the way in which the change from a social infant to social adult is made.

The newborn infant shows fairly consistent and recognizable patterns of behaviour, and will modify these patterns in response to adults' actions.

Upon this foundation his mother imposes modes of interaction at a level of sophistication that the infant is not capable of sustaining alone. Schutz and Luckman (1974) have rephrased this into a phenomenological framework: 'The one confronting him (e.g., his mother) always conducts herself in such a way as to presuppose a certain reciprocity on the part of the child. One of the partners always conducts himself as if it were a genuine we-relation.' Even in later infancy the mother continues to control and interpret the infant's social (Stern, 1974) and communicative contributions (Snow, 1977; Ryan, 1974). His increasingly active participation in social interaction is an integral part of the acquisition of the rules and structures which govern adult language (Bruner, 1975; Cicourel, 1973; Habermas, 1970).

Finally, the events of the first week of a child's life can be viewed as having a significance in themselves. Through processess of mutual modification, mother and infant begin to establish a pattern that will provide the basis for the long development to adulthood. The infant's responses to his mother give specific information about his individual needs. The structure of the hospital setting imposes demands on the pair; individuals will respond in different ways, and the very process of adjusting to these demands will create new and varied situations for the mother and infant to develop satisfying modes of relating to each other. As Stratton reminds us (1977) the most crucial function of the newborn period may be to 'establish in the mother an understanding of her baby and an appropriate set of attitudes toward him'.

ACKNOWLEDGEMENTS

Parts of this study were supported by the Medical Research Council, The Nuffield Foundation, and St. Mary's Hospital Medical School. We would like to thank the many members of staff at St. Mary's Hospital who worked with us, and the mothers and infants who cooperated so readily. We are also grateful for our colleagues who commented helpfully on earlier drafts.

REFERENCES

Abramson, J. H., Singh, A. R. and Mbambo, V. (1969). 'Antenatal stress and the baby's development', *Arch. Dis. Childhood*, 37, 42–49.

Ahrens, R. (1954). 'Beitrag zur Entwicklung des Physiognomie—und Minikerkennens', *Z. Exper. Angew Psychol.*, 2, 412–454.

Ainsworth, M. D. S. (1976). *Infancy in Uganda: Infant Care and the Growth of Love*, Baltimore, Johns Hopkins.

Aleksandrowicz, M., Cayne, L. and Aleksandrowicz, D. R. (1974). 'Obstetrical pain—relieving drugs as predictors of neonate behavior variability', *Child Develop.*, 45, 935–945.

Als, H., Tronick, E., Adamson, L. and Brazelton, T. B. (1976). 'The behavior of the full-term but underweight newborn infant', *Dev. Med. and Child Neurol.*, 18, 590–602.

Apgar, V. (1953). 'A proposal for a new method of evaluation of the newborn infant',

Current Res. Anaesth., **32**, 260.

Bakow, H. (1973). *The relation between newborn behaviour and mother–child interaction*, Paper presented at SSRCD, March 1973.

Barnet, C. R., Leiderman, P. H., Grobstein, R. and Klaus, M. (1970). 'Neonatal Separation: the maternal side of interactional deprivation', *Pediatrics*, **45**, 197–205.

Bayley, N. (1969). *Bayley Scales of Infant Development*, New York, Psychol. Crop.

Beintema, D.J. (1968). *A Neurological Study of Newborn Infants*, Clinics in Developmental Medicine No. 28, London, SIMP.

Bell, R. Q. (1968). 'A re-interpretation of the direction of effects in studies of socialisation', *Psychol. Rev.*, **75**, 81–95.

Bench, J. and Weir, K. (1977). Research in progress.

Bernal, J. F. (1972). 'Crying during the first 10 days and maternal responses', *Dev. Med. and Child Neurol.*, **14**, 363–372.

Bernal, J. F. (1973). 'Night waking in infancy during the first 14 months', *Dev. Med. and Child Neurol.*, **15**, 760–769.

Blehar, M. C., Lieberman, A. and Ainsworth, M. D. (1977). 'Early face-to-face interaction . and its relation to later infant mother attachment', *Child Develop.*, **48**, 182–194.

Bosack, T. N. (1973). 'Effects of fluid delivery on the sucking response of the human newborn', *J. Exp. Child. Psychol.*, **15**, 77–85.

Brazelton, T. B. (1970). 'Effects of prenatal drugs on the behavior of the neonate', *Amer. J. Psychiatry*, **126**, 1261–1266.

Brazelton, T. B. (1973). *Neonatal Behavioral Assessment Scale*, London, SIMP.

Brazelton, T.B., Robey, M.D. and Collier, G.A. (1969). 'Infant development in the Zinacanteco Indians of Southern Mexico', *Pediatrics*, **44**, (2), 274–289.

Brazelton, T. B., Tronick, E., Adamson, L., Als, H. and Wise, S. (1975). 'Early mother–infant reciprocity', in *Parent–Infant Interaction*, CIBA No. 33, Amsterdam, Elsevier.

Brazelton, T. B., Tronick, E., Lechtig, A., Lasky, R. E. and Klein, R. E. (1977). 'The behavior of nutritionally deprived Guatemalan infants', *Dev. Med. and Child Neurol.*, **19**, 364–372.

Brennan, W. M., Ames, E. W. and Moore, R. W. (1966). 'Age differences in infants' attention to patterns of different complexities', *Science*, **151**, 354–355.

Bronson, G. (1974). 'The Postnatal Growth of Visual Capacity', *Child Develop.*, **45**, 873–890.

Brown, J., Bakeman, R., Snyder, P. A., Frederickson, W. T., Morgan, S. T. and Hepler, R. (1975). 'Interactions of black inner-city mothers with their newborn infants', *Child Develop.*, **46**, 677–686.

Bruner, J. S. (1975). 'The ontogenesis of speech acts', *J. Child Lang.*, **2**, 1–19.

Burt, R. A. P. (1971). 'The foetal and maternal pharmacology of some of the drugs used for the relief of pain in labour', *Brit. J. Anaesth.*, **43**, 824–836.

Calder, A. A., Moar, V. A., Ounsted, M. K. and Turnbull, A. C. (1974). 'Increased bilirubin levels in neonates after induction of labour by intravenous prostaglandin E_2 or oxytocin', *Lancet*, (ii), 1339–1342.

Carey, W. B. (1970). 'A simplified method for measuring infant temperament', *J. Pediatrics*, **77**, (2), 188–194.

Carey, W. B. (1972). 'Clinical applications of infant temperament measures', *Behavioral Pediatrics*, **81** (4), 823–828.

Carey, W. B. (1974). 'Night waking and temperament in infancy', *Behavioral Pediatrics*, **84**, (5), 756–758.

Carpenter, G. (1974). 'Mother's face and the newborn', *New Scientist*, 21 March, 742–744.

Chisholm, J. (1977). Paper in preparation.

Christensen, S., Dubignon, J. and Campbell, D. (1976). 'Variations in intra-oral stimulation and nutritive sucking', *Child Develop.*, **47**, 539–542.

Cicourel, A. V. (1973). 'The acquisition of social structure: towards a developmental sociology of language and meaning', in Cicourel, A. V., *Cognitive Sociology*, London, Penguin.

Cohen, L. B. and Salapatek, P. (eds.) (1975). *Infant Perception: From Sensation to Cognition*, London, Academic Press.

Copans, S. A. (1974). 'Human prenatal effects: methodological problems and some suggested solutions', *M. P. Q.*, **20**, 43–52.

Crook, C. K. (1976). 'Neonatal sucking: effects of quantity of the response contingent fluid upon sucking rhythm and heart rate', *J. Exp. Child Psychol.*, **21**, 539–548.

Crook, C. K. (1977). 'Taste and the temporal organization of neonatal sucking', in Weiffenbach, J. (ed.), *Taste and Development: the Genesis of Sweet Preference*, Washington D. C., Government Printing Office.

Crook, C. K. and Lipsitt, L. P. (1976). 'Neonatal nutritive sucking: effects of taste stimulation upon sucking rhythm and heart rate', *Child Develop.*, **47**, 518–522.

Crook, C. K., Burke, P. M. and Kittner, S. (1977). 'Some effects of an exteroceptive stimulus upon nutritive sucking of neonates', *Develop. Psychol.*, **13**(5), 469–472.

Dayton, G. O. and Jones, M. H. (1964). 'Analysis of characteristics of fixation reflex in infants by use of direct current electro-oculography', *Neurology*, **14**, 1152–1156.

De Chateau, P. and Winberg, B. (1976). 'Long-term effect on mother–infant behaviour of extra contact during the first hour post partum', *Acta Paediat. Scan.* (in press).

DHSS (1974). *On the State of Public Health*, Annual report of the Chief Medical Officer of the DHSS for the Year 1973, London, HMSO.

Dubignon, J., Campbell, D., Curtis, M. and Partington, M. W. (1969). 'The relation between laboratory measures of sucking, food intake and perinatal factors during the newborn period', *Child Develop.* **40**, 1107–1120.

Duncan, S. (1972). 'Some signals and rules for taking speech turns in conversation', *J. Pers. and Soc. Psychol.*, **23**, 283–292.

Dunn, J. F. (1975). 'Consistency and change in maternal style', in *Parent–Infant Interaction*, Proceedings of a Ciba Foundation Symposium, No. 33, Amsterdam, Elsevier.

Dunn, J. and Richards, M. P. M. (1977). 'Observations on the developing relationship between mother and baby in the neonatal period', in *Interaction in Infancy: The Loch Lomond Symposium*, London, Academic Press.

Escalona, S.K. (1962). 'The Study of individual differences and the problem of state', *J. Amer. Acad. of Child Psychiat.*, **1**, 11–37.

Escardo, F. and De Coriat, L.F. (1960). 'Development of postural and tonic patterns in the newborn infant', *Pediatric Clinics of N. Amer.*, **7**, 511–525.

Fantz, R. L. (1961). 'The origin of form perception', *Scientific American*, **204**, 66–72.

Fantz, R. L., Ordy, J. M. and Udelf, M. S. (1962). 'Maturation of pattern vision in infants during the first six months', *J. Comp. Physiol. Psychol.*, **55**, 907–917.

Freedle, R. and Lewis, M. (1971). *Application of Markov processes to the concept of state*, Paper presented at the Merrill–Palmer Conference at Detroit, Michigan.

Freedman, D. G. (1969). 'Behavioral differences between Chinese–American and European–American newborns', *Nature*, **224**, 1227.

Friedman, E. A. and Sachtleben, M. R. (1976). 'Neonatal jaundice in association with oxytocin stimulation of labour and operative delivery', *B. M. J.*, **1**, 198.

Garrow, D. H. and Smith, D. (1976). 'The modern practice of separating a newborn baby from its mother', *Proc. Royal Soc. Medicine*, **69**, (1), 22–25.

Gewirtz, H. and Gewirtz, J. (1969) 'Caretaking settings, back ground events, and behavior differences in four Israeli childrearing environments', in Foss, B. (ed.), *Determinants of Infant Behaviour*, Vol. **4**, London, Methuen.

Greenberg, M. and Morris, N. (1974). 'Engrossment: the newborn's impact upon the father', *Am. J. Orthopsychiatry*, **44**, 520–531.

Gregg, C. L., Haffner, M. E. and Korner, A. F. (1976). 'The relative efficacy of vestibular-proprioceptive stimulation and the upright position in enhancing visual pursuit in neonates', *Child Develop.*, **47**, 309–314.

Griffiths, R. (1954). *The Abilities of Babies*, London, Univ. London Press.

Gunther, M. (1955). 'Instinct and the nursing couple', *Lancet*, **1**, 575.

Gunther, M. (1961). 'Infant behaviour at the breast', in Foss B. (ed.), *Determinants of Infant Behaviour*, London, Methuen.

Habermas, J. (1970). 'Towards a theory of communicative competence', in Dreitzel, H. P. (ed.) *Recent Sociology*, No. 2, New York, Macmillan.

Hales, D. H., Lozoff, B., Sousa, R. and Kennek, J. H. (1977). 'Defining the limits of the maternal sensitive period', *Dev. Med. and Child Neurol.*, **19**, 454–461.

Hart, N. and Hart, K. (1976). *Authority and conflict in relationships between hospital doctors and their patients*, paper presented at the British Sociological Assn. Conference.

Hershenson, M. (1965). *Visual discrimination in the human newborn*, Dissertation Abstract, Vol. **26**, 1793.

Horowitz, F. D., Self, P. A., Paden, L. Y., Culp, R., Laub, K., Boyd, E. and Mann, M. E. (1971). *Newborn test and four-week retest on a normative population using the Brazelton newborn assessment procedure*, Paper presented at the SRCD Meeting in Minneapolis.

Hubert, J. (1974). 'Belief and reality: social factors in pregnancy and childbirth', in Richards, M. P. M. (ed.), *The Integration of a Child into a Social World*, Cambridge, C. U. P.

Jaffe, J., Stern, D. N. and Peery, L. C. (1973). 'Conversational coupling of gaze behavior in prelinguistic human development', *J. Psycho-linguistic Research*, **2**, 321–330.

Jeffares, M. J. (1977). 'A multifactorial survey of neonatal jaundice', *Br. J. Obs. Gynaec.*, **84**, 452–455.

Kaye, K. (1977). 'Toward the origin of dialogue', in Schaffer, H. R. (ed.), *Interactions in Infancy*, London, Academic Press.

Kendon, A. (1967). 'Some functions of gaze direction in social interaction', *Acta Psychologica*, **26**, 22–63.

Kitzinger, S. (1975). *Some mothers' experiences of induced labour*, National Childbirth Trust (unpublished).

Klaus, M. and Kennell, J. H. (1970). 'Mothers separated from their infants', *Pediatric Clinics of N. Amer.*, **17**, 1015–1037.

Korner, A. (1969) 'Neonatal startles, smiles, erections and reflex sucks as related to state, sex and individuality', *Child Develop.*, **40**, 1039–1053.

Korner, A. F. and Grobstein, R. (1966). 'Visual alertness as related to soothing in neonates: implications for maternal stimulation and early deprivation', *Child Develop.*, **37**, 867–876.

Leifer, A. D., Leiderman, P. H., Barnett, C. R. and Williams, J. A. (1972). 'Effects of mother–infant separation on maternal attachment behavior', *Child Develop.*, **43**, 1203–1218.

Levy, D. (1958). *Behavioural Analysis*, Springfield, Thomas.

Lewis, M. (1972). 'State as an infant–environment interaction: an analysis of mother–infant interactions as a function of sex', *M. P. Q.*, **18**, 95–122.

Lewis, M. and Johnson, N. (1971). 'What's thrown out with the bath water? A baby?, *Child Develop.*, **42**, 1053–1055.

Lipsitt, L. P. (1970). 'Infant Learning: the blooming, buzzing confusion revisited', in Meyer, M. E. (ed.), *Second Western Symposium on Learning*, Washington,

Little, A. H. (1970). *Eyelid conditioning in the human infant as a function of the interstimulus interval*, Master's thesis, Brown University.

MacFarlane, J. A. (1975). 'Olfaction in the development of social preference in the human neonate', in *Parent–Infant Interaction*, ed. by CIBA, Amsterdam; CIBA Foundation.

MacFarlane, J. A. (1977). *The Psychology of Childbirth*, London, Fontana.

McDonnald, R. L. (1968). 'The role of emotional factors in obstetric complications: a review', *Psychosomatic Med.*, **30**, 222–234.

McGurk, H. (1974). 'Visual perception in young infants', in Foss, B. (ed.), *New Perspectives in Child Development*, Mddx, Penguin Education.

Mills, M. and Melhuish, E. (1974). 'Recognition of mother's voice in infancy', *Nature*, **252**, 123–124.

Moss, H. A. (1967). 'Sex, age and state as determinants of mother–infant interaction', *M. P. Q.*, **18**, 95–122.

Noble, A. D., Craft, I. L., Bootes, J. A., Edwards, P. A., Thomas, D. J., and Mills, K. L. M. (1971). 'Continuous lumbar epidural analgesia using bupivicaine: a study of the foetus and newborn child', *J. Obs. Gynaec. Br. Common.*, **78**, 559–563.

O'Driscoll, K. (1975). 'An obstetrician's view of pain', *Br. J. Anaesthetia*, **47**, 1053–1059.

Osofsky, J. D. (1976). 'Neonatal characteristics and mother–infant interaction in two observational situations', *Child Develop.*, **47**, 1138–1147.

Osofsky, J. D. and Danzger, B. (1974). 'Relationships between neonatal characteristics and mother infant interactions', *Develop. Psychol.*, **10**, 124–130.

Osofsky, J. D. and O'Connell, E. J. (1977). 'Patterning of newborn behavior in an urban population', *Child Develop.*, **48**, 532–536.

Ottinger, D. R. and Simmons, J. F. (1964). 'Behaviour of human neonates and prenatal maternal anxiety', *Psychol. Reports*, **14**, 391–394.

Ourth, L. and Brown, K. B. (1961). 'Inadequate mothering and disturbance in the neonatal period', *Child Develop.*, **32**, 287–295.

Parke, R. D., O'Leary, S. E. and West, S. (1972). 'Mother–father–newborn interaction: effects of maternal medication, labor, and sex of infant', *Amer. Psychol. Assoc. Proc.*, **7**, 85–88.

Parmelee, A. H., Sigman, M., Kopp, C., Haber, A. (1975). 'The concept of a cumulative risk score for infants', in Ellis, H. R. (ed.), *Aberrant Development in Infancy*, New Jersy, Halstead Press.

Parmelee, A. H., and Haber, A. (1973). 'Who is the "at risk infant"?', *Clinical Obst. and Gynac.*, **16**, 376–387.

Prechtl, H. F. R. (1965). 'Problems of behavioural studies in the newborn infant', in Lehoman, D. S., Hinde, R. A. and Shaw, E. (eds.), *Advances in the Study of Behaviour*, London, Academic Press.

Prechtl, H. F. R. and Beintema, D. (1964). *Neurological Examination of the Full-term Newborn Infant*, Clinics in Devel. Med. No. 12, London, SIMP.

Prechtl, H. F. R., Akiyama, Y., Zinkin, P. and Grant, D. K. (1968). 'Polygraphic studies of the full-term newborn', in MacKeith, R. and Bax, M. (eds.), *Studies of Infancy*, London, Heineman Med. Books.

Richards, M. P. M. and Bernal, J. F. (1972). 'An observational study of mother-infant interaction', in Blurton-Jones, N. (ed.), *Ethological Studies of Child Behaviour*, Cambridge, C. U. P.

Richards, M. P. M., Dunn, J. F. and Antonis, B. (1977). 'Caretaking in the first year of life: the role of fathers' and mothers' social isolation', *Child: Care, Health and Development*, **3**, 23–36.

Riley, E. M. D. (1977). 'What do women want?—the question of "choice" in the conduct of labour', in Chard, T. and Richards, M. P. M. (eds.), *Hazards of the New Obstetrics*,

London, SIMP.

Robson, K. S. (1967). 'The role of eye-to-eye contact in maternal–infant attachment', *J. Child Psychol. Psychiat.*, **8**, 13–25.

Robson, K., Pederson, F. and Moss, H. (1969). 'Developmental observations of diadic gazing in relation to fear of strangers and social approach behaviour', *Child Develop.*, **40**, (2), 619–627.

Robson, K. S. and Moss, H. A. (1970). 'Patterns and determinants of maternal attachment', *J. Pediatrics.*, **77**, 976–985.

Rosenthal, M. (1973). 'The study of infant–environment interaction: some comments on trends and methodologies', *J. Child Psychol. Psychiat.*, **14**, 301–317.

Ryan, J. (1974). 'Early language development: towards a communicational analysis', in Richards, M. P. M. (ed.), *The Integration of a Child Into a Social World*, Cambridge, C. U. P.

Sameroff, A. J. (1975). 'Early influences on development: fact or fancy?', *M. P. Q.*, **21**, (4), 267–294.

Sander, L. W. (1969). 'The longitudinal course of early mother–child interaction', in Foss, B. M. (ed.), *Determinants of Infant Behaviour*, London, Methuen.

Sander, L. W., Stechler, G., Burns, P. and Julia, H. (1970). Early mother–infant interaction and twenty-four-hour patterns of activity and sleep', *J. Amer. Acad. of Child Psychiat*, 103–123.

Scanlon, J. W. (1973). 'How is the baby? The Apgar score revisited', *Clinic Pediat.*, **12**, 61.

Scanlon, J. W. (1974). 'Obstetric anesthesia as a neonatal risk factor in normal labour and delivery', *Clinics in Perinatology*, **1**, (2), 465–482.

Scanlon, J. W., Brown, W. U., Weiss, J. B. and Alper, M. H. (1974). 'Neurobehavioral responses of newborn infants after maternal epidural anesthesia', *Anesthesiology*, **40**, (2), 121–128.

Schacter, J., Elmer, E., Ragins, N. and Wimberly, F. (1977). 'Assessment of mother–infant interaction: schizophrenic and non-schizophrenic mothers', *M. P. Q.* **23**, (3), 193–206.

Schaffer, R. (1977). *Mothering*, London, Fontana.

Schaffer, H. R. (ed.) (1977a). *Interactions in Infancy: the Loch Lomond Symposium*, London, Academic Press.

Schaffer, H. R. and Emerson, P. E. (1964). 'The development of social attachments in infancy', *Mon. Soc. Res. Child Develop.*, **29**, (94).

Schutz, A. and Luckman, T. (1974). *The Structures of the Life World*, London, Heineman.

Seashore, M. J., Leifer, A. D., Barnett, C. R. and Leiderman, P. H. (1973). 'The effects of denial of early mother–infant interaction on maternal self-confidence', *J. Pers. and Soc. Psychol.*, **26**, (3), 369–378.

Snow, C. (1977). 'The development of conversation between mothers and babies' *J. Child Lang.*, **4**, 1–22.

Sontag, L. W. (1941). 'Significnace of foetal environmental differences', *Am. J. Obs. Gyn.*, **42**, 996–1003.

Sostek, A. M. and Anders, T. F. (1977). 'Relationships among the Brazelton Neonatal Scale, Bayley Infant Scales, and early temperament', *Child Develop.*, **48**, 320–323.

Stern, D. N. (1971). 'A micro-analysis of mother-infant interaction behavior regulating social contact between a mother and three-and-a-half month-old twins', *J. Am. Acad. Child Psychiat.*, **10**, 501–517.

Stern, D. (1974). 'The goal and structure of mother–infant play', *J. Am. Acad. Child Psychiat.*, **13**, 402–421.

Stern, E., Parmelee, A., Akiyama, Y., Schultz, M. Z., and Wenner, W. H. (1969). 'Sleep cycle characteristics in infants', *Pediatrics*, **43**, 65–70.

Stratton, P. M. (1977). 'Criteria for assessing the influence of obstetric circumstances on later development', On Chard, T. and M. Richards (eds.) Hazards of the New Obstetrics, SIMP.

Swoboda, P. J. (1976). 'Continuous vowel discrimination in normal and at risk infants', *Child Develop.*, **47**, 459–465.

Thalme, B., Belerage, P. and Raabe, N. (1974). 'Lumbar epidural analgesia in labour', *Acta Obstet. Gyn. Scand.*, **53**, 27–35.

Theorell, K., Prechtl, H. F. R., Blair, A. W. and Lind, J. (1973). 'Behavioural state cycles of normal newborn infants', *Dev. Med. and Child Neurol.*, **15**, 597–605.

Thoman, E. B. (1975). 'Sleep and wake behaviours in neonates: consistencies and consequences', *M. P. Q.* **21**, (4), 295–314.

Thoman, E. B., Leiderman, H. P. and Olson, J. P. (1972). 'Neonate–mother interaction during breast-feeding', *Develop. Psychol.*, **6**, 110–118.

Thomas, A., Chess, S. and Birch, H. G. (1969). *Temperament and Behavior Disorders in Children*, New York, NY U Press.

Thomas, A., Chess, S., Birch, H. G., Hertzig, M. E. and Korn, S. (1963). *Behavioral Individuality in Early Childhood*, New York, NY U Press.

Trevarthern, C. (1975). 'Les activites innes du nourisson', *La Recherche*, **6**, 447–458.

Tronick, E., Koslowski, B. and Brazelton, T. B. (1973). *Neonatal behavior among urban Zambians and Americans*, Unpublished paper.

Tronick, E., Wise, S., Als, H., Adamson, L., Scanlon, J. W. and Brazelton, T. B. (1976). 'Regional obstetric anesthetic and newborn behavior: effect over the first 10 days of life', *Pediatrics*, **58**, 94–100.

Turner, B. K. (1956). 'The syndrome in the infant resulting from maternal emotional tension during pregnancy', *Med. J. Australia*, **1**, 222–223.

Uzgiris, I. C. and Hunt, J. M. V. (1975). *Towards Ordinal Scales of Psychological Development in Infancy*, Illinois, U. Illinois Press.

Vulliamy, D. G. (1972). *The Newborn Child*, London, Churchill.

White, B. (1971). *Human Infants*, New Jersey, Prentice-Hall.

White, B., Castle, P. and Held, R. (1964). 'Observations on the development of visually directed reaching', *Child Develop.*, **35**, 349–364.

Wilcox, B. M. (1969). 'Visual preferences of human infants for representations of the human face', *J. Exp. Child Psychol.*, **7**, 10–20.

Wingate, M. B., Wingate, L., Iffy, L., Freundlich, J. and Gottsgen, D. (1974). 'The effect of epidural analgesic upon foetal and neonatal status', *Am. J. Obst. Gyn.*, 1102–1106.

Wolff, P. H. (1966). *The Causes, Controls, and Organisation of Behaviour in the Neonate*, New York, Internat. U. Press.

Wolff, P. H. (1968). 'The serial organization of sucking in the young infant', *Pediatrics*, **42**, 943–956.

Wolff, P. H. (1969). 'The natural history of crying and other vocalizations in infancy', in B. M. Foss (ed.), *Determinants of Infant Behaviour*, vol. **4**. London, Methuen.

Woodson, R. and Woodson, E. daCosta (1977). Paper in preparation.

Wortis, R. P. (1971). 'The acceptance of the concept of maternal role by behavioral scientists: its effects on women', *Am. J. Orthopsychiatry*, **41**, 733–745.

Yang, R. K., Zweigg, R., Donthitt, T. and Federman, E. J. (1976). 'Successive relationships between maternal attitudes during pregnancy, analgesic medication during labour and delivery, and newborn behavior', *Develop. Psychol.*, **12**, 6–14.

Chapter 2

Effects on Development of Medical Interventions and the Separation of Newborns from their Parents

M.P.M. Richards

The last decade has seen an extraordinary growth of interest among the relevant professions, and more generally, in the initial formation of the social relationship between parents and children and in the possible consequences of separation of infants at or soon after birth for their subsequent development. My main aim in this chapter is to discuss the available evidence about the consequences of early separation for children and their parents and to suggest ways in which the negative consequences can be reduced or removed. However, to do this, I think it is essential to set the current discussion of early separation in the context of our changing attitudes towards parents and children. I will begin by attempting to trace some of the reasons for the increasing emphasis on the neonatal period.

The extent to which our attitudes about the earliest stage of our children's lives have changed is well illustrated by the following quotation from Ribble written in the mid 1950s.

In our twentieth-century culture the first years of a child's life are rarely thought of as a period of vital significance for his mental development. The decisive role of parents in promoting the first stage of psychological growth is seldom recognised. Young parents themselves do not usually consider this phase of their lives as one of special psychological creativeness, during which they observe and take a dynamic part in the personality development of their children. On the contrary, there is an unfortunate and widely held concept of those years as being predominantly a time of sacrifice and deprivation, a time to be lived through gracefully or met with fortitude and gotten over.

Ribble, 1955, pp. 6–7.

Of course, Ribble was not alone in the 1950s in urging greater attention to the neonatal period and the first few months of life. Similar sentiments can be found in the writings of Winnicott (e.g. 1958), for example. But what is significant is that, despite the arguments put forward by these writers who were influential in many other ways, there was very little general interest in this aspect of their work.

For those of us professionally concerned with research or practice relating to parents and children it is natural to assume that the changes in attitudes have been brought about by our own research and teaching, but I think this is only partly true. Certainly ideas that originate within the professional community can have very wide influence. But ideas require a receptive climate for their acceptance, and what we have to understand is why the emphasis on the neonatal period gains a much readier acceptance today both within and outside the professional community.

A major factor in changing attitudes is the enormous change in medical practice that has occurred over the last few decades. Both obstetric and paediatric practice have altered in ways which have produced a strong reaction in patients.

Before the advent of the National Health Service in Britain there was very little special provision for sick or preterm infants; few doctors, nurses or midwives specialized in their care and there was little that scientific medicine could offer as a basis for practice. Today all this has changed. Neonatology is now a recognized subspeciality within paediatrics and there have been very significant advances in the understanding of neonatal physiology. Many of the conditions that were invariably fatal for small or sick babies are now routinely soluble problems. Neonatology has created its specialized (and centralized) institutions of the special care and intensive care baby units. The proportion of the recent decline in perinatal mortality that is attributable directly to changing medical practice has come about largely through the improved prognosis for small and preterm babies.

But these improvements in mortality have been bought at some cost because they involve an assumption about the ways in which care for babies is to be provided that ignores their social relationships. The effects of this assumption may damage babies and their parents. When specialized care for newborns was first being developed infection was a major problem and it was taken for granted that babies should be isolated from all but medical and nursing staff. Though today we now understand that the risk of infection from parents and sibling *is* minimal and the infections themselves are much more readily treatable, the belief about the need for isolation still persists.

Neonatology is characterized, by and large, by what Thomas McKeown (1965) has aptly called the engineering approach to medicine. Illness and disease are seen as disordered physiology, malfunctioning machinery to be repaired. Physiological functions are closely monitored, nowadays almost always by electronic devices. All the vital physiological needs, for warmth, for oxygen, for food are closely controlled—again, often by mechanical devices. In the incubator among the tubes and wires of the monitoring devices the baby is lost as a social being, to her or himself and to his parents. The baby is lost to him or herself because the first step in developing autonomy and so a social self depends on the association in time between the expression of changing need and their satisfaction by a caretaker. This requires caretakers who get to know a baby's individual patterns and are ready and able to phase their behaviour with that of the baby. These conditions are seldom satisfied in a special care nursery. Not only are the baby's needs often ignored but large number of different caretakers are usually involved. Prince, Firlej and Harvey (1978) have shown that the crying of babies in incubators was often not responded to and feeding schedules in special care nurseries are almost always determined by the clock. A Canadian study (Minde and coworkers, 1975) found that up to 71 nurses might care for a baby during a stay in a special care nursery.

Though these attitudes of the engineering approach may have seen their greatest development in the intensive care unit, similar changes have occurred in obstetrics in the treatment of both healthy women and healthy babies. The place of birth has shifted from home to hospital and among hospitals towards the consultant obstetric unit (Davis and Kitzinger, 1978). Routine induction and acceleration of labour and administration of anaesthetics and analgesics have robbed parents of the remaining control they have had over the birth of their children. They have become the passive recipients of obstetric management based almost entirely on physiological criteria (Chard and Richards, 1977).

It is not surprising, in the face of these fundamental shifts in medical practice, that there have been attempts by parents to regain control of their own care and to retain responsibility for that given to their children. These attempts have taken place in a context of changing attitudes to medicine in general. The optimism of the 1950s and early 1960s has passed as it has become clear that scientific medicine is unable to solve many current problems and that many of its apparent solutions carry large costs in terms of drug 'side' effects, unnecessary treatments, the medicalization of non-medical concerns and a reduction in control by patients. Complaints about maternity care have been particularly prominent in the growing critique of medicine and there are now several patient pressure groups active in the field. The interest in the area is also shown by the growing number of critical books, articles and programmes on television and radio. What is significant about current lay critiques is that they have gone much further than the earlier demands for humane treatment and have called into question the effectiveness of many practices (e.g. the induction of labour) and have stressed the iatrogenic problems. They have emphasized the divide between medical care in the tradition of the engineering approach and the psychological and social needs of patients.

But reactions to changes in medical practice are only part of the story. This is particularly apparent in the USA where the recent reactions to obstetric and paediatric practice have, if anything, gone much further than in Britain; this in spite of the fact that the engineering approach, especially in obstetrics, had become dominant there several decades ago. Even in the 1950s in the United States a 'normal' delivery of a low risk mother might involve her being restrained throughout labour in the lithotomy position, feet in stirrups and arms strapped to the delivery table, deep in 'twilight sleep', and a baby born by forceps. The mother would be lucky to catch more than a glimpse of her baby for the first 48 hours and after this all contacts were (and often still are) rigidly restricted and controlled by hospital routines. So while in Britain the demands for a new approach to maternity and neonatal care have grown in parallel with the increasing domination of the engineering approach, the same explanation cannot apply in the USA.

At least two other factors are probably important. These are the so-called counter culture of the late 1960s and the rise of the women's movement. Both these, in rather different ways, have led to changing attitudes to childbirth and to children. Among the many manifestations of the 1960s counter culture was the idea that experience and feeling should be accepted and lived through rather than avoided or ignored. The common cry was to 'get into your feelings'. As this generation has had its children these ideas have been applied to childbirth and child rearing. From the late 1960s onwards some of these values have found expression in a whole series of birth books produced in the USA and widely circulated there and in Europe. Several of these combine the values of the counter culture with a critique of medical practice often based on the supposedly 'natural' features of childbirth in other cultures and at earlier points in history. This same 'back-to-nature' theme may be found in books on childcare which urge such things as the continual holding of babies or the family sharing the same bed. A general feature of the birth books is the espousal of home birth, and birth as an experience to be shared among relatives and friends. This has found practical expression in the growth of American lay midwifery and the setting up of birth centres, at first outside, but now also within, the traditional medical institutions.

At some points the arguments and demands arising from the counter cultural tradition run parallel with those coming from the women's movement, but ideologically the two are very separate. Feminists have often argued for, and practised, medical self-help, and have tried to counter the 'mystification' of professional medicine by spreading information about female physiology and experience. A few years ago this tended to concentrate on sexual conduct, contraception and abortion, but increasingly the concern is with childbirth and childrearing. Here the main claims are for women to have control over their own bodies and for choice in childbirth (and recognition of the lack of choice offered by professional medicine). Feminist attitudes toward children are much more varied and often stand in contradiction to those found in the birth books. This can be seen over the issue of the use of analgesics and anaesthetics in labour. The more extreme back-to-nature position is to deny any role to such drugs while some feminists have called for the availability of drugs 'on request' and have dismissed the evidence of the ill effects of most of the commonly-used drugs on babies as a further manifestation of patriarchal values being forced upon women.

These changes in society at large have had their influence on developmental psychology, which in turn has had effects in the wider world. Two shifts within developmental psychology have had particular consequences for the problems of early separation. The first is the gradual rejection of Bowlby's theory of attachment as the guiding principle for studies of parent–child relationships. Bowlby's concern was for the consequences of separation on the child after an attachment had been formed. As this formation was thought to take about six months, by implication early separation was of little consequence and there was no theoretical reason for its investigation. As criticism of this theoretical view has grown, the scope of investigations has enlarged to include the earliest phase of the infant's social relationships. The other important shift in developmental pychology has been the rediscovery of the varied abilities of young infants and an appreciation of what is often referred to as their 'competence'. This has led to a position where it is no longer possible to consider the needs of babies simply in terms of their physiological requirements and has placed renewed emphasis on their social worlds.

Earlier research on parent–child relationships within the Bowlby paradigm has been replaced by work on the developing systems of communication between infants and adults (Richards, 1974; Stern, 1977; Newson Chapter 5, and Jones Chapter 10, this volume) often by detailed analysis of face-to-face interaction situations. Some of these studies have been extended to include sick and preterm infants, (Field, 1977). This research has provided a strong impetus to study the first encounter of parents with their babies and so has drawn attention to the conditions under which these occur. However, in other ways it has been less useful as a background for the consideration of early separation. In particular, as in the earlier attachment work, the psychology of parents is largely ignored and accounts of their feelings and experiences are usually absent in descriptions of the early interactions. Most of the research is very behaviourist in methodology if not in underlying theory. This absence of the discussion of parental feelings has created a theoretical vacuum for practitioners responsible for the care of parents and children. In response to this, a working notion which does not really find any reflection in contemporary research work has been created around the concept of bonding. The term itself is apparently derived from the work of Winnicott, but its meaning today is rather different from his meaning. The contemporary idea of bonding is of a process by which the parents (though usually only the mother is considered) become attached to their newborn. The general assumption is that this process occurs in the first few days of life and, if it is disrupted, there are long-term consequences for the child's social relationships and development in general. In effect, Bowlby's notion of attachment has been given a new name and has been transposed to a much earlier phase in development. It is clear that despite the wide currency of the term bonding, the notion has little theoretical basis.

Klaus and Kennell (1976), who have been largely responsible for the recent promotion of the term bonding, attempt to provide a theoretical framework which is largely based on analogies with the behaviour of newly natched chicks and newborn goats. This kind of argument not only suffers all the usual difficulties of using animal models for human behaviour (see Bernal and Richards, 1973) but ignores the information which we do have on the psychological development of parenthood. As I shall discuss below, this latter evidence may be used to understand and extend the research on early separation.

RESEARCH ON EARLY SEPARATION

Against this background a number of studies have been undertaken in which the progress of groups of separated and non-separated infants and their mothers are compared. The first study was carried out in Cleveland by Klaus and Kennell (1976) but this has been followed by other studies in the USA (e.g. Seashore and coworkers, 1973; Field, 1977), Sweden (de Chateau and Winberg, 1977), Britain (Whiten, 1977) and Latin America (Hales and coworkers, 1977). I have reviewed this research in detail elsewhere (1978) so will only give a brief account here.

These studies have employed varying lengths of separation (from a couple of hours at delivery to several days): they have examined full-term and preterm babies, and social groups as different as American black welfare mothers lacking any proper antenatal care and English middle-class samples. In some the 'contact' mothers (those not separated or only suffering minimal separation) have been given an opportunity to hold their babies with skin-to-skin contact at birth while in other studies they have simply been permitted to visit their children in special care nurseries. But despite these numerous differences and the methodological problems of research in a field like this, the finding of all the studies are broadly similar. Most report changes in the patterns of mother–infant interaction in the first few months after reunion but these, in general, seem to wane, so that by a year they have disappeared or are at least minimal. The main changes in interaction that have been found after separation are a reduction in face-to-face interaction, in affectionate holding, kissing and talking, and close attention to the baby during a paediatric examination. In addition several studies found a reduction in the mother's confidence in her own ability to cope adequately with her baby after discharge from hospital, and reduced success in lactation.

In general, these studies have concentrated on the behavioural characteristics that can be observed in interaction situations: very little attention has been paid to the attitudes and feelings of mothers, and the role of fathers has been almost completely ignored.

Apart from one with a very small sample none of these studies provides any long term follow up. The best data here come from Douglas's follow up of the 1948 national cohort. He found (1975) that hospital admissions in the first six months had much less marked effects than later. But he did note that 'unstable job-patterns among children admitted for a week or less in the first six months were at the same level as those with no admissions, but were raised among children who stayed longer than a week'. In another paper Douglas and Gear (1976) report the findings of investigations carried out at 13 and 15 years on the low birth weight children (< 2000 g) in his sample. Overall the low birth weight children tended to do worse in terms of social adjustment and congnitive development than matched control normal birth weight children. However, the difference only reached statistical significance for the school teachers' rating of nervousness. Comparisons were made of the low birth weight children born and reared at home with those born in hospital (who we may assume suffered more separation). There was a tendency for those born at home to be rated as more nervous and more troublesome by teachers than those born in hospital. Anxiety and shyness has been noticed in other follow-up studies of low birth weight children but it has been suggested (Blake, Stewart and Turcan, 1975) that the incidence of such problems has been reduced since parents were given freer access to children in special care units.

There are of course many follow-up studies of preterm, small for dates and other sick or malformed children (e.g. Drillien, 1964). Most of these show effects persisting through development (though such effects interact strongly with the social conditions of rearing) but it is impossible to say how far such effects are due to early separation, which will be common and often prolonged for such babies or to their neonatal condition.

There are also a number of retrospective studies of various conditions which probably involve altered patterns of parent–child relationships. These have been shown to be more common after perinatal complications that are likely to entail early separation, and include 'failure to thrive' (Shaheen and coworkers, 1968; Fanaroff, Kennell and Klaus, 1972), non-accidental injury (Klein and Stern, 1971; Lynch, 1975) and sudden unexpected death in infancy (Fedrick, 1974). However, it is not clear from these studies that the separation was (or was not) in any way causally related to the later problem. Similarly, Fanaroff and his coworkers (1972) found a marked correlation between frequency of parental visiting and telephone calls to the special care unit during separation and subsequent child abuse. But again it is not clear whether the low rate of visiting of the subsequently abusive parents was an expression of the disturbed relationship with their babies or whether it contributed to the disturbance (or both).

There is another group of studies which have investigated the effects of extra stimulation (e.g. pattern light and music, rocking water beds, extra handling from nurses) on babies in special care units. The general finding (e.g. Kramer and Pierpont, 1976) is that stimulation increases growth rates and develop-mental progress as measured by a neonatal examination. It is difficult to know how to interpret these findings. The general theoretical orientation of those who have carried out these experiments is based on research with rodent species. This has demonstrated that under certain conditions handling and stress soon after birth will accelerate growth and sexual maturity and may enhance performance in some learning situations. In rats and mice these effects appear to be mediated through stimulation of the adrenal hormone system and changed maternal behaviour. We do have human evidence that growth rates may vary with parental behaviour (Pollit, Gilmore and Valcarcel, 1978), and accelerated growth and maturation might account for the better scores in neonatal examinations in the studies with premature babies. It is also possible that a Hawthorn effect may be operating so that the stimulated babies receive more caretaking and perhaps more food. How any of these effects may be influenced by parental visiting is not clear as the appropriate studies remain to be done.

To summarize the empirical work: we have good reason to think that early separation changes patterns of maternal–infant interaction for at least some months and that it reduces maternal confidence. Longer term effects are more doubtful but on general grounds it seems quite likely that in combination with other post-natal adverse factors, long term effects can occur.

How do we explain these effects? To simplify the discussion I am not going to consider direct effects of separation on the infant (of the kind found in the stimulation studies). Though these must always be kept in mind, I think it is much more important to discuss the effects of separation on parents as these are likely to be much more potent in producing long term effects on infants than brief neonatal events.

Recent research does not support the idea that brief episodes are likely to have long term direct effects on infants or children and the frequent attempts to find support for various sensitive periods in development have been largely unsuccessful (q.v. Rutter, 1972). However, it is much more plausible to argue that single events can have relatively long-lasting effects on parental attitudes behaviour towards their children and that such events are likely to be particularly potent during the period when adults are making the transition to parenthood and are first evolving a mode of initiation and response to their babies. As styles of parenthood and caretaking will have a profound effect on a child's development single events acting via the parents' attitudes and behaviour could have very important long term effects for children.

Klaus and Kennell have suggested that early separation produces its effects because the mother is denied contact with her baby during a period when she is particularly sensitive to her baby, and that this period lasts for only a matter of hours after delivery. As I have mentioned already the theoretical basis for their claim is drawn from research with animals. But as Winnicott (1958) has stated 'the study of the mother needs to be rescued from the purely biological'. It is my intention to use the work of Winnicott and others to attempt this exercise and to provide an explanation of early separation effects in terms of parental psychology.

Current work on parental relationships is of minimal help in the discussion of early separation because it is so little concerned with the psychology of parents or parenthood. Indeed the problem of separation shows up the urgent need to build such a psychology upon the foundations laid by workers like Winnicott. In the paper I have just quoted, Winnicott puts forward his notion of 'primary maternal preoccupation'. 'It is my thesis that in the earliest phase we are dealing with a very special state of the mother, a psychological condition which deserves a name, such as *Primary Maternal Preoccupation.* I suggest that sufficient tribute has not yet been paid in our literature, or perhaps anywhere, to a special psychiatric condition of the mother, of which I would say the following things:

It gradually develops and becomes a state of heightened sensitivity during, and especially toward the end of, the pregnancy.

It lasts for a few weeks after the birth of the child. It is not easily remembered by mothers once they have recovered from it.

I would go further and say that the memory mothers have of this state tends to become repressed.'

'I do not believe that it is possible to understand the functioning of the mother at the very beginning of the infant's life without seeing that she must be able to reach this state of heightened sensitivity, almost an illness, and to recover from it. (I bring in the word 'illness' because a woman must be healthy in order both to develop this state and to recover from it as the infant releases her. If the infant should die, the mother's state suddenly shows up as illness. The mother takes this risk.)'

Winnicott described the devotion to and identification with the baby that occurs in this phase to the exclusion of other interests, 'in a way that is temporary and normal'.

'The mother who develops this state ... provides a setting for the infant's constitution to begin to make itself evident, for the developmental tendencies to start to unfold, and for the infant to experience spontaneous movement and become the owner of the sensations that are appropriate to this early phase of life.'

'Only if a mother is sensitized in the way I am describing can she feel herself into her infant's place, and so meet the infant's needs. These are at first body-needs, and they gradually become ego-needs as a psychology emerges out of the imaginative elaboration of physical experience.'

'There comes into existence an ego-relatedness between mother and baby, from which the mother recovers, and out of which the infant may eventually build the idea of a person in the mother. From this angle the recognition of the mother as a person comes in a positive way, normally, and not out of the experience of the mother as the symbol of frustration. The mother's failure to adapt in the earliest phase does not produce anything but an annihilation of the infant's self.'

I have quoted from Winnicott at some length because he is one of the few theorists who have given serious consideration to what happens to the mother in the initial phase of her relationship with her child and he provides us with a position from which we may begin to understand what happens in early separation. Like other psychoanalytic writers Winnicott also stresses the continuity of the various phases of the reproductive cycle and the way in which each phase is created from the earlier one. This is elaborated in detail by Deutch (1947). She describes how the fantasized image of the child developed during the later part of pregnancy becomes modified and transformed by the first contacts with the baby after delivery as the mother moves into the primary maternal preoccupation. The fantasy children created during pregnancy often include both idealizations and fears of abnormality and malformation.

The ideal conditions for successful negotiation of these phases involve a continuity of support from the father and/or other relatives and friends, and a period of unhurried calm after delivery in which the mother can explore and get to know the baby. The latter opportunity is also needed by the father so that he is able to develop an identification with the baby which can from the basis of the primary paternal preoccupation. The reality of a normal delivery and post partum care in an average maternity hospital is likely to be very far from these ideal condtions; when the baby is small and/or sick and separated from the parents through admission to a special care unit conditions may be so far from the ideal as to create a crisis which could have very long term effects on the parent's view of their child.

When a delivery goes badly and a baby has medical problems the worst fears of pregnancy may seem to be realized. It is not surprising therefore that the birth of a low birthweight baby can represent a severe emotional crisis (Caplan, Mason and Kaplan, 1965). Though at present the evidence is largely anecdotal, similar reactions may occur with other kinds of abnormal births (see Klaus and Kennell, 1976). Another factor that may increase the parents' distress is that they may feel guilty that things they have done are the cause of the abnormal birth. If one assumes that any admission to a special care unit, as well as the birth of a low birth weight or malformed baby is likely to confirm the parent's fears, about one in five of all deliveries in Britain is abnormal from the parents' point of view.

The crucial question concerns the effect of separation from the baby in this already fraught situation. Most studies tend to see parental visiting of babies in special care units solely in terms of its possible influence for the development of the child. But as Minde and his colleagues (1975) have pointed out, it can also be seen as an indication of the degree to which parents have resolved their fears and conflicts over an abnormal birth and are able to begin the phase of identification with their baby. Where parents' access to their newborns is limited or completely removed, we can hypothesize that their whole attitude and response to the baby may be changed by a number of processes.

As we have seen, there is good evidence that a separated mother is less likely to feel confident in being able to look after her baby. This is hardly surprising because when a baby is removed from a mother, she is in effect being told that she is incapable of caring for her baby, and that this care must be entrusted to experts. It may be days or even weeks before a mother or father gets a chance to be alone with their baby and, in any sense, to get to know him or her. The continuity of the stages of pregnancy, delivery and the lying-in period is broken.

Many parents comment that they did not really feel that the baby belonged to them until he or she was discharged home from the special care unit. If 'owner-ship' (or the opportunity for the growth of devotion and identification) is deter-mined by who has responsibility for the baby's care, parents are obviously correct in their perceptions. The lack of opportunity to get to know the baby and take responsibility for his or her care are likely to increase these feelings of not belonging.

When a baby spends more than a few days in a special care unit, the mother is likely to be discharged home without him. Many parents find this a very difficult period. Friends and relatives (as well as the parents themselves) will expect the mother to return home with a baby. Parents may become very distressed at the frequent need to provide explanations of what has happened. If the mother is at home for an extended period without her baby, she may tend to resume a life that does not make provision for a new baby. When her baby does eventually arrive home, it may be relatively difficult to make 'space' for him or her. Or to put it in Winnicott's terms, the special conditions of the post partum period may pass without the mother having an opportunity to become preoccupied with her baby. Even when regular visiting is possible for parents, this may not be sufficient either to create parental identification with the baby or to hold the parents' feelings in 'cold storage' until the baby is with them.

When guilt is attached to the birth of a less than perfect baby by the parents, the removal of the baby may be seen as a punishment and this, in turn, can become translated into resentment directed towards the baby. Separation also can allow the conversion of the fantasized child of pregnancy into a grotesque monster and parents may then stay away from their baby for fear of having their fantasies confirmed. Often when the baby is seen there is a sense of relief that the baby is not as bad as they feared. Several units now provide parents with photographs of their separated babies, and these do seem to reduce the more fearful fantasies and at least provide a realistic image for identification.

It seems likely that fathers may have a particular part to play in coping with the crisis that so often marks the birth and postnatal period of a baby who requires treatment in a special or intensive care nursery. In many cases, as for example, when a mother is recovering from a caesarian section, a father may be in a better position than a mother to visit the baby frequently and to take primary responsibility for caretaking. ·A father's initial responses to the baby may often suffer less than those of a mother from the feelings of guilt that can attend an abnormal birth. Furthermore, fathers, in general, are less intimidated by the machinery and clinical atmosphere typical of a special care unit. However, at the same time their caretaking can be inhibited by the still widely held belief that the care of babies is the business of women. This often seems to cause them to hold back from close involvement and to become self-doubting in their ability to provide adequate care. In overcoming these doubts the attitude of staff in special care units can be crucial. All too often, though father's visiting may be encouraged, his role as a caretaker is not taken very seriously. He is expected to show his pride and concern for his child, but from a distance and the particular problems of fatherhood are seldom appreciated. In a study of parental visiting in a special care nursery (Hawthorne, Richards and Callon, 1978) it was found that a significant minority of fathers did become very involved in the care of their sick or preterm children and it was the observers' impression that in these cases the mothers had an easier time than those whose spouses had remained more distant. There is also much anecdotal evidence to suggest that where a father becomes deeply involved in care in the postnatal period his heightened interest tends to persist, to the benefit of all family members. Or to describe it in Winnicott's terms, where fathers have the opportunity and support to develop their devotion and identification with their newborn children, they may be much more likely to remain involved and caring parents.

Part of the expectations built up by parents during pregnancy may include an idealized image of the baby. This is likely to be of the chubby full-term variety so prominent in the baby food advertisements before the dangers of overfeeding were taken seriously. If parents have an image of this kind, the sight of a low birth weight or malformed baby could be very upsetting, especially if it is enclosed in an incubator and attached to several wires and tubes. In situations like this, the initial contact can be very difficult for parents, but we have been surprised how quickly, with frequent visiting and sensitive support, parents seem to be able to accept their baby as he or she is. Of course, for a few babies there is a real question about their survival and general prognosis. Even where a baby has subsequently died, many parents seem to be glad to have seen and handled their child. In a few cases parents do not wish to have close contact until they are sure that their baby will survive. Here nothing is likely to be gained by forcing the issue.

It is not simply the appearance of preterm or sick babies that may increase difficulties for parents, the relative disorganization of their behaviour may make close identification more problematic. State change may be very rapid and erratic and these babies are often much slower to develop regular cycles of waking, sleeping and feeding. They often do not show the extended period of quiet attention immediately after delivery which is characteristic of healthy newborns so that, even without separation, it may take parents much longer to develop a sense of knowing their baby and being confident in their ability to recognize his or her needs correctly.

What I hope these brief comments will make clear is that there is every reason to expect that early separation (not say a 'normal' hospital delivery) can have an effect on the initial adaptation process of parents to their newborn and this in itself is enough reason for those responsible for maternity and neonatal care to reduce separation to the barest minimum compatible with good physical care. However, we must also acknowledge that parents, like babies, have immense powers of recuperation and adaptation. Every early separation would not be expected to create a life-long disarrangement of the parent–child relationships. However, recuperation does require a positive and supportive environment, and where separation is coupled with other problems we may expect more persistent difficulties.

An important point which has yet to receive detailed consideration is the variable effects of early separation. Why do some parents and children come through the most adverse and difficult circumstances unscathed while others seem to be profoundly affected by much more benign situations? The obvious direction to look for the origins of the variations in parental capacities for recovery and recuperation is to the parents' own childhood and relationships with their own parents. As an hypothesis, it seems reasonable to suggest that a childhood which provided support for growing autonomy and open emotional relationships with both parents is most likely to provide the most secure basis for the transition to parenthood and the greatest resistance to early separation and other adverse situations. In addition, social and emotional support at the time of the adversity is likely to be important.

We must also guard against the possibility of creating the expectation for parents of persistent difficulties after separation. Here we have the danger of self-fulfilling prophecies. Also, there is perhaps the temptation of overdramatizing the possible effects of separation, in the hope that this will bring about a more rapid change in obstetric and paediatric practice. But even without any evidence of persisting ill effects of separation, I think there are very good reasons for changing practice if only because parents, in general, resent and dislike separation. It is they who carry responsibility for their children and this is a good enough reason for trying to arrange things in ways that meet their needs.

It would be too simple to believe that the problems arising from early separation would be minimized if parents were granted free access to their babies in all special care nurseries though this of course, would be a desirable first step. Much more important is the general atmosphere of maternity hospitals and special care units and, in particular, the needs of parents to retain a sense of responsibility for their children, to feel that they can exercise genuine choice in how they are to be cared for and to find peace and privacy in which to get to know their children and build their social relationships with them. We should not underestimate the extent of changes required to achieve this and the demands that it will make on all professional staff concerned. Parents' complaints about the treatment they and their babies receive are often explained by positing a 'lack of communication'. However, to accept this would be a trivialization of the problem and would be to ignore the overwhelming influnece of complex social institutions like hospitals with their hierarchical structures and the commitment of staff to physical care on relationships between parents and children. Reducing these influences will be very difficult.

There are two problems that deserve particular attention. First, there is the question of hospital routines. Clearly, complex institutions like hospitals will run more smoothly if all patients do the same thing at the same time. But the effect of enforced routines may have a profound influence on patients. Individuality, and so a sense of self, is likely to be reduced. If one is not allowed retain responsibility for oneself, it becomes more difficult to develop responsisibility for someone else—especially a strange and demanding newborn. This is an area in which the aim must be to allow for as wide individual choice as possible. Some mothers will appreciate the freedom from responsibility that a hospital stay can provide while others will find the subjugation to routine exhausting and demoralising.

The second point is closely related and concerns the attitudes of staff to maternity patients. Here the need is for support which does not damage self-confidence. Too often attempts to provide this result in a style of care that essentially infantilizes the patients. At worst mothers are treated as ungrateful and recalcitrant children who are unable to know what is best for themselves. This kind of atmosphere offers no support at all for adults who are making the transition to parenthood.

To offer the kind of care that is required in a maternity hospital makes great demands on staff and raises problems that go far beyond issues of technical expertise. Deep feelings and conflicts may be aroused for the staff and opportunities need to be created where these can be expressed and examined.

Treatment in maternity hospitals is governed by the principle that control and intervention are always necessary in case things go wrong. Or to put it in terms of the usual obstetric cliché, a delivery is only normal in retrospect and a potential disaster in prospect. Such a view is an obvious consequence of the engineering approach to medicine. Somehow this must be replaced by the view that every delivery is normal until complications are apparent and that the medical needs in the narrow sense of a normal delivery and lying-in period are minimal and certainly should not be an overriding factor in the organization of care. As one distinguished obstetrician has put it, the most valuable thing every obstetrician has to learn is to stand with his hands in his pockets. We need to develop a system of 'potential' medical assistance where the social and psychological needs of parents and babies remain paramount. Just because a proportion of deliveries are abnormal and require extensive intervention, we must not let an interventionist approach predominate for the majority. Such a situation would be unlike that which predominates in hospital medicine, and would require large changes in attitudes in doctors, midwives and nurses. The caring and non-invasive support role which is required from staff makes great psychological demands and there will be constant tendencies to avoid it and to reduce it to the exercise of technical skills on a routine basis premised on the supposed physiological or medical needs of mothers and babies. In order to stand against these pressures to allow the engineering approach to dominate, staff themselves will need emotional and psychological support. There is much that could be learnt from the kinds of supports for professional staff that have been developed elsewhere (e.g. in social work) where similar problems arise.

There is much that is unsatisfactory in the present organization of special and intensive care for babies (Brimblecombe, Richards and Roberton, 1978). Present admission policies for special care units mean that nationally a large proportion of the babies admitted are healthy and do not require the kinds of treatments that are only available in these units. A modification of admission (and discharge) policies so that only the babies likely to benefit medically spend time in these units is likely to almost halve the current admission rates (Richards and Roberton, 1978) and would make an enormous reduction in the current extent of separation. Changes in booking policies are needed and we must ensure that except in exceptional circumstances mothers and babies are always cared for in the same hospital. Too often at present when it is necessary to transfer a baby to another hospital for admission to a special care nursery, the mother is left behind. Especially with the current low demand for maternity beds, every attempt should be made to transfer babies with their mothers.

But even when all these changes have been achieved, there will still be a need for intensive and special care and we must look closely at all units to ensure that they are both places where the highest possible standard of medical care is available and where parents can find peace and quiet and support to develop their relationships with their children. Perhaps the crucial thing is a recognition that 'contact' is not enough: parents must feel a continued responsibility for their babies and a real sense of involvement in their care. This means that wherever possible routine care must remain with parents and staff need to adopt an enabling and supportive role. It is very easy to reduce a parent's fragile sense of confidence by a demonstration of technical skill and efficiency. It is much more difficult to provide support and knowledge for a parent who is learning to look after a small and/or sick newborn. But the latter should be the predominant role for staff in special care nurseries and they need support and training to achieve it. This role is particularly demanding for them because in addition to this supportive role they do, of course, require a high degree of technical skill and efficiency.

CONCLUSION

In this chapter I have argued that early separation can have at least short term effects. I have suggested that these effects can be best understood in terms of a view of parental psychology that emphasizes the continuity of pregnancy, delivery and the initial development of the relationship with the child; and, which, in addition, pays especial attention to parents' needs for peace and calm with their newborn and responsibility for his or her care so that the evolution of the primary parental preoccupation is enhanced. The postnatal period can be viewed as a sensitive period for the establishment of the social relationship with the child provided that it is realized that the length of any such period is extremely variable and is not a simple once-and-for-ever process.

The kind of care that parents and babies often receive in maternity hospitals may operate in a number of ways to make the establishment of the parent–child relationship more difficult and these adverse factors are likely to be much more prominent when a delivery is abnormal and/or the baby is sick or preterm. Social and psychological considerations must be predominant in the provision of maternity care. A view of medicine based on the engineering approach is insufficient and distorting. There is no reason to think that there are conflicts between the provision of the best possible physical care and psychological considerations, but to achieve this ideal will require major changes in the roles of staff and hospital organization.

ACKNOWLEDGEMENTS

I am grateful to Judy Dunn and Alan Russell for their comments on a draft of this paper and to Phyllis Osbourn for her many secretarial skills.

REFERENCES

Bernal, J. F. and Richards, M. P. M. (1973). 'What can the Zoologist tell us about human development?', in Barnett, S. A. (ed.) *Ethology and Development*, Clinics in Developmental Medicine, London, SIMP/Heinemann Medical Books.

Blake, A., Stewart, A., Turcan, D. (1975). 'Parents of babies of very low birthweight: long-term follow up', in Porter, R., O'Connor, M. A. (eds.) *Parent–Infant Interaction*, Ciba Found. Symp. No. 33 (new series), Amsterdam, Elsevier.

Caplan, G., Mason, E. A., Kaplan, D. M. (1965). 'Four studies of crisis in parents of prematures, *Comm. Mental Health*, **1**, 149–161.

Chard, T. and Richards, M. P. M. (eds.) (1977). *The Benefits and Hazards of the New Obstetrics*, Clinics in Developmental Medicine, London, SIMP/Heinemann Medical Books.

Davis, J. and Kitzinger, S. (eds.) (1978). *The Place of Birth*, London, Oxford University Press.

de Chateau, P. and Winberg, B. (1977). 'Long-term effect on mother–infant behaviour of extra contact during the first hour post partum. I. First observations at 36 hours. II. Follow-up at 3 months', *Acta Paediat. Scand.*, **66**, 137–143 and 145–151.

Deutch, H. (1947). *The Psychology of Women, Vol. 2 Motherhood*, London, Research Books.

Douglas, J. W. B. (1975). 'Early hospital admissions and later disturbance of behaviour and learning', *Developm. Med. Child Neurol.*, 17, 456–480.

Douglas, J. W. B. and Gear, R. 1976. 'Children of low birthweight in the 1946 National Cohort', *Arch. Dis. Child.*, 51, 820–827.

Drillien, C. M. (1964). *The Growth and Development of the Prematurely Born Infant*, Edinburgh, Livingstone.

Fanaroff, A., Kennell, J. H. and Klaus, M. H. (1972). 'Follow-up of low birthweight infants—the predictive value of maternal visiting patterns', *Paediat.*, 49, 287–290.

Fedrick, J. (1974). 'Sudden unexpected death in infants in the Oxford Record Linkage Area', *B. J. Prev. Soc. Med.*, 28, 164–171.

Field, T. M. (1977). 'Effects of early separation, interactive deficits, and experimental manipulations on infant–mother face-to-face interaction', *Child Developm.*, 48, 763–771.

Hales, D. J., Lozoff, B., Sosa, R. and Kennell, J. H. (1977). 'Defining the limits of the maternal sensitive period', *Developm. Med. Child Neurol.*, 19, 454–461.

Hawthorne, J. T., Richards, M. P. M. and Callon, M. (1978). 'A study of parental visiting of babies in a Special Care Unit', in Brimblecombe, F. S. W., Richards, M. P. M. and Roberton, N. R. C. (eds.), *Early Separation and Special Care Nurseries*, Clinics in Developmental Medicine, London, SIMP/Heinemann Medical Books.

Klaus, M. H. and Kennell, J. H. (1976). *Maternal–Infant Bonding*, St. Louis, Mosby.

Klein, M. and Stern, L. (1971). 'Low birthweight and the battered child syndrome', *Am. J. Dis. Child.*, 122, 15–18.

Kramer, L. I. and Pierpont, M. E. (1976). 'Rocking waterbeds and auditory stimuli to enhance growth of preterm infants', *J. Pediat.*, 88, 297–299.

Lynch, M. A. (1975). 'Ill-health and child abuse', *Lancet*, 2, 317–319.

McKeown, T. (1965). *Medicine in Modern Society*, London, Allen and Unwin.

Minde, K., Ford, L., Celhoffer, L., Boukydis, C. (1975). 'Interactions of mothers and nurses with premature infants', *Canad. Med. Ass. J.*, 113, 741–745.

Pollitt, E., Gilmore, M., and Valcarcel, M. (1978). 'Early mother–infant interaction and somatic growth, *Early Human Developm.*, 1, 325–336.

Prince, J., Firlej, M. and Harvey, D. (1978). 'Contact between babies in incubators and their caretakers', in Brimblecombe, F. S. W., Richards, M. P. M., Roberton, N. R. C. (eds.), *Early Separation and Special Care Nurseries*, London, SIMP/Heinemann Medical Books.

Ribble, M. A. (1955). *The Personality of the Young Child*, Columbia University Press.

Richards, M. P. M. (1974). 'First Steps in Becoming Social', in Richards, M. P. M. (ed.) *The Integration of a Child into a Social World*, London, Cambridge University Press.

Richards, M. P. M. (1979). 'Possible effects of early separation on later development in children', in Brimblecombe, F. S. W., Richards, M. P. M. and Roberton, N. R. C. (eds.), *Early Separation and Special Care Nurseries*, London, SIMP/Heinemann Medical Books.

Richards, M. P. M. and Roberton, N. R. C. (1978). 'Admission and discharge policies for Special Care Units', in Brimblecombe, F. S. W., Richards, M. P. M. and Roberton, N. R. C. (eds.), *Early Separation and Special Care Nurseries*, Clinics in Developmental Medicine, London SIMP/Heinemann Medical Books.

Rutter, M. (1972). *Maternal Deprivation Reassessed*, London, Penguin Books.

Seashore, M. J., Leifer, A. D., Barnett, C. R., Leiderman, P. M. (1973). 'The effects of of early mother–infant interaction on maternal self–confidence', *J. Person. Soc. Psychol.*, 26, 369–378.

Shaheen, E., Alexander, D., Truskowsky, M. and Barbero, G. S. (1968). 'Failure to thrive–a retrospective profile', *Clin. Pediat.*, **7**, 255–261.

Stern, D. (1977). *The First Relationship: Infant and Mother*, London, Fontana/Open Books.

Whiten, A. (1977). 'Assessing the defects of perinatal events in the success of the mother–infant relationship', in Schaffer, H. R. (ed.), *Interactions in Infancy*, London, Academic Press.

Winnicott, D. W. (1958). *Collected Papers*, London, Tavistock.

Chapter 3

Neurobehavioural Findings in Preschool and School-aged Children in Relation to Pre- and Perinatal Complications

A. F. Kalveboer

INTRODUCTION

Early risk factors have been the topic of intensive study and reflection during the last decade. Initially, simple main effect and interaction models were adopted to account for the possible effects of early somatic and environmental risk factors on children's neurobehavioural development. However, during ontogeny, there is a continuous reorganization of behaviour in relation to changing environmental demands. It is necessary to think in terms of behaviour environment systems in order to understand the complex determination of problem behaviour. No easy predictions about children's neurobehavioural status at a later age can be made on the basis of isolated, specific early risk factors.

This is one of the main conclusions from the follow-up project, from which some data are presented in this report. This study focuses on the implications of pre- and perinatal complications for children's later neurobehavioural status at preschool and school age.

In itself this particular study has important limitations, which include a large age gap between successive assessments and little detailed evaluation of the children's social setting (although key-measures of the social–educational level of the families are included).

The aims of the study when originally planned were:
a) to give *an indication* about the possible significance of suboptimal obstetric and early neurological conditions for children's later neurobehavioural development, in order
b) to provide background data for the formulation of more precise questions (c.q. hypotheses) which could be tested in more intense follow-up studies where the implications of specific early neurobehavioural handicaps (such as lack of motor and postural control, inconsistency in motor functions,

apathy, etc.) could be analysed as functions of the interaction between the developing organism and relevant aspects of the social and physical environment.

In this project comprehensive methods for the neurological and behavioural assessment have been applied. Items were selected on the basis of their relationship to neurological function and behavioural patterning.

CONTEXT OF THE STUDY

This study is one of a series of follow-up projects which started in 1956 in the Department of Developmental Neurology in Groningen, the Netherlands. In earlier reports, data have been presented on relationships between obstetric risk and neurological condition in the newborn (Prechtl, 1968) between newborn neurological status and neurological status at preschool age (Touwen, 1972) and between neurological findings and free-field behaviour at age of 5 (Kalverboer, 1975).

The present report focusses on possible implications of obstetrical complications and early neurological dysfunctions for children's adaptive behaviour at preschool and school age. Obstetric and neonatal neurological data are related to free-field behaviour at 5 and school performance and task orientation measures at age 8. In addition certain data will be presented on relationships between free-field activity measures at preschool age and school performance and task orientation measures at age 8.

METHODS AND MEASURES

Standardized techniques for obstetric, neurological and behavioural assessment at various ages have been developed in the department. They have been described in detail by Prechtl, 1968 (obstetrical optimality), Prechtl and Beintema, 1964 (neurological examination of the newborn), Touwen and Prechtl, 1970 (neurological assessment at preschool age) and Kalverboer (direct observation of free-field behaviour at preschool age).

The following measures are included in the analyses reported here:

1. *Obstetric risk score.* A total of 42 factors obtained through direct observation and standardized interview are considered. The index is described in detail by Prechtl (1968).

2. *Neonatal neurological optimality score.* The score represents the number of items considered to be in the optimal range. The maximum score is 42. This score is regarded by us as an index of the integrity of the central nervous system (Prechtl, 1968).

3. *Scores on three neonatal neurological syndromes,* namely: hyperexicitability, apathy and hemisyndrome (Prechtl and Beintema, 1964). Definitions of these syndromes are given in Table 3.1.

Table 3.1 Classification of neonatal syndromes †

---

1. Hyperexcitability syndrome:

    (a) Moro   : low threshold
    (b) Tremor   : high amplitude
                           low frequency
    (c) Biceps reflex   : very exaggerated contraction going on to
                           clonus or
    Knee-jerk reflex: exaggerated response with at least a few beats of clonus

2. Apathy syndrome:

    The following responses are absent or of low intensity recoil of the arms, rooting, sucking, palmar grasp reflex, plantar grasp reflex, labyrinthine reflexes, headlift in prone.

3. Hypotonia:

    Resistance against passive movements completely lacking (−) or barely discernable (+) in neck, trunk, shoulderjoints, elbow joints, wrists, hips, knees, ankles (Prechtl and, Beintema, p. 24).

---

†Definitions and coding according to *The Neurological Examination of the Fullterm Newborn Infant*, Prechtl and Beintema, 1964.

4. *Scores at preschool age* (age range 4 yr 11m–5yr 4m) (a) Neurological optimality score. The number of items from a predefined set in which scores are within the optimal range (items and optimal ranges are presented in Appendix 3.1). This neurological optimality score is regarded by us as a general measure for the integrity of the central nervous system at preschool age. Maximum score 52.

(b) Scores for six neurological subgroups, labelled as sensorimotor, postural, choreiform dyskinesia, motor coordination, functional maturation, response maturation, see Appendix 3.1 (details are given in Kalverboer, 1975).

(c) Free-field behaviour scores derived from individual observations in a specially designed playroom under standard conditions and sequence:

   (i) Mother—together with mother in the novel empty room (3 min)
  (ii) Alone 1—alone in the empty room for the first time   (3 min)
 (iii) Blocks—with blocks and a passive observer   (10 min)
  (iv) Alone 2—in the empty room for the second time   (3 min)
   (v) Vartoys—alone with a variety of toys   (15 min)
  (vi) One toy—alone with one non-motivating toy   (5 min)

Ratings of the following were derived from videotape records (see Kalverboer, 1975). Contact behaviour (visual, verbal, tactile) exploratory activity, passive waiting, play at various levels of complexity, consistency, general motor activity.

5. *Scores at school age.* At the age of eight (range 8yr 2m—8yr 8m), teacher's reports were obtained about children's school performance and task orientation and were compared to control subjects, matched for sex, age and socioeconomic class (standardized questionnaires). 'School performance' ratings were based on teacher's descriptions from a questionnaire in which children were scored as being in the highest, intermediate, or lowest quartile of their class. 'Task definition' ratings were based on teacher descriptions from a questionnaire containing items on distractibility, inattentiveness, fluctuations in quality and speed of work, and hyperactivity.

Further data have been collected on the social and educational status of the family, the occurrence of interval complications, etc.

COMPOSITION OF THE SAMPLE

The primary criteria for the selection of subjects was 38–42 weeks gestation, birth weight more than 2,500 g, no severe neurological disorder diagnosed during the 1st month, and the availability of a complete record of obstetric and neonatal records.

The records of children born in the Academic Hospital in 1962 and 1963 were examined and 180 cases which fulfilled the above criteria were selected for further study. Thirty children dropped out for various reasons (see Kalverboer, 1975, p. 15 for details). This left us with a final sample at preschool age of 150 children, 75 boys and 75 girls. Teacher's reports were obtained from 142 children, 72 boys and 70 girls.

As hospital delivery in the Netherlands generally occurs on medical or social grounds (about 60%) it follows that the present group of children carried a slightly higher risk for obstetric and neurological complications than the Dutch population in general. Socioeconomic state was slightly below those of the Dutch population in general, again a consequence of the criteria usually required for referral to a University Hospital for delivery.

The distribution of neonatal neurological scores is presented in Table 3.2. The children who were included in this analysis were either high in apathy, or high in hyperactivity; that is, there was no overlap between the syndromes.

RESULTS

In this group of 150 children, only weak relationships were found between obstetric risk and neonatal neurological optimality with correlations as low as 0.26 in boys and 0.24 in girls (one-tailed test). In previous analyses, reported by Prechtl in 1968, much stronger relationships were found between obstetrical and neonatal neurological data. This difference may be due to the lower incidence of brain disorder in the present sample.

No significant correlations were found between scores for obstetrical risk

Table 3.2 Frequency of neonatal syndromes in original sample

1. Hyperexcitability–syndrome

	Boys (N:75)		Girls (N:75)		Total group (N:150)	
	no.	%	no.	%	no.	%
0 Hyperexcitability syndrome absent	58	77.3	63	84	121	80.7
1 Incomplete hyper excitability syndrome	58	10.7	10	13.3	18	12
2 Fully developed hyper excitability syndrome	9	12	2	2.6	11	7.3

2. Apathy–syndrome

	Boys (N:75)		Girls (N:75)		Total group (N:150)	
No. of symptoms	no.	%	no.	%	no.	%
0	37	49.3	33	44.0	70	46.7
1–2	25	33.3	33	44.0	58	38.7
3–4	8	10.7	5	6.7	13	8.7
5 or more	5	6.6	4	5.3	9	6.0

3. Hemisyndrome

	Boys (N:75)		Girls (N:75)		Total group (N:150)	
No. of symptoms	no.	%	no.	%	no.	%
0	45	60	46	61.3	91	60.7
1–2	4	5.3	3	4	7	4.7
3–14	2	2.6	3	4	5	3.3
5–6	1	1.3	4	5.3	5	3.3
7–8	23	30.7	19	25.3	42	28

and neonatal neurological optimality on the one hand and neurological and free-field behaviour measures at preschool age on the other. In a group of 57 boys, who had not suffered from interval complications between the newborn period and the time of the preschool assessment (such as head trauma, meningitis and encephalitis), a low correlation was found between neonatal and follow-up neurological optimality scores ($r = 0.28$, $p < 0.03$). Small but significant correlations were found between scores for *apathy* and *hyperexcitability* in the newborn period and directly observed *free-field activity* at preschool age. (See Table 3.3 and also Kalverboer, Touwen and Prechtl, 1973).

Table 3.3   Behaviour/task orientation at 5 and 8 years of age significantly related to
obstetric risk/neonatal neurological state ($N = 102$)

Perinatal	5 y (free-field)	8 y (school)
obstetric risk		—
neurological optimality		—
apathy	*less* exploration ($p < 0.05$) *more* contact and body manipulation ($p < 0.02$) in novel environment *less* high level play ($p < 0.03$) *longer* periods of no play activity ($p < 0.05$)	task orientation *worse* in boys ($p < 0.10$)
hyperexcitability	duration of play longer ($p < 0.05$) more high level play ($p < 0.05$)	task orientation *better* in boys ($p < 0.05$)

Mann–Whitney U test
P = two-tailed significance
See Kalveboer (1975, Appendix p. 54–61) for definition of behaviour patterns in the freefield observation.

'*Apathetics*' ($N = 22$) showed *less* exploratory activity ($p < 0.05$) and *more* contact behaviour and manipulation of body and clothes ($p < 0.02$) in the novel environment with the mother (Stage 1 of the testing situation) than optimal controls. They also showed less constructive play ($p < 0.03$) in a condition in which a variety of toys was presented, whereas they had slightly longer periods of inactivity ($p < 0.05$) than optimal controls ($p < 0.05$). Interestingly enough, hyperexcitable boys played longer and at a higher level than optimal controls in a condition with just one non-attractive toy left in the room ($p < 0.05$).

In a condition with a variety of toys present, no differences were found between level and duration of play activity between hyperexcitables and controls.

Apathetic boys had slightly lower task orientation scores at school age, ($p < 0.10$), whereas task orientation scores of hyperexcitable boys were slightly higher than in optimal controls ($p < 0.05$).

In summary, only weak relationships are found between obstetric neonatal neurological scores on the one hand, and neurological and behavioural follow-up data obtained at preschool age and school age on the other. Intriguing correlations were found with respect to hyperexcitability and apathy, which may be important as a background for designing more intense follow-up studies. Correlations are too low for any prediction to be made for individual children.

Data on relationships between neurology and behaviour at preschool age on the one hand and school achievement and task orientation at 8 on the other are given in Table 3.4 for the group as a whole ($N = 102$) and in the Tables 3.5A and 3.5B for boys and girls separately.

Table 3.4 School performance and task orientation at 8 in relation to neurology/behaviour at 5 years of age

Total group ($N = 102$) (Speaman correlation)

5y	School performance	8y Task orientation
Neurology:		
—neurological optimality	0.28 (0.01)	—
—maturity of functions	0.27 (0.01)	0.26 (0.01)
—sensorimotor	0.29 (0.01)	0.20 (0.05)
Free-field behaviour:		
—exploration activity	− 0.24 (0.05)	− 0.20 (0.05)
—low level play	− 0.23 (0.05)	—
—high level play	0.24 (0.05)	—
I.Q.: (Stanford-Binet)	0.43 (0.001)	0.39 (0.001)
Sex:	0.35 (0.001) (boys lower)	0.24 (0.05) (boys lower)

p = two-builed significance

In the total group, a significant but low correlation is found between the neurological optimality scores at 5 and school performance at 8 ($r = 0.28$, $p < 0.01$). This is mainly due to a substantial correlation in the subgroups of boys ($r = 0.35$), a correlation which is absent in the girls.

At preschool age, optimality scores were given for six subgroupings of neurological signs: sensorimotor, posture, coordination, dyskinesis, maturation of functions, and maturation of responses. (See Appendix 3.1). In the boys only weak relationships were found between the subgroups: 'sensorimotor' and 'coordination' on the one hand and measures for subsequent school performance at the age of 8 (0.33 and 0.25). In girls only a weak relationship was found between 'maturation of functions' at 5 and 'task orientation' at 8 (0.27, $p < 0.10$).

Free-field behaviour scores obtained in the variety-of-toys condition were correlated with the school measures. In boys as well as in girls, low significant correlations in the expected direction were found between play behaviour on the one hand and school performance on the other. In the boys these play measures also had a relationship to the task orientation scores, in that a lower level of play activity was related to lower task orientation scores. In girls this last relationship was lacking. In the girls only, exploratory activity in a novel environment was negatively correlated with school performance at 8. None of the correlations is high enough to allow for any prediction about individual children.

The best preschool age predictor of school age variables is the child's I.Q.

Table 3.5   School performance and task orientation at 8 in relation to neurology and
behaviour at 5 and parent education

A	Boys ($N = 60$) (Spearman rank correlation)	
5 y	School performance	8y Task orientation
Neurology:		
—neurological optimality	0.35 (0.01)	—
—sensorimotor	0.33 (0.01)	—
—coordination	0.25 (0.05)	—
Free-field behaviour		
—low level play	− 0.23 (0.05)	− 0.20
—high level play	0.24 (0.05)	0.18 (0.08)
I.Q. (Stanford-Binet)	0.36 (0.01)	0.30 (0.01)
School education mother	0.23 (0.05)	—
School education father	0.30 (0.01)	—

B	Girls ($N = 42$)	
5y	School performance	8y Task orientation
Neurology:		
—neurological optimality	—	—
—maturation of functions	—	0.27 (0.10)
Free-field behaviour:		
—exploratory activity	− 0.25 (0.10)	—
—high level play	0.25 (0.10)	—
I.Q. (Stanford-Binet)	0.52 (0.001)	0.45 (0.001)
School education mother	6.25 (0.10)	—
School education father	0.25 (0.10)	—

The correlations between Stanford–Binet scores at preschool age and school
measures range from 0.30 (I.Q.—task orientation in boys) to 0.52 (I.Q.—school
performance in girls). Also significant correlations were found between indices
for the parents' school education and children's school performance at 8
(see Table 3.6).

DISCUSSION

In this report some obstetric, neurological and behavioural data are collected
at different times or the child's development. Correlations are generally low,
most of them are insignificant. They do not allow for any prognosis about
individual children.

Table 3.6   I.Q. at preschool age in relation to neurology, behaviour and parent education

	Total group	Boys (N = 60)	Girls (N = 42)
		(Specaman rank correlation)	
Neurology:			
—neurological optimality	—	—	—
—maturity of functions	0.27 (0.01)	—	0.28 (0.10)
—sensorimotor	—	—	—
Free-field behaviour:			
—exploratory activity	− 0.20 (0.05)	—	− 0.32 (0.05)
—low level play	− 0.29 (0.01)	—	− 0.32 (0.05)
—high level play	0.26 (0.01)	0.38 (0.01)	0.25 (0.10)
Education level mother	0.34 (0.01)	0.34 (0.01)	0.34 (0.05)
Education level father	—	—	0.57 (0.001)

Low correlations between early obstetric and neurological measures and behavioural measures at later ages are not surprising. Correlations between neurological and behavioural measures obtained at the same age (even on the same day) were shown to be weak in a neurobehavioural study at preschool age (Kalverboer, 1975) in which neurological status only accounted for 4–8 per cent of the variance in free-field behaviour. Neurobehavioural relationships at preschool age were, to a large extent situation-specific, and intra- and interindividual variablity was one of the main findings.

The correlation between neurological optimality in the neonatal period and at age five was not significant for the groups as a whole (Touwen, 1971). However in boys who had not suffered any interval complication there is a significant correlation between the two diagnostic assessments. But since the correlation is as low as 0.28 ($p < 0.03$) it is not, therefore, useful for any individual prognosis.

In earlier studies in the Department of Developmental Neurology, stronger relationships has been found between neonatal and obstetrical neurological factors (Prechtl, 1968) as well as between neonatal neurological data and follow-up neurological data (Dijkstra, 1960; Touwen, 1971).

The higher correlations in the previous groups might be attributable to the shorter period between neonatal and follow-up neurological examinations (Dijkstra had examined the children between 18 months and $3\frac{1}{2}$ years of age and Touwen at the age of 4), partly to changes in obstetrical practice, such as a decline in the number of instrument deliveries. The variance of neonatal optimality scores is lower in this group than in the previous groups, with a lower base rate for organic brain disorder in the present sample. It may be that non-organic factors are more important 'determinants' of behaviour in later development in groups with a good neurological status than in groups with a higher incidence of brain dysfunctions.

The application of 'overall neurological optimality scores' may have obscured relationships between specific neurological and behavioural measures at early and later ages. This is indicated by the relationships between specific neurological syndromes (hyperexcitability and apathy) in the newborn period and free-field behaviour at 5 and task orientation at the age of 8. Evidently different neurological dysfunctions, such as hyperexcitability, apathy, hypotonia, have different implications for the child's neurobehavioural development. In our analyses apathy and hyperexcitability have quite opposite connections to later behaviour. Such relationships will be obscured if non-optimal items, belonging to different 'syndromes', are included in one overall (non-)optimality score.

An additional problem in neurobehavioural follow-up studies is the lack of unequivocal criteria for the distinction between 'variations within the normal range of nervous functions' and 'neurological dysfunctions'. This is indicated in this study by the relatively favourable behavioural findings at preschool age in children, diagnosed as 'hyperexcitables'. Detailed inspection of the data strongly suggests that quite a few of the 'hyperexcitable' children in our sample were in fact healthy newborns, characterized by vigorous, lively, motor reactions to relatively weak stimuli. This findings may illustrate one of the most important functions of follow-up programs: to contribute to the establishment of more valid criteria for the distinction between 'real disorders or dysfunctions' and 'variations within the normal range'.

The follow-up findings with respect to neonatal apathy and hyperexcitability may indicate the function of this follow-up study for further research.

Apathy in the newborn periods relates to a lack of exploratory activity, more contact seeking behaviour and a lower level of playing at preschool age and lower task orientation scores at eight. Although weak, this relationship is remarkable in view of the relatively mild neurological symptomatology in the newborn period, the favourable socialeconomic conditions of the children in our sample and the wide age-gap between neonatal and follow-up examinations. Phenomena at preschool and school age are rather similar to those commonly mentioned as signs of the childhood depression syndrome (Watson, 1977); the findings suggest that in essence this is a motivational problem ('lack of initiative').

Various models can be suggested for the explanation of these relationships. A simple 'main effect' model would suggest an organic brain disorder, present from birth on, that manifests itself directly in a low level of responsiveness. According to this model the lack of initiative would be unaffected by environmental factors. As a general explanation this seems unlikely. It is a well-established finding that interaction between organism and environment strongly affects behavioural outcome, particularly in children from a favourable socialeconomic background (Sameroff and Chandler, 1975). There is strong evidence that early neurological syndromes are a much stronger handicap for children in less favourable socialeconomic conditions (Werner, Bierman and French, 1971).

A simple 'interaction' model would possibly suggest that the lack of responsiveness of children with the apathy syndrome directly affects the behaviour of the caretaker; there may be too little appeal for stimulating and contacting those children who are inactive or disorganized. A more complex interaction model would suggest that, in such children, stimulation would not only be less frequent but also less adapted to the structure of the infant's own activity. Disorders in the child's behavioural patterning may contribute to the development of a lack of contingency between actions of the child and the social partners. Non-contingent stimulation may interfere with learning and with the development of initiative (Watson, 1977; Papousek, 1977). Apathetic children and children who have inconsistent states and an inconsistent temporal organization of their motor behaviour ('real hyperexcitables') may be particularly prone to an exposure to non-contingent stimulation. The situation may be complicated by differences in the ability of caretakers to find the most suitable reciprocal relationship. Exploratory studies in our laboratory suggest great differences between mothers in their ability to adapt finely their behaviour to that of the infant during breast-feeding. In conclusion, the patterning of the child's own activity may basically affect its emotional and cognitive development ('perception of control', 'operant conditioning'). Children with neurologically-based disorders in the temporal and spatial organization of their behaviour may be highly vulnerable for the development of problem behaviour.

'Apathetic' children seem to be a group at risk. Behavioural problems at preschool age suggest a vulnerability for the development of depressive symptoms. Probably, negative effects of early apathy would be much stronger in children living in less favourable social conditions. The background of problems becomes even more complex when the nutritional condition of child and/or caretaker is bad, or when mothers suffer from depression themselves (Ferreira, in press). Precise studies on different educational and hygienic conditions of specific risk groups in carefully analysed social environments are lacking. The few studies available until now, have been carried out in seriously deprived groups in which social, economical and hygienic deprivation were all present. Perhaps different models are appropriate for different conditions. This can only be tested in close follow-up studies in which organism–environment interactions and relationships are included in the design. This follow-up study may provide background knowledge for the designing of such studies.

Appendix 3.1   Functional categories of neurological items[1]

Sensorimotor:

     resistance to passive movements
     tendon reflexes of the arms
     tendon reflexes of the legs
     abnormal skin reflex
     threshold tendon reflexes of the arms
     active power

Appendix 3.1 (*contd.*)
    skin reflexes of the leg on the toes
    type of grasping
    threshold tendon reflexes of the legs
    position of the arms in forward extension
    plantar response
Posture:
    posture of the feet, standing
    walking
    standing ability
    posture of the legs, standing
    posture of the feet, sitting
Coordination:
    Romberg
    kicking
    following object, sitting
    response to push, standing
    fingertip–nose test
    rebound
Choreiformity:
    choreiformity in finger muscles
    choreiformity in eye, tongue and face musculature
    choreiformity in arm and trunk muscles
Maturation of functions:
    heel-toe gait
    raising into sitting
    walking on heels
    walking on tiptoe
    hopping
    standing on one leg
    diadochokinesis
Maturation of responses:
    planter grasp
    Mayer
    Lery
    Galant

[1] Details on assessment and evaluation in Touwen and Prechtl (1971). *The Neurological Examination of the Child with Minor Nervous Dysfunction*, Heinemann, London.

REFERENCES

Dijkstra, J. (1960). *De Prognostische Betekenis van Neurologische Afwijkingen bij Pasgeboren Kinderen*, Groningen, Thesis.

Ferreira, M. C. R. (in press). *Interactions of Nutrition and Socio-cultural Conditions and their Effect on Mental Development*, Department of Psychology and Education, University, Sao Paulo.

Kalverboer, A. F., Touwen, B. C. L., and Prechtl, H. F. R. (1973). 'Follow-up of infants at risk of minor brain dysfunction', *Annals of the New York Academy of Sciences*, **205**, 172.

Kalverboer, A. F. (1975). *A Neurobehavioural Study in Pre-school Children*, Clincs in Developmental Medicine, 54.

Prechtl, H. F. R. (1968). 'Neurological findings in newborn infants after pre- and perinatal complications', in Jonxix, J. H. P., Visser, H. K. A. and Troelstra, J. A. (Eds.), *Aspects of Prematurity and Dysmaturity*, Leiden, Stenfert Kroese.

Prechtl, H. F. R. and Beintema, D. J. (1964). *The Neurological Examination of the Full-term Newborn Infant*, Clinics in Developmental Medicine, No. 12, London, SIMP/Heinemann.

Sameroff, A. J. and Chandler, M. J. (1975). 'Reproductive Risk and the Continuum of caretaking casualty', in Horowitz, F. D., Hetherington, M., Scarr-Salapatek, S. and Siegel, G. (eds.), *Review of Child Developmental Research*, Vol. 4, University of Chicago Press.

Touwen, B.C. L. (1971). 'Neurological follow-up of infants born after obstetrical complications', in Stoelinga, G. B. and Van der Werfften Bosch, J. J. (eds.), *Normal and Abnormal Development of Brain and Behaviour*, Leiden, University Press.

Touwen, B. C. L. (1972). 'The relationship between neonatal and follow-up findings', in Saling, E. and Schutte, F. J. (eds.) *Perinatal Medizin*, II Stuttgart, Thieme.

Touwen, B. C. L. and Kalverboer, A. F. (1973), 'Neurologic and Behavioural assessment of children with 'Minimal Brain Dysfunction', in Waltzer, S. and Wolff, P. (eds.) *Minimal Cerebral Dysfunction in Children, Seminars in Psychiatry*, 5, 79.

Touwen, B. C. L. and Prechtl, H. F. R. (1970) *The Neurological Examination of the Child with Minor Nervous Dysfunction*, Clinics in Developmental Medicine, No. 38, London, SIMP/Heinemann.

Werner, E. E., Bierman, J. M. and French, F. E. (1971). *The Children of Kauai*, Honolulu, University of Hawaii.

Chapter 4

The First Year of Life: Continuities in Individual Differences

Judy Dunn

The wealth of recent research on infancy has amply confirmed what parents and those who care for babies know so well—that young babies differ markedly from one another. But the question of how far these individual differences can be shown to continue into later childhood and beyond is one that poses obvious and intractable problems. The central difficulty is that in the course of the astonishingly fast development from birth to the second year, the new cognitive, social and motor skills the child acquires transform his behaviour. A response may appear to be identical at different ages, but its meaning and the circumstances or motives which elicit and influence it may in fact be very different. The crying of an 18 month old whose toy is taken by another child is obviously a response to forces very different from those that provoke the crying of a hungry 3 month old.

STRATEGIES OF RESEARCH

Psychologists have used a number of different strategies in the face of these obstacles to assessing the continuity of individual differences from infancy onwards. One approach, that for example of Thomas and coworkers in their longitudinal study of New York children (1963), has been to look for continuities in the *style* of the individual's behaviour, to look not at *what* the child did, but at *how* he did it. Several recent studies have employed their relatively global classification which distinguishes different aspects of temperament, such as activity level, quality of mood, rhythmicity, adaptability, intensity of reaction, approach–withdrawal, threshold of responsiveness, attention span and distractability (Carey, 1970; Graham, Rutter and George, 1973, Garside and coworkers, 1975). Thomas, Chess and Birch suggested that individual differences in these traits were stable from early infancy, and further analysis showed that particular patterns of temperament from 12 months on were associated with an increased rate of later disturbance.

A different approach has been to use direct behavioural measures of stable individual differences at one age, and then to examine individual differences in measures of quite different aspects of behaviour at a later age: Bell, Weller and Waldrop (1971) for instance looked at measures reflecting 'optimal' functioning in the newborn period, and then compared these with a broad range of measures of preschool behaviour. With this approach there may be little initial conceptual assurance on what links there might be between individual differences in behaviour at the ages studied; the correlations which are found can be used to generate hypotheses about the traits which link the behaviour at the different ages.

Another strategy is to look for continuity in the physiological differences which are thought to underlie differences in temperament. Here the interest has been very much in the use of autonomic indices (Richmond and Lipton, 1959; Lipton and coworkers, 1961). A fourth possibility is to study the development of particular processes. Here the research is carried out within a more clearly-defined conceptual framework, and relationships are looked for between aspects of behaviour which may be topographically very different. An example of this approach is Kagan's (1971) study of differences in a dimension of reflection/impulsivity.

When we look at recent work carried out within any of these research orientations, three particular issues recur insistently. The first is the problem of assigning meaning to behaviour, and thus assessing the implications of individual variability in the first year. This problem arises whether the behaviour is described at a fine-grain level, such as changes in heart rate, or at a more general level such as 'activity' or 'irritability', and it is of central importance in the use of global categories of temperament, which attempt to aggregate a number of distinct responses. The second issue concerns the relation between individual differences in babies and individual differences in their caretakers, and the possible basis of continuities or discontinuities we find in the stability of such individual differences. The third issue is the importance of the nature of the sample studied, and how this affects the problem of prediction. These three issues will be discussed in the light of some recent research.

CATEGORIZING AND DESCRIBING BEHAVIOUR: THE MEANING OF BEHAVIOUR

The New York Longitudinal Study was designed to test the hypothesis that 'personality is shaped by the constant interplay of temperament and environment' (Thomas, Chess and Birch, 1970). It was not assumed that a child's temperamental traits were immutable; rather, it was suggested that the environment in which a child developed could heighten or diminish his reactive style, and that a given environment would not have the same meaning for different children. It was a long term investigation of the differences in behavioural reactions of a sample of middle-class children, based on structured interviews in which the interviewers were careful to code only descriptions of the way the infant responded in particular situations. The parents were asked about the child's behavioural style during day-to-day routines.

From this interview data Thomas, Chess and Birch developed broad interpretative categories of temperamental traits, classifications of reactivity which were thought to be appropriate for characterizing children from birth to early childhood. For instance, the rhythmicity of biological functions was assessed in terms of the child's sleep–wake cycle, the regularity of his appetite and so on, his adaptability in terms of how he reacted to altered circumstances. Each of the nine behavioural traits which they identified was rated on a 3-point scale. It was found that certain characteristics of the traits clustered together, and the authors derived three general types of temperament. First, an 'easy' group, characterized by positive mood, regularity of body functions, adaptability etc.; second, a 'difficult' group, intense in reaction, irregular in bodily function, slow to adapt to change, and negative in mood. A third group were termed 'slow to warm up'. These children were low in activity level, and tended to withdraw and to be slow to adapt.

The study has been extremely important in drawing attention to the significance of differences between children, and has generated much further research, demonstrating for instance an association between temperamental traits and behaviour disorders in older children (Graham, Rutter and George, 1973; Thomas and Chess, 1977). It is one of the very few studies which has followed children in detail from early infancy. But interpreting the findings does present considerable difficulties. The distribution of scores on the temperamental traits was extremely skewed, information was combined for different ages, and the general pattern of individual stability of each temperamental train decreased markedly as the gap between ages of assessment increased. For instance, 24 out of 28 correlations involving adjacent age periods were significantly positive, but only 2 out of 7 correlations between age period one (mean 5.9 months) and age period five (mean age 27.3 months) reached significance.

The broad categories of temperement used in the New York study are inevitably interpretative, and there is a real problem in using these sorts of categories to describe the behaviour of babies in the first year, when the meaning of a particular item of behaviour, change of behaviour or intensity of response is often ambiguous or obscure, and when it may well change markedly over the first 12 months. Much of the recent work on individual differences in infants then has involved the use of more focussed and detailed measures of behaviour, rather than ratings of broad traits. Where these are used as indices of broader categories the results often suggest that we should define just what we imply in using the categories, and just why we presume them to be appropriate, with greater precision. To illustrate the way in which close examination of the broad temperamental traits has raised further developmental

issues of great importance I want to look briefly at some of the recent research
into three of the temperamental traits: attention span, intensity of response,
and activity.

Attention

There has been a great deal of recent research into the distribution of attention, and the response to novelty in infancy. Much of this work has been carried
out in the context of studies of congnitive development. The infant's reaction
to familiarity, novelty, and incongruity and his displays of interest, surprise,
wariness or declining interest have been seen as particularly sensitive indicators
of the child's cognitive structures. Since what is novel and what is familiar
depends upon the experience and the cognitive capacity of the child, not upon
any external criteria of the stimulus properties, we can begin to understand how
the child's congnitive capacity is changing by studying the changes in these
patterns of attention over time. The developmental changes in habituation
and in response to discrepancy are now being mapped out by employing a
variety of behavioural and autonomic indices (McCall, 1971). But for the
assessment of continuity of individual differences, these age changes present
considerable problems. The patterns of response to a particular situation may
change markedly over quite a short period. In different phases of development
we find very different reactions to the outside world and to people; these
responses may reflect particular adaptations to that phase of development,
and individual differences at that phase may not *necessarily* relate in any
consistent way to individual differences at later stages. Before examining the
evidence for continuity in individual differences in attentive behaviour, the
considerable problems involved in measuring attention must be discussed.

Measurement of attention

Attempts have been made to define attention more carefully through physiological measurements, such as heart rate changes, vasodilation in the
head and vasoconstriction in the extremities, and skin potential changes,
and through behavioural observations of activity changes, orienting behaviour,
and decreases in sucking and vocalization. Cardiac responses have been a
particular focus of attention. The general idea that individual differences in
measures of rate of habituation to a stimulus, and in response to discrepancy
may reflect individual differences in rate of information processing, in sensitivity to environmental change, or in basic cognitive functioning is an attractive
one. It is certainly plausible that individual differences in such broad constructs
would significantly influence the child's early experience, and thus
affect the particular course of his development. However, McCall, one of the
most experienced researchers in this field notes that the latest studies suggest

that we should be extremely cautious about extrapolating from individual differences in particular indices of attention or habituation to such constructs.

Will a child who is a rapid habituator for one set of stimuli at one age also be a rapid habituator for another set of stimuli and/or at a later age? The available data (all unpublished) suggest that, while different patterns of habituation can be replicated across stimuli and across assessment occasion, infants are not always found in the same habituation pattern group. That is, there is replicability for different habituation styles across stimuli, age and response measure; but there is no individual stability or habituation trait.

(McCall, 1975)

There is a great deal that we do not yet know about the relationship between the different facets of attention distribution, even at a single age. For instance, infants who show rapid habituation to a stimulus are more likely to respond relatively rapidly to a new discrepant version of the stimulus, but the response which predicts the rapidity of this reaction to the novelty will vary with different modalities of stimulation: cardiac habituation for instance predicts best the change in response to auditory stimuli, but visual fixation habituation the change in response to visual stimuli (McCall, 1971). While autonomic measures do show much individual stability in the newborn period (Lipton and coworkers, 1961; Clifton and Graham, 1968) and are in some situations more sensitive indices of changes in response than visual fixation, the various autonomic measures do not always correlate well. For instance, heart rate and skin conductance have been shown to covary directly, indirectly or not at all, depending on the circumstances (Taylor and Epstein, 1968). The heart rate response is influenced by many factors. Physical activity during orientation, for example, may considerably alter the cardiac response (Lewis, 1974). Lewis points out that the heart rate response itself should not be taken as a unitary measure, since the different parameters used to describe it do not always generate the same result. Each index of autonomic activity reflects the functioning of a particular physiological system, and these systems serve different functions. It has been noted in a number of studies that we need to understand these particular biological functions more fully before we can clearly relate the measures to behavioural observations (Venables, 1975).

Longitudinal studies of differences in attentive behaviour

The problems of identifying appropriate response measures become all the more acute with studies of the longitudinal stability of individual differences, and the value of a strong theoretical framework for guiding research becomes correspondingly apparent. In his longitudinal study of children from 4 months to 44 months, Kagan was interested in individual differences in a dimension of reflection/impulsivity. In looking for continuity of a psychological construct dealing with 'the capacity to become involved with interesting stimuli', he chose to study different dimensions of attention involving the response to visual stimuli, play with objects, and activity changes. When he selected children at the 27 month stage on an index of play 'tempo', defined in terms of the length of acts of sustained directed activity, he found this was correlated with habituation measures and smiling to stimuli at 4 months, and with long involvement with play objects at 8 months. The *behaviour* measures were very different, but the links could plausibly be interpreted as support for continuity in rhythms of attention over this period.

Wilson and Lewis (1971) examined the relations between a number of different measures of attention to visual stimuli, in a longitudinal study of children between 6 and 44 months, using a principal component analysis. They identified two components of attention, an 'orienting' factor (visual fixation, HR deceleration, and decreased activity) and an 'affect' factor (smiling, vocalizing, and HR deceleration), and found that although some of the measures forming the two components were similar at the different ages, other measures were less consistent. At the younger ages, for instance, many discrete looks was related to high attention (much looking, decrease in HR, and little activity), but by 44 months many looks was related to low attention. There was not a consistent pattern of individual differences over the age period 6 to 44 months. Rather, there was consistency from each age point in the study to the next.

Some aspects of attentive behaviour show very marked changes with age. Schwartz, Campos and Baisel (1973) examined the heart rate changes to the 'deep' side of a visual cliff, and found that 5 month olds showed heart rate deceleration, the pattern associated with alerting and interest, while 9 month olds showed heart rate acceleration, the pattern associated with wariness or fear. Sroufe (1974) has demonstrated several comparable discontinuities in the development of affective responses. That such discontinuities coincide with periods of very rapid development is shown by Emde and colleagues (1976) in a longitudinal study of the development of emotional expression in infancy. They provide evidence, from data on sleep, wakefulness, EEG and affect expression, that development proceeds at uneven rates, with two periods of rapid change—from birth to $2\frac{1}{2}$ months, and from 5–9 months—which represent major changes in developmental organization.

Not only do these age changes raise again the issue of precisely how to interpret a particular response, but they remind us that rate of development may well contribute to the individual differences in behaviour found at any one age. This is particularly important during the very rapid development of the child's first year.

Since heart rate response measures change dramatically around the middle of the first year, we should not be surprised by the pattern of discontinuity and continuity for heart rate responses which Kagan found in his longitudinal study. There was no stability in individual differences from 4 months to 27 months, but 'moderate' stability from 13 months to 27 months. This **measure** was more stable for boys. Kagan argued that the disposition to 'excitedly attend' was reasonably stable for both boys and girls from the second half of the first year, but that the continuity was reflected through vocalisation for girls (which showed greater stability in their case) and through heart rate deceleration for boys. He cited as support for this interpretation a pattern of correlations which showed that boys who showed large deceleration at 8, 13, and 27 months were more attentive at play at 2 years than boys who were low decelerators, a difference which was not apparent for girls.

A major difficulty in assessing the significance of the different autonomic indices during the first year is that with the exception of Kagan's study and those of Lewis (Wilson and Lewis, 1971) there is so little information on the stability of the individual differences beyond the early months. Lewis (1970) showed consistent differences in heart rate and variability from foetal measures through to 56 weeks. But we do not know what significance we should place on these early heart rate differences. Schachter and colleagues (1975) showed for example that black infants had higher heart rate levels than white infants, a difference that could not be accounted for by the perinatal variables studied. Now there is some evidence that hypertensive disease is more common among adult black Americans than it is in the white population, but Schachter and colleagues stress that the idea that elevated heart rate at birth is directly linked with later hypertensive disease is highly speculative. Similar caution was urged by Kittner and Lipsitt (1976), who demonstrated a relationship between obstetrtic factors and the heart rate response of newborns. As we will see in a later section, the long term significance of newborn differences varies very much according to the nature of the sample of children studied.

Intensity of response

The study of attention during early infancy then suggests that it is particularly important to take precise account of the child's changing nature, to take account of the possibility that variation may be due to differences in rate of development, and to be aware of the extent to which different facets of attention vary independently of one another. Another aspect of individual differences in temperament which has been conceptualized as a single dimension is intensity of response, characterized by Yang and Halverson (1976) as 'high magnitude, energy-expending activity'. But here too recent research suggests that the nature of the longitudinal relationships can be clarified if the single dimension is examined more criticially. In 1971 Bell, Weller and Waldrop had reported that measures of optimal functioning as newborns (rapid rate of sucking, and prompt response to the removal of a pacifier) was associated with lethargic, inattentive, inactive and non-participatory behaviour at the preschool age. Yang and Halverson (1976) tested this hypothesis in two ways. First they reconstituted the measures of intensity which Bell, Weller and Waldrop had used at both periods, and secondly they selected new variables which they felt on conceptual grounds would be related to intensity. In analysing the preschool data, they selected variables on an *a priori* basis as having positive or negative connotations for development. The measures with negative connotations, all highly correlated, concerned frenetic hyperactive play, and negative peer interaction. Measures of total intensity, *a priori* positive and *a priori* negative intensity were adopted. When the longitudinal relations between the factors derived from these measures, and conceptually related factors of intensity for newborns were examined, the results confirmed some of the original results, but they also considerably extended and clarified the original findings. It was found that measures of 'reactive intensity' and 'basal intensity' in the newborn period were correlated negatively with the factor of negative intensity at $2\frac{1}{2}$ for boys, and failed to correlate with the factor of positive intensity. That is, only the 'socially negative' aspects of intensity at the preschool stage related negatively to the assessment of newborn intensity. There is, then, no need to invoke the puzzling 'inversion'. It was 'based on the presumption that optimal and socially valued behaviour was indexed at the newborn and nursery phases in some unitary way.' (Yang and Halverson, 1976).

Activity

Assessments of a dimension of activity have been included in several studies (e.g. Thomas and coworkers, 1963; Kagan, 1971; Birns, Barten and Bridges, 1969; Wilson and Lewis, 1974), although only the first two of these include measures both from the first year and from later ages. The ways in which 'activity' was measured operationally differed greatly from one study to another. Thomas and coworkers define activity in terms of the 'proportion of active/ inactive periods in the day', as well as in terms of mobility during regular events in the child's day. Birns and colleagues treat activity as the amount and vigour of bodily activity when the child is not asleep or crying. Wilson and Lewis, and Kagan include both measures of mobility, and measures of changes in activity. Given this wide range of measures it is not surprising that there is disagreement about the stability of a dimension of activity. Kagan found little stability in his measure of mobility, and concluded that a tendency to 'run around' independent of context was not a stable disposition between the ages of 8 months and 27 months. He found more convincing evidence of stability of individual differences in the 'tempo' dimension discussed earlier, where tempo was defined in terms of the length of acts of sustained directed activity.

Wilson and Lewis did find that high mobility in a play room at 13 months was correlated with high mobility at 25 months, and Halverson and Waldrop (1976) found evidence for a considerable degree of stability in an activity dimension between the ages of $2\frac{1}{2}$ and $7\frac{1}{2}$ years. These findings provide another example of how the use of a unidimensional construct can mislead us. They showed that ratings of 'vigorous high-active play' at $2\frac{1}{2}$ years were associated with individual differences in both 'social participation', and in 'impulsive high activity', and that these two groups were related to *different* groups of behaviour measures at the age of $7\frac{1}{2}$ years. It was the 'impulsive activity level' factor, not the 'high activity associated with social participation', which carried negative implications for intellectual development. The social behaviour associated high activity at $2\frac{1}{2}$ was positively related both to social participation at $7\frac{1}{2}$, and to verbal intelligence and high scores on tests of field independence.

In considering activity then we face problems similar to those raised by the research on attention. Should we for instance class toy-change activity as being regulated by an information-processing dimension, or as being regulated by an 'activity' dimension? How we interpret it will inevitably govern our choice of variables to examine at later ages. The 'meaning' of toy-change behaviour at a particular age, in a particular context, must be investigated by examining its relationship to other behaviour at the same and later ages, and to behaviour in other contexts.

Problems of interpretation

This discussion has touched on just three of the broad temperamental traits. But it is already apparent that there are two sorts of problems in relating the results of direct observational studies to the broad traits. The first is that the unidimensional traits may mask more complex interrelationships between response systems, and the second is that it is not always clear, when we find reliable measures of individual differences between babies which do relate to later individual differences, how these should be labelled, or to which trait if any they should be assigned. It is not clear how we ought to *understand* the relationship which we have uncovered in this way. In his study of the development of wariness or fear, Bronson found evidence for consistent individual differences over the early months. A few infants consistently cried at a stranger at 4 months. In the earlier weeks these same babies had reacted with more distress and 'startle' to being bathed, and to a sudden looming stimulus (Bronson, 1972). Bronson discusses these individual differences in terms of 'reactivity'. How closely differences in such response measures relate to the differences in responsiveness which Bell, Weller and Waldrop termed intensity differences, or to the 'threshold' differences reported by Carey (1974) we do not yet know.

DISCONTINUITIES

Bronson's study provides a further illustration of the need to take account of the changes in the child's conceptualizing of his enviornment around the middle of the first year of life. Individual differences in wariness were not stable by $6\frac{1}{2}$ to 9 months. During the second half of the first year the infant's social experience and the context of the encounter with the stranger had an increasing effect on the baby's response, and new patterns of indivudal differences emerged, although some differences which Bronson attributed to temperament were still apparent. It is striking how important such demonstrations of discontinuity have been in helping us to understand the nature of the child's response in the first year. We have learned a great deal about a pattern of behaviour at one particular age, about changes in its meaning and the processes underlying it, by discovering the nature of stability and instability of individual differences in the behaviour over time. Another interesting example here is the relationship which has been found between individual differences in children's behaviour during D.Q. testing, in the first year, and later I.Q. measures. Repeated studies have failed to show any correlation between performance on infant mental development tests and later I.Q. (other than between vocalization and verbal items for girls), but quite substantial correlations have been found between ratings of the persistence and enjoyment with which a baby approaches a test item and later I.Q. (Birns and Golden, 1972). It is this 'unexpected' relationship over time, supported by other findings (Lewis and Rosenblum, 1976) which has suggested the value of a new approach to understanding infant intellectual development in the first year, an approach which emphasises the motivational aspects of the infant's behaviour.

The main obstacle to gauging the importance of these early differences is that so few studies have followed children from the first year, and that so few studies until now have combined assessment of the more global traits with behavioural observation, or combined fine-grain measurement of autonomic differences with behavioural observations over a long enough time span to make developmental assessment possible. Extremes on a continuum of rhythmicity/regularity in behaviour for instance have been implicated in the later development of disturbance (Graham, Rutter and George, 1973; Tutter and coworkers 1964), but I can find no published work using behavioural observations during the 1st year which can extend or clarify this finding, nor any work with autonomic measures that could help us to understand its basis. Until we have more information we are left unable to decide, when our direct behavioural indices fail to show continuity, whether this is because of our 'frail methodology' as Kagan has suggested, or whether the unifying trait they are supposed to index is an oversimplified construct in the mind of the psychologist. But in other cases, where several studies of different samples have found comparable relationships over time, there are grounds for more confidence. Three separate studies, for instance, have now suggested that newborn differences in sucking and in reactivity are related to differences in reaction patterns that continue into the third or fourth year (Bell, Weller and Waldrop, 1971; Yang and Halverson, 1976; Dunn and Richards, 1977). The question which we will now consider is how these continuing individual differences are related to the child's relationships with his family, and to the social environment in which he grows up.

INDIVIDUAL DIFFERENCES AND EARLY SOCIAL INTERACTION

Hereditary factors

Discussion of temperamental differences in children sometimes carries the implicit assumption that these differences are in some sense constitutional characteristics of the children, differences which can be modified by different styles of parental care, but which are essentially 'endogenous'. It must be noted however that Rutter, Korn and Birch (1963) specifically comment that their use of 'primary reaction patterns' 'in no sense implies innate or simple genetic determination of the observed individual differences'. There are a few suggestions from behavioural genetics that are interesting here: Freedman and Keller (1963) and Repucci (1968) have both found the early smiling behaviour around 4 months of age to show heritability, and Kagan suggests that this may be linked with the attention patterns of his 'slow tempo' trait. Throughout the first year his slow tempo children smiled more than the fast tempo children. He also suggests that this trait may be linked to the tendency towards inhibition rather than spontaneity which Gottesman (1966) and Scarr (1969) found to be heritable.

Torgersen (1974) carried out a study in Bergen comparing the temperamental traits of a sample of 53 same-sexed dizygotic and monozygotic twins, using an assessment based on the protocol of the New York Longitudinal Study. She assessed the twins at 2 months and at 9 months; at 2 months the differences between members of dizysotic twin pairs were significantly greater than the differences between monozygotic twins for only two traits (regularity and intensity) but by 9 months the differences between members of dizygotic pairs were significant for all nine traits. Comparing the findings at 2 and 9 months, Torgersen found that the differences between the dizygotic pairs were much increased at the later age. Since this assessment was based on mothers' reports, it is important to note that the 'majority' of mothers in the study are said not to have known the zygosity of their infants. This study certainly indicates that there is an important genetic component in temperamental differences during the first year.

Rutter, Korn and Birch (1963) analysed the information on the twins and siblings included in the New York Longitudinal Study, and found some evidence for genetic components in the categories of activity, approach/ withdrawal, and adaptability, during the first year. They also found that these were the least stable of the reactivity categories, and the evidence for genetic components was much less strong after the first year.

Continuity and patterns of social interaction

For most examples of continuity in individual differences in young children however we are simply not in a position to tell how far the stability reflects continuity of environmental variables, or how far it is 'endogenous'. It is clear for instance that differences between newborn babies are closely associated with differences in the caregiver's behaviour. Osofsky and Danzger (1974) showed that there were consistent relationships between a mother's behaviour to her baby during a feed in the newborn period, and the characteristics of the baby as assessed in the Brazelton Neonatal test. The attentive mothers tended to have responsive babies, and the baby who was alert and responded to auditory measures in the Brazelton test also looked at the mother a great deal during the feed. Dunn and Richards (1977) found that a group of measures reflecting maternal affectionate attention to the baby during feeds (looking at, smiling at, talking affectionately to the baby) was correlated with the behaviour of the baby during an assessment of the baby's non-nutritive sucking behaviour, and with his response to the removal of a pacifier. These measures were the same as the measures of latency to respond and rate of sucking which Bell took to reflect intensity of reaction. We found that a high rate of this non-nutritive sucking, in the test situation, was positively correlated with the group of measures of maternal affectionate interest during the feed. Now we did indeed trace continuities from these neonatal measures, and one example will illustrate the point that this continuity could not be assigned to the behaviour of mother or baby independently. The frequency of vocal demands made by the child at 14 months, and the mother's responsiveness to the baby's vocalizations were positively correlated with the neonatal measures (Dunn, 1977). The relationship could be expressed either as an association between the 14 month measures and the newborn maternal affectionate variables or the infant suck rate measures, and it seems better justified to express the continuity as one of interactive style rather than as a continuity of either mother or baby behaviour.

We also now know that many of the aspects of newborn behaviour discussed in relation to the individual differences in attention, and reactivity are in fact importantly related to the course of labour and delivery (e.g. Kittner and Lipsitt, 1976; Bowes and coworkers, 1970; Brackbill and coworkers, 1974). The possibility cannot be ruled out that there may be other differences between the mothers who had these more difficult deliveries, and those with easier deliveries, differences which may have affected their babies either pre- or postnatally, and which could contribute to the continuity of differences between the babies.

Many of the examples of continuity found in Kagan's longitudinal study could have arisen from continuity in individual differences between mothers, or in interactive style between mother–baby pairs. Kagan found for instance, that 21 of his 4-month-old children were particularly irritable and restless when presented with a visual display. Each of the 21 irritable children was matched with a baby who never fretted in the experimental situation, and the pairs were compared at 8, 13, and 27 months. The 12 irritable girls behaved at

13 and 27 months as if they were more advanced than the non-irritable controls. They looked longer at discrepant stimuli, vocalized more to auditory stimuli, showed less stereotyped play, and at 27 months were more talkative. Now it would be quite reasonable to hypothesize that these differences might be related to a maternal style that was consistently different from that of the control mothers—a highly stimulating, intrusive and responsive pattern of interaction for example.

In the normal family situation then it is very difficult to separate the effects of continuity of individual differences in children from those in mothers. Some preliminary findings from a study at the Matera Baby Centre at Athens do suggest, however, that a marked change in environment may well affect the stability of 'temperamental' differences between children. For babies remaining in the Institution, there were correlations between scores on the Brazelton assessment in the newborn period, and temperamental characteristics at 6 and 9 months, assessed on the Thomas, Chess and Birch interview. But for a small group of babies who were adopted at 3–4 months, the 9 month temperament assessment showed no relationship with the neonatal assessment (Tsitsikas, pers. comm.). And in a study we are carrying out with children aged between 18 months and 3 years we find that for some of the temperamental traits the child may behave very different members of the family. Adaptability, intensity of reaction, and mood may all be scored differently if questions are asked in relation to the child's style of behaviour with the father, or grandmother, as opposed to the mother.

Discontinuities

If we do take account of the potential importance of continuities in the caregiver's response in contributing to the stability of individual differences in children, it must also be noted that there may well be *discontinuities* in interaction patterns at particular stages in the child's development. Data from the Cambridge longitudinal study suggest that the point at which children begin to talk may be a stage at which continuities in maternal responsiveness, which have been stable during the first year, disappear. Consistent individual differences between the mothers in their interest in talking to their babies, in engaging them in play and in responding to the babies' noises were found throughout the first year. Now it is just these aspects of communication between mother and child which one might assume to be good predictors of later intellectual development. But there was no association between these indices of maternal response and the children's I.Q. at 4 years. There was however a link between I.Q. at 4 years and another aspect of the maternal behaviour at 14 months—a measure not of *whether* the mother responded to the child, but of *how* she responded. The children who scored highly on the I.Q. test at 4 had mothers who at 14 months had been particularly *accepting* of their verbal response to the child's word or actions. (This category of 'acceptance' has been shown to be related to some aspects of rapid language acquisition (Nelson, 1973).) A new pattern of individual differences between the mothers appears, then, when their children begin to talk, and to understand speech, and the mothers react in different ways to this new development (Dunn, 1977). If this pattern of discontinuity in individual differences in adult responsiveness is at all general it could well contribute to the greater stability of individual differences in children found after the first birthday.

NATURE OF THE SAMPLE AND THE PROBLEM OF PREDICTION

It is likely that the nature of the sample of children studied will profoundly affect the degree of stability of individual differences which is found over time. Inclusion of children of very low I.Q. can for instance increase the stability of individual differences. Exceptionally low scores on infant tests do have some predictive significance from the first months (McCall, Hogarty and Hurlburt, 1972), while average or high scores in the first year have no predictive power (McCall, 1976; Willerman and Fiedler, 1974). Where a sample includes children whose behaviour is extreme, it is possible that these children will continue to differ markedly from the rest of the sample. Kagan's study includes several examples where patterns of individual differences stable over time could be demonstrated for children scoring at the extreme of whatever behavioural measure was under scrutiny. For instance 12 boys scoring as extremely slow or fast tempo children showed impressive continuity from 8 to 36 months.

It is thus entirely possible that patterns of stable individual differences found in a sample may mask different patterns of continuity for different subgroups within the sample. Certainly we should hesitate to generalize broadly from studies of samples that may be rather special. The sample of children studied by Thomas, Chess and Birch for instance was a very homogeneous group of upper middle class children, largely drawn from the families of physicians and theatre people. In addition the researchers commented that 42 out of 141 (29%) 'presented problems that called for psychiatric attention' (Thomas, Chess and Birch, 1970).

Recently, comparisons have been made using the New York Longitudinal Study interview, or the Carey questionnaire based on it, with babies from different subcultural groups, and these have shown marked differences between the groups. Thomas and Chess (1977) compared a group of Puerto Rican babies with their middle class sample, and Sameroff and Kelly examined 220 4-month old children in Rochester (quoted in Thomas and Chess, 1977), comparing also the black and white children within the low SES group. The major differences they found between the ethnic groups must raise questions about the interpretation of questionnaire differences in such cross-cultural comparisons. Sameroff and Kelly suggest that scores from the Carey questionnaire should be used only for comparison within subcultures.

Differences in class, race, gender and culture probably influence the pattern of continuities in a number of different and important ways. The major impact of class differences probably comes after the first year, with the development of language (Golden and Birns, 1976). Kagan for instance found that the correlations between the child's social class and his reactions to the experimental situation increased steadily with age. For the girls in his sample parental education and social class were linked to attentiveness, language and problem-solving behaviour. The class indices were not however related to excitability or activity. Continuity in those aspects of behaviour associated with class differences, then, is likely to be clearer from the second year onwards. A new pattern of individual differences emerges as the child enters a new phase of development, and others in the child's social world respond to these new developments in different ways. The effects of the class differences are so massive that for some aspects of behaviour differences which were apparent in the first year are swamped. Sameroff and Chandler (1975) have reviewed several studies showing that the effects of perinatal trauma on intelligence quotients disappear unless they are combined with *continuing* severe social conditions.

These findings are paralleled by several of the results from the Cambridge longitudinal study, which was carried out with a medically low-risk sample, selected on stringent perinatal criteria. The children's behaviour during a Stanford-Binet I.Q. test, given when they were 4 years old, was rated on a dimension of distractibility-absorption, on a 3-point scale. First, there was a significant association between social class and the child's absorption in the tasks ($\chi^2 = 4.27$, $N = 55$, $p < 0.05$); in fact all the children from social class I and II were rated high or average on their attentiveness. But within the group of children from social classes 3 and 4, there was a significant relationship between the rating of attentiveness and neonatal measures. For instance, a rate of 'distractible' in the test situation was associated with a very short latency on the neonatal measure of reactivity from the sucking test. (Mann–Whitney U test: distractible at 4 yrs, median latency of response to removal of teat = 7 secs; absorbed at 4 yrs, median latency of response to removal of teat = 31 secs, $p < 0.01$ (2nd babies).) Results from another study, looking at children aged between 18 months and 2 yrs (Dunn and Wooding, 1977), have shown that the extent to which a parent pays attention to a child's activities can have an important effect on the child's own pattern of attention. This study found, moreover, social class differences in the amount of attention which the parent paid to the child's ongoing activity. Middle-class children received much more attention during their play. It seems possible that the effects of such differences in parental attention may overwhelm the variation due to differences between the children which can be traced from the neonatal stage.

In the Cambridge longitudinal study, the children's behaviour in school was assessed at $5\frac{1}{2}$ years by their teachers, who rated them on the Bristol Social Adjustment Guide (BSAG). A pattern of findings similar to the results on distractibility/attentiveness emerged. While there was no significant association between the scores on the BSAG and the neonatal measures for the sample as a whole, or for social classes I and II, among the children from social classes 3 and 4 it was found that a high score (representing more difficulties of adjustment) was positively associated with the neonatal reactivity measure (Mann–Whitney U test; high score on BSAG median latency = 6 secs; low score on BSAG median latency = 20 secs, $p < 0.01$). And a similar pattern of results was found when the children's responsiveness to the psychologist during the Stanford-Binet test was examined. A 3-point rating scale of responsiveness was used; all the children from social classes I and II scored as quickly responsive, but among the children from social classes 3 and 4 there was a tendency for the children who had been quickly reactive as newborns to be most responsive in the test situation. (Mann Whitney U test; quick to respond at 4 yrs, median latency = 12 secs; slow to respond at 4 yrs, median latency = 19 secs, $p < 0.06$). There was also a significant association, within classes 3 and 4, between the level of education the mother had received, and the child's response to the psychologist. (Mothers who had taken O-levels were more likely to have children rated as responsive; $\chi^2 = 4, p < 0.05$.)

Many of the measures of newborn behaviour discussed here have shown differences between ethnic groups: scores on the Brazelton Neonatal assessment have been found to differ between American samples and samples of Chinese–American, Uruguayan, and Mexican babies (Brazelton, 1973). Differences in response to soothing, and in self-quieting were particularly marked. The origins of these differences is not known, nor is their long term significance, but it is clear that they may well influence the pattern of interaction with caregivers. We know too that there are differences between cultures in the way that caregivers respond to babies, and in the value placed on different temperamental traits. Caudill and Weinstein (1969) in a study comparing Japanese and American middle-class mothers and babies showed marked differences between the cultures in the caretaking of the 3 month old babies and in the behaviour of the babies. The American babies were more active, more vocal, and more exploratory than the Japanese babies. Parallel differences were found in the mothers: the American mothers had a stimulating and lively approach. An important difference between the two groups was found in the links between the behaviour of baby and mother. The American mothers responded to happy noises from their babies by stimulating them further with talking and playing. The Japanese mothers interacted with their babies to soothe them when they were fretful, and did not respond in the same way to the happy vocal behaviour. It is not known how far these early differences set up particular patterns of responsiveness in the children which continue beyond the first year. (Rebelsky and Black's (1972) study of Dutch and American babies found that there were differences in social behaviour between the two groups of babies in the early months, and the Dutch babies were developmentally behind, but that by the end of the first year the differences had disappeared.) But it is certainly important to consider the extent to which any pattern of continuities of individual differences may reflect particular features of the group studied.

Early differences and later disorder

Much of our interest in continuities of individual differences from the first year stems from the hope that we will learn how to predict which children are particularly likely to develop difficulties later. In the New York Longitudinal Study, comparisons were made between the children who were referred for psychiatric help and the rest of the sample (Rutter, Korn and Birch, 1964). There were no significant differences, during the first year, in the rank on temperamental characteristics of the 21 children who were later referred for help, and those of the other 71 children. During the second year, however, patterns of temperamental characteristics did significantly differentiate the clinical cases, though prediction on the basis of any one category would have been unsatisfactory. A pattern of irregularity, high intensity, unadaptability, and negative mood was particularly likely to be associated with later problems. Even so, two-thirds of the children later referred did not fit this pattern.

The same association between this pattern of temperamental characteristics and later behaviour disorder was found in a more recent study (Graham, Rutter and George, 1973), which was based on a group of families where one parent was receiving psychiatric care. The children who were most likely to show disorder one year later were those with irregular sleeping and feeding, who were unadaptable, lacked fastidiousness and who tended to be negative in mood and intense in their emotional expression. When these attributes were combined to form a 'temperamental adversity index', it was found that children with high scores were three times more likely than those with low scores to show psychiatric disorder later (Rutter and coworkers, 1977).

Other chapters in this volume discuss the consequences of various perinatal problems, and the incidence of behavioural problems associated with them. Some findings from the medically low risk sample in the Cambridge study (Richards and Bernal, 1972; Dunn and Richards, 1977), illustrate both the possibilities and the problems of predicting the development of difficulties in a sample of normal infants. By 14 months, the most common problem causing concern to parents was that of sleeping difficulties. The group of children who were regular night wakers at 14 months had not only consistently slept less than the rest of the sample from the first postnatal week, but during the early post-natal days had cried more frequently, woken more frequently, and on the sucking test had responded with significantly shorter latency to the removal of the teat. Their deliveries had tended to be more difficult (though still in the

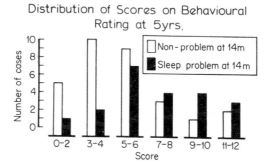

Figure 4.1 Distribution of scores on behavioural
rating at 5 years

normal range on defined perinatal criteria) (Bernal, 1973). At five years of age
it was found that children who had been sleep problems at 14 months
were significantly more likely to score above the median on a rating of behaviour
problems, based on Richman and Graham (1977) (Figure 4.1). (Sleep problem
group median score = 7.5; rest of sample median score = 4.5; $\chi^2 = 6.9$,
$p < 0.01$.) However it must be noted that several individuals who scored
relatively highly on the problem rated at 5 had not been sleep problems at
14 months, and vice versa. We would not use the fact that a child was a sleep
problem at 14 months as a predictor of any great power, although it does perhaps
suggest that sleep problems in the second year are worth some attention from
the clinician.

Autonomic measures have been discussed earlier in the context of the research
on attention. It is perhaps even more important to know more about individual
differences between babies in these autonomic indices in the context of possible
links between individual differences in psycho-physiological responses to
stressors and the development of disease. But as Venables (1975) noted, we do
not yet know the answers to several key questions here. How reliable are these
measures, and how far do they remain characteristic of the person? And how
soon in his life are these measures characteristic of a person, assuming they
are stable characteristics? Until we know more about the answers to these
questions we shall not be in a position to judge how useful the autonomic
indices will prove for predicting high risk groups during the first years of life.

CONCLUSIONS

The first year of life presents particular difficulties for those looking for
stable patterns of individual differences. The difficulties of interpreting infant
behaviour, and thus assigning it to more global categories are great, the develop-

mental changes are so rapid that an important source of variation at any one age may well be the rate of development itself, and we are a long way from understanding the significance of differences in autonomic indices in the early months. But lack of stability may not simply reflect problems of measurement. There may be important changes in behavioural organization during the first year which lead to major discontinuities in development. Too few studies follow children in detail from the early months until the second or third year, and when the information from those studies which do is carefully examined it is clear that we remain free to stress either the continuities, or the lack of stability, according to our own prejudices. Thomas, Chess and Birch's emphasis on patterns of stable individual differences that could be linked to behavioural problems was of great importance, at a stage when little recognition was given to the 'nature of the child as an organism'. Their study grew out of an explicit 'concern over the apparent one-sidedness of the prevalent approach to the development of personality'. Kagan, too, specifically commented that he had deliberately chosen to emphasize the continuities in his data, while it would have been open to him to stress the modest size of the correlations, and the inherent instability. In Figure 4.1 either the continuing differences between our two groups of children over a period of four years, or indeed the evidence for the change in some individuals could be emphasized. Evidence for the flexibility of developmental processes is of course encouraging for those concerned with clinical problems, and there is now a growing interest in theoretical models which take account of the adaptability in development. We find that developmental models such as Waddington's epigenetic process which allow for considerable flexibility, are discussed in the context of both early personality development (Bowlby, 1973) and of perceptual and cognitive development (Bower, 1974). These theoretical models seem potentially much more useful than earlier more rigid notions, and would not conflict with the evidence that dramatic changes in environment even after the first two years can have a marked effect (Kagan, 1976; Tizard and Rees, 1975). If we are to understand the developmental importance of individual differences in infancy, what we need is research that draws imaginatively on the different ways of studying the children, on the understanding of clinicians and of developmental psychologists, research which takes account of the complexity of mutual influences within the family, and of the overriding importance of seeing development as an essentially long term process.

ACKNOWLEDGEMENTS

This chapter was written while the author was supported by the Medical Research Council. I am grateful to Robert Hinde and John Dunn for their helpful comments on the manuscript.

88 THE FIRST YEAR OF LIFE

REFERENCES

Bell, R. Q., Weller, G. M., and Waldrop, M. F. (1971). 'Newborn and preschooler: organization of behaviour and relations between periods', *Monogr. of the Soc. Res. Child Devel.*, **36**(1–2) no. 142.

Bernal, J. F. (1973). 'Night-waking in the first 14 months', *Developmental Medicine and Child Neurology*, **15**, 760–769.

Birns, B., Barten, S., and Bridges, N. (1969). Individual differences in temperamental characteristics of infants', *Transactions of the New York Academy of Sciences*, **31**, 1071–1082.

Birns, B. and Golden, M. (1972). 'Prediction of intellectual performance at 3 years on the basis of infant tests and personality measures', *Merrill-Palmer Quarterly*, **18**, 53.

Bower, T. (1974). *Development in Infancy*, Freeman, San Francisco.

Bowes, W. A., Brackbill, Y., Conway, E., and Steinschneider, A. (1970). 'The effects of obstetrical medication on fetus and infant', *Monogr. of the Soc. Res. Child Devel.*, **35** (4) no. 137.

Bowlby, J. (1973). *Attachment and Loss: 2. Separation, Anxiety and Anger*, Hogarth Press, London.

Brackbill, Y., Kane, J., Manniello, R. L., and Abramson, D. (1974). 'Obstetric premedication and infant outcome', *American Journal of Obstetrics and Gynecology*, **118**(3), 377–384.

Brazelton, T. B. (1973). *Neonatal Assessment Scale*, Heinemann Medical Books, London.

Bronson, G. W. (1972). 'Infants' reactions to unfamiliar persons and objects', *Monogr. of the Soc. Res. Child Devel.*, 148, **37**, no. 3.

Carey, W. B. (1970). 'A simplified method for measuring infant temperament', *Journal of Pediatrics*, **77**, 188–194.

Carey, W. B. (1974). 'Night waking and temperament in infancy', *Journal of Pediatrics*, **84**, No. 5, 756–758.

Caudill, W. and Weinstein, H. (1969). 'Maternal care and infant behaviour in Japan and America', *Psychiatry*, **32**, 12–43.

Christie, M. (1975). 'The psychosocial environment and precursors of disease', in Venables P. and Christie M. (eds.), *Research in Psychophysiology*, Wiley, London.

Clifton, R. K. and Graham, F. K. (1968). 'Stability of individual differences in heart rate activity during the newborn period', *Psychophysiology*, 5, 37.

Dunn, J. F. (1977). 'Patterns of early interaction: continuities and consequences', in Schaffer H. R. (ed.), *Studies in Parent–Infant Interaction*, Academic Press, London.

Dunn, J. F. and Richards, M. P. M. (1977). 'Observations on the developing relationship between mother and baby in the newborn', in Schaffer H. R. (ed.), *Studies in Parent–Infant Interaction*, Academic Press, London.

Dunn, J. E. and Wooding, C. (1977). 'Play, learning and interaction with the mother', in Tizard B. and Harvey D. (eds.), *The Biology of Play*, Heinemann Medical Books, London.

Emde, R. N., Gaensbauer, T. J., and Harmon, R. J. (1976). *Emotional Expression in Infancy*, Psychological Issues, x, 37, International Universities Press, New York.

Freeman, D. G. and Keller, B. (1963). 'Inheritance of behavior in infants', *Science*, **40**, 196.

Garside, R. F., Birch, H., Scott, D. M. I., Chambers, S., Kolvin, I., Tweddle, E. G., and Barber, L. M. (1975). 'Dimensions of temperament in infant school children', *Journal of Child Psychology and Psychiatry*, **16**, 219–223.

Golden, M. and Birns, B. (1976). 'Social class and infant intelligence', in M. Lewis (ed.), *The Origins of Intelligence*, Plenum Press, New York.

Gottesman, I. I. (1966). Genetic variation in adaptive personality tests, *J. Child Psychol. Psychiat.*, **7**, 199–208.

Graham, P., Rutter, M., and George, S. (1973). 'Temperamental characteristics as predictors of behaviour disorders in children', *American Journal of Orthopsychiatry*, **43**(3), 328–339.

Halverson, C. F. and Waldrop, M. F. (1976). 'Relations between preschool activity and aspects of intellectual and social behaviour at age $7\frac{1}{2}$', *Developmental Psychology*, **12**, no. 2, 107–112.

Kagan, J. (1971). *Change and Continuity in Infancy*, Wiley, New York.

Kagan, J. (1976). 'Emergent themes in human development', *American Scientists*, **64**, 186–196.

Kittner, S. and Lipsitt, L. P. (1976). 'Obstetric history and the heart rate response of newborns to sound', *Developmental Medicine and Child Neurology*, **18**, 460–470.

Lewis, M. (1974). 'The cardiac response in infancy', in Thomson R. F. and Patterson M. M. (eds.), *Methods in Physiological Psychology*, Vol. Ic, Academic Press, New York.

Lewis, M. and Rosenblum, L. A. (1976). *The Origins of Intelligence*, Wiley, New York.

Lewis, M., Wilson, C., Ban, P., and Baumel, M. (1970). 'An exploratory study of resting cardiac rate and variability from the last trimester of prenatal life through the first year of postnatal life', *Child Development*, **41**, 799–811.

Lipton, E. L., Steinschneider, A., and Richmond, J. B. (1961). 'Autonomic function in the neonate. IV. Individual differences in cardiac reactivity', *Psychosomatic Medicine*, **23**, no. 6, 472–484.

McCall, R. B. (1971). 'Attention in the infant: avenue to the study of cognitive development', in Walcher D. and Peters D. (eds.), *Early Childhood: the development of self-regulatory mechanisms*, Academic Press, New York.

McCall, R. B. (1975). Commentary in F. D. Horowitz (ed.) 'Visual attention, auditory stimulation and language discrimination in young infants', *Monogr. of the Soc. Res. Child Devel.*, **39**, (5–6), no. 158.

McCall, R. B. (1976). 'Toward an epigenetic conception of mental development', in Lewis M. (ed.), *Origins of Intelligence*, Plenum Press, New York.

McCall, R. B., Hogarty, P. S., and Hurlburt, N. (1972). 'Transitions in infant sensorimotor development and the prediction of childhood I. Q.', *American Psychologist*, **27**, 728.

Mednick, S. and Schlusinger, F. (1968). 'Some pre-morbid characteristics related to breakdown in children with schizophrenic mothers', in Rosenthal D. and Kety S. S. (eds.), *The Transmission of Schizophrenia*, Pergamon Press, Oxford.

Nelson, K. (1973). Structure and strategy in learning to talk, *Monogr. Soc. Res. Child Devel.*, No. 149.

Osofsky, J. D. and Danzger, B. (1974). 'Relationships between neonatal characteristics and mother–infant interaction', *Developmental Psychology*, **10**, no. 1, 124–130.

Rebelsky, F. and Black, R. (1972). 'Crying in Infancy', *Journal of Genetic Psychology*, **121**, 49–67.

Repucci, C. M. (1968). *Hereditary influences upon distribution of attention in infancy*, unpublished doctoral dissertation, Harvard University.

Richards, M. P. M. and Bernal, J. F. (1972). 'An observational study of mother–infant interaction', in Blurton Jones N. (ed.), *Ethological Studies of Child Behaviour*, Cambridge University Press, Cambridge.

Richman, N. and Graham, P. J. (1971). 'A behavioural screening questionnaire for use with 3 year-old children: preliminary findings', *Journal of Child Psychology and Psychiatry*, **12**, 5–32.

Richmond, J. B. and Lipton, E. L. (1959). 'Some aspects of the neurophysiology of the newborn and their implications for child development', in Jessner L. and Pavenstedt E.

(eds.), *Dynamic Psychopathology in Childhood*, Grune and Stratton, New York.

Rutter, M., Birch, H., Thomas, A., and Chess, S. (1964). 'Temperamental characteristics in infancy and the later development of behavioral disorders', *British Journal of Psychiatry*, **110**, 651–661.

Rutter, M., Korn, S. and Birch, H. (1963). 'Genetic and environmental factors in the development of "primary reaction patterns"', *British Journal of Social and Clinical Psychology*, **2**, 161–173.

Rutter, M., Quinton, D., and Yule, B. (in press). *Family Pathology and Disorder in Children*, Wiley, London.

Sameroff, A. N. and Chandler, M. J. (1975). 'Reproductive risk and the continuum of caretaking casualty', in Horowitz F. D., Hetherington, M., Scarr-Salapatek S. and Stegel G. (eds.), *Review of Child Development Research*, Vol. 4., University of Chicago Press, Chicago.

Scarr, S. (1969). Social introversion–extraversion as a heritable response, *Child Development*, **40**, 823–832.

Schachter, J., Kerry, J. L., Wimberley, F. C., and Lachin, J. M. (1975). 'Phasic heart rate responses: different patterns in black and white newborns', *Psychosomatic Medicine*, **37**, No. 4, 326–332.

Schwartz, A. N., Campos, J. J., and Baisel, E. (1973). 'The visual cliff: cardiac and behavioural correlates on the deep and shallow sides at five and nine months of age', *Journal of Experimental Child Psychology*, **15**, 85–99.

Sroufe, L. A., Walters, E., and Matas, L. (1974). 'Contextual determinants of infant affective response', in Lewis M. and Rosenblum L. A., (eds.), *The Origins of Fear*, Wiley, New York.

Taylor, S. P. and Epstein, S. (1968). 'The measurement of autonomic arousal', *Psychosomatic Medicine*, **29**, No. 5, 514–525.

Thomas, A. and Chess, S. (1977). *Temperament and Development*, Brunner/Mazel, New York.

Thomas, A., Chess, S., Birch, H. G., Hartzig, M. E., and Korn, S. (1963). *Behavioral Individuality in Early Childhood*, New York University Press, New York.

Thomas, A., Chess, S., and Birch, H. G. (1970). 'The origin of personality', *Scientific American*, **223**, No. 2, 102–109.

Tizard, B. and Rees, J. (1975). 'The effects of early institutional rearing on the behaviour problems and affectional relationships of four-year-old children', *Journal of Child Pcyshology and Psychiatry*, **16**, 61–73.

Torgerson, A. M. (1974). Temperamental differences in infants: Illustrated through a study of turns. Paper presented at a conference on Temperament and Personality, Warsaw.

Venables, P. (1975). 'Progress in psychophysiology: some applications in a field of abnormal psychology', in Venables P. and Christie M. (eds.), *Research in Psychophysiology*, Wiley London.

Willerman, L. and Fieldler, M. F. (1974). 'Infant performance and intellectual precocity', *Developmental Psychology*, **45**, 483.

Wilson, C. D. and Lewis, M. (1971). *A developmental study of attention: a multi-variate approach*, Paper presented at the Eastern Psychological Association, New York, April 1971.

Wilson, C. D. and Lewis, M. (1974). *Temperament: a developmental study in stability and change during the first four years of life*, E. T. S. Bulletin, Princeton.

Yang, R. K. and Halverson, C. F. (1976). 'A study of the "inversion of intensity" between newborn and preschool-age behavior', *Child Development*, **47**, 350–359.

Chapter 5

Intentional Behaviour in the Young Infant

John Newson

This chapter is concerned with the development of communication competence between young babies and their consistent caregivers during the period of early infancy. In the course of a series of studies at Nottingham (Newson, 1974; Newson and Shotter, 1974; Newson, 1977) we have become more and more impressed with the normal infant's capacity to engage in very complex and sophisticated social interactions, and the focus of the work, which began with infants between 10 and 18 months, has inevitably shifted downwards along the age-scale to the first 6 months of life. Our notions about the nature of communicative competence have, during these studies, become increasingly refined: the focus is now almost exclusively upon strategies of communication at the strictly pre-verbal level. Our concern is, then, with the establishment of a code of communication between mother and child at an age when even the passive understanding of words addressed to the child is clearly impossible. The studies are focussed upon the infant's ability to react reciprocally to patterns of sound and movement, upon the development of imitation and upon those mysterious processes which underlie the baby's capacity to share states of feeling with those around him. The attempt, in short, is to investigate and understand something about the ontogenesis of human empathy.

The approach we adopted is one which sees 'mothering' less as an unanalysable gift and more as a skilled performance which arises out of first-hand experience in interacting with babies. It is therefore not exclusively the prerogative of mothers or even of the female sex. The skill is manifest in the moment-by-moment adjustments one makes when confronted with a pre-verbal infant with whom one is trying to relate communicatively and needs to be analysed in micro-detail if we are to understand how complex the reactions of both parties are, during the course of normally unselfconscious interaction.

The actions which babies emit have characteristic forms which are apparently pan-cultural. They move their heads, wave their arms and legs, breathe heavily, vocalize, blow raspberries, screw up their faces and shift their visual regard, etc.

in ways which are clearly biologically preprogrammed. Individual movements are also integrated into coordinated action-patterns which 'run-off' in sequences of activity interspersed with natural breaks in a typical 'burst–pause' pattern. When closely examined in temporal perspective the stream of behaviour is clearly organized with intrinsic periodicity and in accordance with certain universal and fundamental rhythms. We probably respond to certain action patterns as wholes only because our own attentional mechanisms are 'tuned' to be sensitive to precisely similar cyclic and rhythmic patterns as those of the baby.

From birth human infants are responded to by their normal mothers as beings already able to communicate to other persons fairly directly, at least at the level of being able to indicate that they have urgent wants and discomforts, or that they are relaxed and content. More strikingly, however, infants are so organized that they are able to participate both actively and effortlessly in conversation-like exchanges within a format which conforms to a two-way alternating dialogue. Typically the infant and his regular adult caregiver come to operate according to a turn-taking sequence in which each partner first acts and then attends to the activity of the other (Schaffer, 1974).

There is controversy about whether this alternation of activity indicates some intrinsic predisposition towards turn-taking in the baby, or is an artefact of the controlling influence exerted by the more conversationally experienced partner. As already suggested, however, much neonatal activity follows a burst-pause cycle; if the adult merely filled in the infant's own pauses with his own bursts of activity a turn-taking pattern of activity would appear.

When an infant is faced with an 'object' which is responsive to his own activity, it is an interesting fact that he may easily become locked into a sustained sequence of interactive functioning. His movements give rise to effects which compel his visual and auditory attention, eliciting an 'orienting response'. As a result of this his previous movements are inhibited, but soon his attention begins to falter and he starts once more to indulge in active bodily movement. If this again produces external change his attention is once more commandeered and the cycle commences all over again. In this way dyadic interaction is naturally self-sustaining. An easy way to demonstrate the persistent engagement which can thus take place between an infant and an 'environmentally responsive' device is to link the infant's limb with some visible display which responds variably with an appropriate time delay. When, for example, a string attached to the child's wrist is linked to a mobile placed clearly within his view, thus causing it to be disturbed whenever he waves his arms, it has been reported— and we ourselves have independently confirmed this—that even babies as young as six weeks seem to be constrained to 'work' at operating the device so that the child's attentive involvement is characteristically sustained over long periods of time (Papousek, 1967; Kalnins and Bruner, 1973).

The precise feedback characteristics which facilitate such 'self-rewarding' activity are still but little understood, but they obviously include an optimal time delay between action and consequent reaction, and a variable, but not entirely unpredictable, outcome in the form of some consequent effect to which the infant does in fact attend. This optimal time delay may be related to the natural rate of signal exchange. This turns out to be about 30 signals for each partner per minute or 1 per sec. for both.

A mobile is, however, only sensitive to the infant's actions to a very limited degree, in this case being merely responsive to gross arm movements above a certain minimum amplitude. As an 'environmentally responsive feedback system', a human caregiver is a lot more sophisticated. Firstly, such an individual will emit behaviour which is peculiarly liable not only to recruit the baby's full attention, but also to elicit gestural responses from him which are characteristically of a formally similar kind. Under optimal conditions, mouthing and vocalizing at the baby will cause him to respond with conversation-like expressive gestures. These include limb movements and mouthings appropriate for vocalization even when no sound is forthcoming. More specifically, tongue poking has been shown to elicit tongue poking, more easily during the first two months than later (Maratos, 1976) and certain forms of rhythmic auditory stimulation including the human voice can induce a baby to respond with sympathetic synchronous whole body movements (Condon and Sander, 1974). All these facts make it marginally less surprising that adult and infant are able to regulate their joint activity harmoniously and are soon able to produce a very adequate simulation of mature human discourse.

To understand how intentional behaviour arises it is necessary first to project oneself into the role of someone who is trying to communicate with the infant. Such a person is bound to respond selectively to precisely those actions, on the part of the baby, to which one would normally react *given the assumption that the baby, like oneself, is in essence a communicating being or person.* In other words, the caregiver, being already well practised in the art of communication, will not respond indiscriminately to all aspects of the infant's activity. Instead, he or she will selectively attend to those actions to which one would habitually attach significance as gestures which are normally meaningful in ordinary human discourse. Ordinary 'mothering' thus implies a selective monitoring function which constantly seeks to understand what is commanding the attention of the other. Being continuously influenced by the infant's direction of regard, intensity of gaze and gesticulations is therefore characteristic of the sensitive human caregiver. Other changes in the infant's facial expression will also be watched for and noted, because they will automatically be interpreted as changes in state which the infant is assumed to be experiencing. If he begins to look 'pained' it will be assumed that he is suffering distress. Similarly, right from the moment of birth, one automatically finds oneself distinguishing between uncoordinated spasmic movements which seem to overtake the infant and coordinated hand swipes apparently aimed with some degree of intention towards objects in the external world.

The response mechanisms of the ordinary human communicator are, however, so delicately tuned that we are able to respond, in anticipation, to what might be called meaningful actions in the making. For example, when a mother sees the beginnings of a turned-down mouth in the facial expression of her child, she may immediately act to distract him *before* his lower lip begins to tremble, and thus may succeed in diverting him before his discomfort irrevocably engages his attention. In this instance the action is deliberately prevented from running its 'normal' course. It is in fact a taken-for-granted aspect of normal mothering that distress in an infant may be cut short by using such distraction strategies. Somewhat less obviously, perhaps, actions which the mother values may skilfully be drawn out of the infant. Thus, by judicious anticipation allied with angling for the baby's attention at the right moment, full-blown smiles may be got from a baby by building upon the first incipient smile-like gestures which the mother thinks she is able to detect. What eventually leads her to distinguish between a mere grimace and a true social smile is probably that the latter can be reliably elicited in a ritual consisting of nodding and smiling at the infant. In other words, it is the context and timing of the baby's gesture, in relation to the mother's attempt to bring it out as an integral part of a *social exchange*, which is critical in determining whether a smile is considered 'social'. It follows that the meaning of a smile, as a social gesture, is inseparably bound up with the infant's ability to use it in a socially appropriate manner, i.e. at precisely the right moment within a dialogue of social interaction.

What is being argued here is that, whenever he is in the presence of another human being, the actions of a baby are not just being automatically reflected back to him in terms of their physical consequences. Instead they are being processed through a subjective filter of human interpretation, according to which some, *but only some*, of his actions are judged to have coherence and relevance in human terms—either as movements born of intentions, or as communications (or potential communications) addressed to another socially aware individual. It is thus only because mothers *impute* meaning to 'behaviours' elicited from infants that these eventually do come to constitute meaningful actions as far as the child himself is concerned. Actions achieve this status to the extent that they are capable of being used as communication gestures which he knows how to produce, on cue, in the context of a social exchange between himself and someone else. In a real sense, therefore, gestures only acquire their *significance* in so far as they can be utilized as currency within social dialogues.

In summary, what is being argued here is that mothers, by treating their infants as beings already capable of some communication and by assuming that they are continuously developing an ever-expanding corpus of shared understanding with them, about actions that can be performed, and happenings of which they are both aware, tend to perform a 'scaffolding function' by which intentions are imputed or attributed as a stage towards their subsequent acquisition by the infant. The term 'scaffolding' was first used in the context of mother–child interaction by Bruner; as an analogy it is of course dangerous to use, but seems particularly apt here. For the builder a scaffold is something which is erected one step at a time ahead of the actual building; it is clearly necessary in constructing the edifice, it closely mimics the form which the building will eventually have, yet at the end of the process it can be dismantled entirely leaving no trace of itself, while the structure remains entirely self-supporting. Numerous examples could be given of the way mothers operate to facilitate the building of the child's fundamental structures of thought and feeling using the scaffolding technique. The same basic process is seen in the phenomenon of pseudo imitative behaviour (e.g. the process by which the mother teaches her child to bang the table in rhythmic alternation with herself); in engaging him in game-like repetitive rituals such as 'walky round the garden ...'; in assisting her baby to play an appropriate reciprocal role in transactions such as offering an object for him to take or encouraging him to give something back; in leading him towards the appropriate use of a pointing gesture; etc. etc. In each and every one of these instances the mother first attributes to the child the intention to perform some act in its appropriate context as a necessary step towards inducing genuine intentionality into his future repertoire of meaningful actions. As a necessary background the concept of an assumed 'conversation without words', and the format of a turn-taking dialogue, seem to be a necessary prerequisite for giving the child a secure foothold within that socially shared structure of ideas, concepts, implicit understandings and emotional feelings which constitute our particular human culture.

In the context of this volume, with its concern for the significance of the first year for later development, the concept of this 'conversation without words' does something to explain why consistency and continuity in care-giving is so essential to early human development. It is one aspect of the general notion that adequate mothering is essential to the human infant since the process of mediating the culture to the child is a progressive and cumulative matter. It takes time and close attention-giving for an adult to establish a viable code of communication with any pre-verbal infant. Disruption of the relationship could be expected to set the child back to square one, by robbing him of the one person with whom he is beginning to establish all sorts of shared understandings both cognitive and emotional. It takes many hours of sustained interpersonal interaction to build that kind of rapport with any infant in the first year of life and the code that is established is bound to be idiosyncratic in content until the unifying constructs of verbal language begin to take over. These in turn however seem to be grounded on a firm sediment of shared intentional structures.

The studies to which I have referred have been based on video-tapes of sensitive caring and predominantly middle-class volunteers, whose babies are not obviously in any 'at risk' category. They have not included any incidents of conflict and frustration between mothers and babies, however it can be argued that these, too, generally involve treating the infant as a responsive individual, so that even if a baby is seen as diabolically wilful or unreasonably demanding he is still probably being reacted to as one party within a dialogue and is being credited with intentions which he may subsequently acquire. It must also be stressed that the mothering 'skill' we are studying is not one which will necessarily be improved by making mothers in general unusually self-conscious about the delicate and intricate patterns which can be seen to underlie the way most normal persons are able to pace their signals and time their interventions, whenever they engage in ordinary two-way social exchanges. We do play our recordings back to parents and we do learn a lot from our discussions with them when reviewing particular incidents, but the 'participant mode' of understanding interaction is hugely expanded when both participant and investigator are able to analyse the process from an 'observer stand-point' as well; it is the bringing together of these two modes of apprehending that seem to be essential if our knowledge of communication processes is to be extended fruitfully.

REFERENCES

Condon, W. S. and Sander, L. W. (1974). 'Neonate movement is synchronised with adult speech: interactional participation and language acquisition', *Science*, **183**, 99–101.

Gray, H. (1978). 'Learning to take an object from the mother', in Lock, A. (ed.) *Action, Symbol and Gesture: The Emergence of Language*, Academic Press, London.

Jones, O. H. M. (1977a). 'Mother–Child Communication with Pre-Linguistic Down's Syndrome and Normal Infants', in Schaffer, H. R. (ed.), *Infant Interaction*, Academic Press, London.

Jones, O. H. M. (1977b). *Mother–Child Communication with Young Down's Syndrome and Young Normal Children*, Ph.D. Thesis, Nottingham University.

Mogford, K. (1972). *Communication of Young Severely Handicapped Children*, Internal circulation, Child Development Research Unit, Nottingham University.

Newson, J. (1974). 'Towards a Theory of Infant Understanding', *Bull. Br. Psychol. Soc.*, **27**, 251–257.

Newson, J. and Shotter, J. (1974). 'How Babies Communicate', *New Society*, **29**, 8th August. Also republished in *Growing up: A New Society Social Studies Reader*, IPC Magazines Ltd., 1976.

Newson, J. and Newson, E. (1976). 'On the Social Origins of Symbolic Functioning', in Varma, V. P. and Williams, P. (eds.), *Piaget, Psychology and Education*, Hodder and Stoughton, London.

Newson, J. (1977). 'An Intersubjective Approach to, the Systematic Description of Mother–Infant Interaction', in Schaffer, H. R. (ed.), *Infant Interaction*, Academic Press, London.

Newson, J. (1978). 'Dialogue and Development', in Lock, A. (ed.), *Action, Symbol and Gesture: The Emergence of Language*, Academic Press, London.

Newson, J. and Newson, E. (in press). 'People as Playthings: Some Research Background', in *Toys and Playthings in Development and Remediation*, Penguin Books Ltd., Harmondsworth.

Chapter 6

Child Development Research Findings and Psychoanalytic Theory–An Integrative Critique

Arnon Bentovim

INTRODUCTION—AN INTEGRATIVE CRITIQUE—LEGITIMATE OR ILLEGITIMATE

The first question that has to be asked is whether it is legitimate to attempt to integrate child development research and psychoanalytic theories. There has been considerable opposition to such attempts. Slater (1975) criticized depth psychologies and by implication psychoanalysis, as being subjective, endopsychic, and unscientific. Bowlby (1969 and 1973) found psychoanalytic theories non-biological and based on an out-dated Lamarkian view of evolution. Dare (1976) has pointed out that psychoanalytic theories are of necessity post-dictive rather than predictive, as they arise from a treatment situation in which the psychoanalyst is attempting to help a patient make sense out of his present life, in terms of his past experiences. Dare has also attempted to separate psychoanalytic theories from developmental theories by describing psycho-analysis as concerned with the ontogeny of the way the individual experiences himself and his world, that is to do with the development of subjective experi-ence. Slater (1975) allies such concern with the subjective to disciplines such as the humanities, aesthetics, economics and education rather than to scientific disciplines. In these subjects complex problems arise which are not open to the empirical solutions of scientific method, but do need theories to provide the internal certitude which helps the worker to continue. Slater also observed that Freud's theories were especially well adapted to sustain what he feels is a 'necessary delusion'.

Such views might appear to indicate that integration of a scientific discipline, with a discipline concerned with the subjective is an attempt to marry incompa-tibles. However, even necessary delusions may be open to empirical observa-tions, and the suggestion that psychoanalytic theories are not equivalent to scientific theories has been rebutted by Kelk (1977), who questioned Popper's assertion (Popper, 1972) that scientific endeavour must be based on falsification of theories rather than proof. The phenomenologists (Gorman, 1975) feel that scientists too have an essential subjective aspect to their work. They have paradigms (Kuhn, 1970) and theories which may be held onto as tenaciously as any psychoanalyst holds to his theory despite 'evidence' to the contrary. Slater says that scientists are 'rooted in the ideologies of their era, brain washed by their teachers, blinded by prejudices and at times even tend to cheat and lie', that is to reject falsifications in order to prove their strongly-held theories. Although he asserts that such actions are those of some scientists rather than science itself, it may be permissible to consider a subjective component as vital to scientific thinking, so that psychoanalytic theories and propositions about subjective experiences must be taken seriously. Such theories may be helpful in explaining empirical findings and in directing further tests to examine the strength of the hypotheses. Wisdom (1968) set out to explore this possibility by setting out a methodology to compare what he called the 'cabbage' (or tabula rasa) theory of the infant's experience with a theory of early infant competence. Eysenck and Wilson (1973) also defended their examination of experiments on Freudian theories, by pointing out that deductions and experiments based on Palovian or Hullian theory could as easily be dismissed, as their scientific construction was less rigorous than might be considered desirable. Fisher and Greenberg (1977) have recently stated that 'We have been amused by the fact that while there is the stereotyped conviction widely current that Freud's thinking is not amenable to scientific appraisal, the quantity of research data pertinent to it that has accumulated in the literature grossly exceeds that available for most other personality or developmental theories'.

Although the assertion that there is compatability, and possible exchange between child development research and psychoanalytic theory, has not been proven, there seems to be more than sufficient basis to continue the examination.

PSYCHOANALYTIC THEORY AND CHILD DEVELOPMENT RESEARCH—PAST AND PRESENT

If we examine the influence of psychoanalytic theories historically on child development research, we find a number of child development researchers including Schaffer (1971) and Mussen, Conger and Kagan, (1969) pointing out that Freud's theories about the development of the infant and young child were an important antidote to James' (1890) concept of the new born infant in disarray, 'assailed by eyes, ears, nose, skin and entrails all at once, feels it all as one great blooming, buzzing confusion'. Freud's view by comparison emphasized organization, order and meaning, however primitive, from the beginning. Dare (1976) summarized three characteristics of Freud's theory of development as

1. phasic, with libidinal stages moving from the oral through the anal to the phallic.

2. concerned with the growth of 'thinking', developing from 'primary' to 'secondary' process thought.
3. concerned with the growth of the self or 'ego' developing from birth.

Using these concepts, psychological dysfunction is then seen as a disturbance or disruption of these developmental stages and processes. Anna Freud (Freud, 1965) has developed these ideas further in her concept of development lines. Although Schaffer (1971) and Caldwell (1964) have pointed out that there is no single study available which firmly and without ambiguity demonstrates that specific experiences at particular times leave permanent effects, they also note that the basic fault of many studies is to disregard the infant—the 'experiencing' child—as a key variable. If the focus of research has now moved from the impact of caretaker on infant to 'the effect of the infant on the caretaker'. (Bell, 1968, Lewis and Rosenblum, 1974), child development research may well need a set of theories which focus on the subjective phenomena of the experiencing infant to lend a structure to the numerous observations now being described.

'ORAL ATTACHMENT' TO OBJECT RELATIONSHIPS

One psychoanalytic theory concerning the growth of the infant's subjective experiences has been evaluated extensively. This is the secondary drive or 'cupboard love' theory of attachment. This puts forward the proposition that the figure who provides relief of the infant's hunger and tension through a good feeding relationship will also act as a first object of the infant's love. The 'object' used in this sense is a concept which first emerged from Freud's instinct theory (1905) and is used in the sense of 'the object of my passion or hatred' (Laplanche and Pontalis, 1973). The object of an instinct or an impulse, is the agent through which the instinctual aim is achieved. This is usually through another person or a part of them. Thus the first object is seen to be an 'oral' one, with the infant having the aim of seeking satisfaction from hunger through the breast. Classical psychoanalytic theory thus sees the infant born without an idea of the social world, that is 'objectless', and gradually forming ideas about this world through frequently repeated satisfactory experiences at the breast (described as a 'part-object') and a gradual appreciation of the whole object, the person who feeds. Differentiation and separation of self and other is thus seen as occurring through a lengthy process of repetition of good experiences and gradual maturation. Such views have been developed by theorists of the 'ego-psychology school' (e.g. Blanck and Blanck, 1972; Mahler, 1968; Freud, 1965; Mahler, Pine and Bergman, 1975.)

Bowlby (1958, 1969 and 1973) and Ainsworth (1969) have considered this model in detail and have found it lacking in explanatory power to account for the growth of the infant's recognition, identification and subsequent relationship to the major figures in the infant's social world. In its place Bowlby (1969 and 1973) has put forward an alternative model of social development—attachment theory. This theory is congruent with present day biological and ethological ideas. The social relationship between mother and infant is not seen to be based on good feeding and its results, but on a number of species-characteristic behaviour systems which bring about social relationships. From the beginning these systems are activated and terminated by stimuli emanating from the participants in that relationship. Signal behaviour, such as crying or smiling bring about closeness and contact, whilst rooting, grasping, and postural adjustments tend to maintain physical contact. Out of proximity, attachment, bonding and a feeling of security emerge, and from there, exploration of the world and the growth of autonomy. Bowlby (1977) has recently discussed the implication of his theories for clinical practice and developmental research.

Other psychoanalysts have also developed theories based on the notion of the infant having an active social competence from birth, and have like Bowlby been less concerned with the idea of relationships arising from feeding alone, or from the relief of distress. Melanie Klein (1952), although focusing on the feeding relationship, for instance, described infants as young as three weeks old interrupting their sucking to look at the mother's face, or responding with a smile to her voice. This was interpreted as indicating that the gratification was as much related to the person who gives the food as to the food itself. Klein felt that there was no 'objectless' state and that from the beginning the infant's experiences were directed to 'objects'.

Spitz (1950) and Spitz and Wolff (1946) made observations concerning the social smile, and stranger anxiety occurring during the first year of life, which supported views of an early occurrence of social responses. Other psycho-analysts such as Fairburn (1952 and 1956) also developed theories about the world being quickly experienced as containing figures with particular pleasur-able and unpleasurable affects attached to them. Such theories, known in psychoanalytic writings as 'object relations theories' (Klein, 1952, Segal, 1964), see the infant's experience of the world as his perception of important figures in his life, which are associated intimately with pleasure and unpleasure. The infant is felt to be endlessly attempting to come close to and even 'take over' what are perceived as good objects, to 'incorporate' them and to attempt to void or project and expel whatever is felt to be bad and unpleasurable. This drama is seen as played out through an intense interaction with the mother, filled with feelings of love and hate for her as she is perceived first as a good then as a frustrating figure. These theories see every experience as having a particular inner experience or phantasy attached to them, and the figures and phantasies, which may arise from within the infant or from without, are experi-enced as real concrete parts of the infant's world. Such theories propose that a confusion arises between the experiences of the world as it is felt to be inside the baby's mind, and as it really is. Many of the baby's actions are thus seen as defensive attempts to act on a persecutory world as he sees it.

There has been a good deal of controversy about such views of the infant's perceptions, and of his competence to manipulate the world in his thinking. Padel (1976) noted Klein's own note of disbelief (Klein, 1952) when she described the infant from 'six to twelve months trying to destroy the mother (seen as bad and frustrating) by every means at the disposal of its sadistic trends—with its teeth, nails, and excreta and with the whole of its body transformed in phantasy into all kinds of dangerous weapons—presents a horrying, not to say unbelievable picture in our minds'. Bowlby (1969) has in particular criticized the antibiological nature of Klein's theory of normal development, based as it is on guilt and a need for reparation for aggression of the attacks described. He sees life preservation, rather than guilt or reparation, as the fundamental building block of development.

Bowlby (1969) has reinterpreted some of the psychoanalytic evidence of such theories, and he uses different models to account for them. Such incompatibility in theory building may well arise through the sources of data used to make observations. Melanie Klein's theories were based on the analysis of disturbed children and adults; as a result her theories were of a post-dictive nature. Bowlby's formulations have been based more on the evidence and predictive theories of child development research.

However, to do away with such theories of a post-dictive type may well hinder an understanding of the infant's experience, and of the parent's experience in relating to him when there is severe disturbance. For instance, to understand a severely abused infant and his mother, both terrified and living in a persecutory world, a developmental model which includes persecutory elements in its stages may well be required (Bentovim, 1977). There may be discontinuities between normal and pathological developmental systems which can give rise to very different developmental theories and which may be helpful in interpreting both normal and pathological phenomena.

Other psychoanalytic theorists interested in object relationships such as Balint, M. (1968) and Balint, A. (1969), and Winnicott (1960) emphasized the role of the environment extensively in their theories of development in a manner which parallels that of Bowlby. This emphasis derives from their experience of observing mothers and infants directly rather than viewing infancy through the eyes of the older child or adult. Relationships are seen as emerging from a setting provided by a parent whose 'sensitive adjustment to the infant allows innate development to unfold', rather than resulting from the satisfaction of oral needs, or the reparation of destructive impulses. Winnicott (1960) describes the mother's preoccupation and care, which allows the infant to gather experiences 'into his omnipotence' or self control. The child needs to develop a theory of the world which enables him to explore and cope with necessary failures of care, to find the resources for the full potential of the self to be realized. Winnicott develops a theory of pathological development based on failures of care in early infancy. Essential to this theory is his concept of the 'transitional object' (Winnicott, 1953). The transitional object, which is unique to the child who uses one, is often a blanket or soft toy used in a particular way—sucked or stroked at times of stress and tension. Winnicott describes it as 'self', and yet 'not-self'; it represents the care provided by the 'other' one in their absence at a time of stress—recapturing the moment of 'good enough care'. Out of the use of such 'transitional' objects, relationships with others are represented and the world of animate and inanimate objects can be confronted, and controlled in the child's mind.

Psychoanalysts have been increasingly interested in their theories in the way that the infant finds ways of representing the other one—the mother, the external object—inside his mind during her absence. Bick (1968) has described the identifications by gestures and movements, repeated in the mother's absence, but formed during mother–infant interaction. It is suggested that out of the parent's role in providing a 'containing relationship' (Bion, 1970), an internal object—a model of the other in the child's mind—is developed, enabling the infant to identify with the parents and find optimal security. Such theoretical formulations have arisen not only from the traditional source, or analytical treatment including autistic children (Meltzer and coworkers, 1975) but also from direct infant observations (Bick, 1964). They suggest a continuity of experience from early infancy to later stages of development.

Psychoanalytic writers themselves have tested theories about continuities from infancy to later childhood. Brody and Axelrad (1970) described the continuity between the quality of relationships observed during feeding and later social relationships.

PSYCHOANALYTIC AND COGNITIVE THEORIES—AREAS OF OVERLAP AND CONVERSION

Current psychoanalytic preoccupations with the way the individual develops a representation of himself, his objects and his world (Kernberg, 1970; Horner, 1975) have many parallels with current interest in the development of perception and cognition in child development research. Ainsworth (1969) saw as a strength of psychoanalytic approaches to early relationships the emphasis on the interlocking between cognitive and social development, that is the way the infant takes in the reality of his experience, and from this develops a model of the world which shapes the way he will see and respond to future experience and by his actions shape events in turn. (see the 'Transactional view of development', Sameroff and Chandler, 1975.)

Current views of cognitive development, e.g. Baldwin (1968) and Kohlberg (1968), express a similar view about the way that perception develops. They propose that representational processes are present from early on in the life of the infant, and that to account for the infant's perceptual and behavioural competence central structures of an enduring nature must be hypothesized. They argue that the infant takes a highly active part in organizing his experience, and determines which stimuli he will attend to, from those to which he is exposed. The observed stimuli are compared, it is suggested, with representations that the infant already has in his mind. These representations are built up and develop through experience, and through continuing interchange with the environment they create an increasingly elaborate model of the world. This model does not necessarily include as an essential feature the satisfaction or frustration of basic needs or memories of distress. It is proposed that even the neonate may have a structure which predetermines the way in which he will apprehend the external world, and a stimulus barrier which exerts considerable selection. The infant has to adapt to continuous changes, so that gradually transformations take place in the existing pattern of structure in his mind and new modes of responsiveness emerge (Schaffer, 1971). This description of the interaction between the infant and his environment is very reminiscent of the intense interaction between mothers and infants that has concerned psychoanalytic theorists, particularly those who have an interest in the very earliest development of object relationships in the infant's mind.

Such ideas about underlying structure are strongly influenced by Piaget's theories of cognition (Piaget, 1953 and 1955). In particular, Piaget's ideas about alternating phases of equilibrium and disequilibrium and the alternating mechanisms of accommodation and assimilation which result in the development of new structures and schemes in the infant and growing child's mind. A number of psychoanalytic writers (e.g. Anthony (1957 and 1976), Wolff (1960) and Sandler (1975)) have attempted to link psychoanalytic systems of development with Piagetian stages of cognitive development. However Sandler (1975) has pointed out that such ideas are difficult to link because of differences in the timing of stages between the two systems. Piaget does not consider the infant can have a fixed concept of the object, whether human or non-human, in its absence until around the ninth month of life. Psychoanalytic observers argue that their observations suggest that the younger infant can hold a picture of his mother in his mind, even when she is not present, at least for a limited period of time. Recent explorations of Piaget's ideas by Bower (1974) and by Bryant (1976) suggest that some sort of object permanence may develop earlier than Piaget had suggested, supporting the idea that the very young infant may be able both to discriminate what he sees and to hold it in his mind as a permanent cognitive structure. The use of a wider range of methods to monitor the infant's responses has helped to support theories of early infant competence in social responsiveness.

Schaffer (1971) described the infant in the first three months of life scanning his environment with intense curiosity, not confusion, and in the last three months of the first year scanning his internal environment of cognitive structure and representations of previous experience, to 'match' the people he meets and the situations he encounters. This 'matching' process influences the way he responds. Schaffer argues that it is the strength of the attachment bond between infant and mother that enables the child eventually to leave his mother. This is dependent on the infant's growing ability to represent the other person to himself in her absence, so that the internalized image provides him with the security which formerly only her physical presence provided.

'The more soundly the internal representation is established, the more easily the child can evoke it, the greater are the gaps of time he can be away to venture forth into unknown territory.'

(Schaffer, 1971).

Such a description can be paralleled by Stierlin's (1969) psychoanalytic description of the functions of inner or internal objects. Internal objects are the ideas of the other one in the mind experienced as if they are real. Stierlin described the functions of such inner objects as referants or files for mental recall and adaptation to new situations. He sees them as guide-posts or gyroscopic steering for interpersonal relationships—anticipatory sets—which narrow down the selection of external objects or people in the environment. Lastly, they are seen as aiding autonomy, providing support when the individual is alone.

VISUAL SYSTEM PRECOSITY FOR OBJECTS

The theories outlined above throw far more emphasis on the image in the child's mind, and by implication on visual than on oral pathways. Previously, it was felt that visual pathways were immature and undeveloped and that the infant only used receptors of such as touch and proprioception in his examination of the world. These views may well have been based on the immaturity of the infant's motor system at birth. The infant's actions appear uncoordinated, and poorly directed, and give an illusion that the infant is unable to perceive or discriminate visually. In Piaget's theory the infant builds up cognitive structure by his repeated actions on the external world. Piaget proposes that at first he is limited to structures based on sucking, mouthing and smelling, without a visual model of the world. Butterworth (1976), however, in a review of Piaget's theory of perception points out that the infant could not perceive objects around him, even primitively, unless he had some cognitive structure to relate his perception to, no matter how poor is his ability to act on such perceptions. Bruner (1957) argues perception and therefore cognition requires mechanisms of inference and categorization, implicating some organized way of seeing and organizing the world from early on. Such ideas are supported by Bower's (1974) somewhat controversial observations of the infant's abilities to discriminate different sizes and shapes of objects. He has described specific hand and arm movement responses indicating an ability to discriminate objects as early as eight days of age.

Butterworth (1976) noted that in some respects the space of hand and eye appear to be mapped onto each other before the infant has had experience of the hand in his visual field. It is suggested that the body acts as a basic frame of reference in relationship to which perceptual judgements can be made.

The emergence of the idea of the body as a first frame of reference in cognitive theory has similarities to earlier psychoanalytic theories which viewed the first self—the primitive ego—as a body ego. Hoffer (1949 and 1950) described the emergence of relationships between self and other out of the focus of eye and hand, and mouth activity. Winnicott (1960) also described the infant's psychosomatic existence as a 'limiting membrane', he felt that the foundation for a body scheme comes from the experience of having an inside and an outside, with a personal or inner-psychic reality emerging from this innate given. Bick's (1968) idea about the skin's function in holding the personality together in the beginning, has some similarities to this.

Butterworth (1976) has extended his description of the self and the non-human object world to social relationships. He argues that the first frame of reference bearing an invariant relationship to the self would be another person. The infant is required only to recognize the match between self and other to place his own actions in correspondence. The notion of 'intersubjectivity' in infancy is discussed by Trevarthen (1977a) and Newson and Newson (1976) (see Chapter 5 this volume).

Research on infants as young as two weeks old (Moore and Meltzoff, 1975) indicates that infants can match movements of part of their face to the corresponding actions of another person, and Scaife and Bruner (1975) have shown that infants appear to follow the other person's line of regard, matching their behaviour to that of the other.

The psychoanalytic writers Winnicott (1971) and Lacan (1949) have both described the way that the infant finds himself in his mother's face as if her face was a mirror. If the infant does not find himself reflected back and 'confirmed' to himself, distress can result. Winnicott's ideas about 'false-self' development (Winnicott, 1965) developed from the notion that the infant, to avoid the unbearable anxiety of being 'unconfirmed', identifies or conforms in a false way to the view of himself expected by the parent.

Child development research (Brazelton and coworkers, 1975 and Carpenter, 1974) has explored the infant's response to violation of expectations. Brazelton and coworkers (1975) asked mothers of infants between 2 and 20 weeks not to reciprocate and respond to their infants' approach in their usual way, but to stop themselves instinctively imitating and mirroring the infants responses in interacting with them. The mothers were asked instead to remain still and to attempt to maintain an unresponsive expression. Transient states of stress and then a sense of helplessness were observed in the infants as their mothers failed to reciprocate and feedback the infants' expressions to them. This was in considerable contrast to the normal chain of interaction seen when mothers respond to their babies.

A similar state of distress and avoidance of mother's face and regard was also noted by Brazelton in a group of babies who were failing to thrive. Their mothers failed to pick up and respond to the infants' cues, yet it was startling to note that such infants could respond in a lively way to a new non-human object, such as a novel toy. It was also noticed that when the mothers became less depressed and withdrawn with treatment, a rapid change was noted in the infants' mood and liveliness, coupled with rapid weight gain.

Similar sensitivity to changes of responsiveness was noted by the Papouseks (1975), who described a similar degree of distress when an infant's expectations of his mother were violated. In their experiments they carried out unexpected sudden separations from the mother by brief periods of darkness, or by dividing a mother's face by black lines drawn on glass and placed between the mother and infant. It was noted that after such an experiment was repeated the infant gradually rejected the mother's attempt to renew contact with him, and remained listless and whining. The creation of distressed persecutory and depressive mood states similar to those proposed in Kleinian theory suggests that such responses can occur over the long-term in more extreme pathological situations when an infant's needs and expectations of positive social interactions are not met.

Clearly, the development of relationships and of social understanding in infancy involves extremely complicated interactions between the visual perceptual system, other sensory modalities and experiences and the emotional responsiveness of the infant. In particular the caretaker's role in helping and involving herself in her infant's developing and growing relationships is a key one.

THE MOTHER'S ROLE IN THE INFANT'S DEVELOPMENT

In discussing the mother's role as a source of stimulation for the infant's perception and an object for his emotional life, a number of different aspects of mothering need to be considered. Schaffer (1971) has drawn attention to the physical qualities of the mother. He noted that objects that move, which are three dimensional and which produce noise and change shape, are watched with particular attention by infants. Such qualities attract the infant far more than any static object. From such evidence Schaffer (1971) suggests that the human face with all these positive qualities may well exert a compelling fascination for the infant from the moment of birth. In particular, it has been noted that the infant pays attention to the mother's eyes. Robson (1967) has noted the stimulus richness of the eyes, their remarkable array of interesting qualities, such as shininess, mobility, variability of size of pupil, width of fissure. The mother who fails to allow her infant to make eye contact with her soon after birth may well be the one who fails to make a satisfactory relationship, resulting in possible abuse as described by Kempe (1976).

Klaus and Kennell (1976) have recently summarized other aspects of mothers which contribute to the interaction between themselves and their infants. In particular they have drawn attention to the importance of mother and infants being brought together to facilitate the growing relationship, and bonding processes. As well as giving physical birth to the infant, the mother has to give psychological birth too; she has to externalize the object that she has been carrying within her, and give birth to it both physically and psychologically. The first hours and days after birth may well be particularly sensitive periods for this process. Klaus and Kennell have called this a 'maternal sensitive period' and feel that the infant in the first hours of life may be more alert and responsive than later on. Winnicott (1966) described this as the stage of primary maternal preoccupation—a heightened state of awareness on the mother's part to enable her to adjust herself to her infant's needs with all the sensitivity and responsiveness that these require in the earliest stages of life. A similar heightened state of awareness may also be present during birth itself. Lang (1972) described the excitement accompanying 'natural' childbirth which carries over from mother to the other members of the family present. During this excitement psychological boundaries between people dissolve and the process, described by Freud and recently summarized by Sandler, Holder and Dare (1976), of 'falling in love' or first 'object-love' can occur between mother and infant if the psychological atmosphere is right. Klaus and Kennell's work in facilitating contact between mother and infant at birth and observing the long term effects of such intervention on mother-child's attachment and development has suggested that the first hours and days of life may well have a highly important emotional significance for later relationships.

When these first hours and days are interrupted because of infant illness or handicap, or if the mother's sensitivity or preoccupation is affected by current or past life stresses, then clinical observation suggests that the optimum sequence of events do not occur. The infant, particularly the one that is handicapped, is not 'fallen in love with'. The parents feel damaged by the loss of the expected perfect infant (Bentovim, 1975). The common fear of a birth of a damaged infant is realized, and the newborn infant may well not only be rejected but also be seen as rejecting in turn. Newson and Newson (1976) have described the way that the mother has to give meaning to the infant's actions and responses from the first minutes of life; they show that it is out of this meaning that the child categorizes and understands the world in turn. With a bad start it is easy to see how a negative interactive process may develop, and a conversation of rejection and anger grow.

A sequence of species—specific touching of the infant by mother has been described, in which the mother begins with fingertip touching of the infant's extremities and proceed to massaging, stroking and encompassing palm contact of the trunk (Klaus and Kennell, 1976). This is accompanied by a high pitched voice—appropriate for the infant's sensitivity to high frequency ranges

(Lang, 1972)— and an odour from the skin and breast milk which is unique and recognized by the infant by the fifth day of life (MacFarlane, 1975).

There is a growing general interest in the importance of the way that a mother feels about her baby both during his pregnancy and during the birth and the first days of life. Lynch (1975) and Lynch and Roberts (1977) have pointed to the significance in child abuse onset of factors around the newborn period. Although the infant may not respond in a consistent way to separations from his caretaker in the first days of life, there is no doubt that mothers have a powerful emotional response when their care of their infant is interrupted by separations. It may well be that if a loving, good view of a baby is to be maintained, protecting him from all the intense feelings of frustration that every mother experiences in meeting an infant's demands, then a sense of continuity through pregnancy and the newborn period is necessary. Once the infant is perceived in a negative way because of separation, illness or handicap, then this view formed at a highly sensitive point in time may well persist very strongly for the mother.

THE INFANT'S ROLE IN EARLY OBJECT RELATIONSHIPS

In earlier sections it has been established that the infant can respond actively to the objects he meets and has considerable competence through the use of visual and other perceptive channels. Social responsiveness through observations of the smiling response has been noted for some time (Spitz and Wolff, 1946; Ahrens, 1954). Recently Goren and colleagues (1975) have demonstrated that response to a facial configuration may not develop from contact with a person; rather, it appears to be an innate form preference. In their experiments newborns showed preference for facial forms minutes after birth, even before there had been an opportunity for the infant to see human faces. The social smile itself is released in an increasingly differentiated way by specific people, with the development of differentiation of stranger and familiar figures, and with separation anxiety occurring in the absence of the familiar. These responses mark the gradual differentiation of the social world and the increasing complexity of the internal representation of it.

Klaus and Kennell (1976) feel that smiling and visual interaction helps to cement proximity between mother and infant. Although Bowlby and Ainsworth differentiated executive behaviours, such as rooting and grasping, from signal behaviours such as crying and smiling, Klaus and Kennell suggest that signal and executive behaviour probably act in conjunction in promoting the reciprocal interaction described as 'entrainment'. One of the most fascinating developments in child development research is the growth of the study of mother–infant interactions and its subtleties described by Brazelton, Koslowski and Main, (1974), Trevarthen (1977b), and Stern (1974). Out of the intense interaction comes 'entrainment'—the setting off of the interaction between parent and infants so that the process once begun seems to have a life of its own, and a momentum to which both have contributed. The analysis of video recordings of mothers and infants has demonstrated the remarkable degree of synchrony, rhythm, meshing and pattering between the two. Turn-taking occurs in many ways between mothers and infants, whether in the field of feeding, sucking, smiling, touching or attracting and rejecting.

Psychoanalytic observations of mothers and infants have long stressed the intensity of the interaction between mother and infant (Boston, 1975). Winnicott (1960) describes the process of mothers identifying with their infants, providing 'holding and alive adaptation to needs, following minute to minute, day to day changes that belong to the infant's growth and development'.

Winnicott felt that many of the activities between mothers and infants which were not to do with caretaking had a quality of playing about them if development was going well (Winnicott, 1971). He suggested that play had an essential function in the infant's development, and mutual play a central role in the interaction between self and other. Out of this interaction Winnicott described the growth of the transitional object which stands for the interaction and presence of the other. Mutual play was seen as important too in the development of dreaming and the creativity which allows for the creative gesture to become part of the self. Winnicott also developed his theory of therapeutic action from the same base of mutual playing (Bentovim, 1977).

Stern (1974) writing within a quite different frame of reference also focusses on play as a central component of mother–infant interaction and development. He presents the goal of play activities as the maintenance of an optimal level of arousal between mother and infant which is affectively positive. The mother contributes to this regulation by altering her behaviour using changes in the infant's behaviour as cues. The infant elicits from the mother variations of normal adult social interpersonal behaviour with exaggerations and sloweddown tempos. Such activities are carefully matched to the infant's state, and enhance his understanding of communication and of object relationships. Stern feels that this regulation is carried out through the control of gaze. The infant seeks out mother's gaze when he wishes to play and interact, and averts from her look when he wishes the interaction and arousal to stop. A cycle of orientation, greeting, play dialogue and then disengagement occurs, maintaining the infant's state within an optimal range. He acquires through such play activities and dialogue, experience of interaction and the precursors of interpersonal coping and defensive operations.

THE EMERGENCE OF INDIVIDUAL DIFFERENCES

Given an infant with normal capacities and 'good enough' mothering, social relationships seem predestined to develop—given the range of the infant's competence and the innate responses of both partners. Clinicians are interested in individual differences, and in why one individual's experience gives rise to object relationships and views of the world which are negative and fearful, whilst another individual is confident and optimistic. If mothers perceive their infants in adult terms, attributing meaning and purpose to their behaviour, then it is not surprising that a model of interaction habitual to the parents' own repertoire of perception and interaction and object relationships will develop. This model in turn may influence the pattern of entrainment between mother and child, and the resulting model of the world which the infant later develops (see Hinde's development of Laing, Philipson and Lee's Interpersonal Perception Theory (1976)). Brody and Axelrad (1970) have described the anatomy of mothering and the components which lead to different styles of interaction.

The infant too brings unique qualities to the relationship which affects his caretaker in turn. Thoman (1975) described the development of a relationship between a mother and an infant where the infant appeared to reject face to face contact. Als and coworkers (1976) observed the response of mothers to babies who were born small-for-dates, and showed that these 'unorganized' infants provided considerable difficulties for caretakers unless they were very experienced. Sander quoted by Bernal (1974) noted the considerable sensitivity of the infant to different caretakers and Bell (1975) observed that individual differences in speed and strength of sucking by the infant also affects the interaction with the caretaker. Detailed observations of differences in perceptual style, sensitivity, and patterns of interaction have grown considerably in recent years from both the child development and psychoanalytic research (e.g. Escalona, 1969; Brody, Axelrad and Moroh, 1976; Beckwith and coworkers, 1976; Sameroff and Chandler, 1975).

Ainsworth's use of the stranger situation at twelve months to differentiate the least and most secure children, in terms of both attachment and of object relationship, has been developed as a satisfactory tool (Ainsworth and coworkers, 1974) to relate to events of the first year to the later emotional development of the infant. In her own research she found that the degree of sensitivity the mother showed in perceiving and responding promptly to the infant's signals and communications during the first year, turned out to be the key variable in influencing the infant's later security. However she was not able to bring events of the first days and hours of life into her analysis, nor to examine early individual differences in the infants themselves.

One of the problems in describing differences between mothers, or between children is that by focussing on one or the other of the enmeshed partners important aspects of the interacting system itself may be left. Attempts have been made not only to describe the synchrony of mother and infant, but to describe differences in the interaction patterns that emerge. Brazelton, Koslowski and Main (1974) described the complex development of the rules that emerge from mother–infant interactions; they argue that the interdependency of rhythm seems to be at the root of attachment and communication. Complex statistical models are being developed to capture the qualities of the system. Straus's systems analysis of the way that violence can arise between members of the family (Straus, 1973) is an illustration of the way that interaction can lead to the development, reinforcement and internalization of violent models and perceptions of self and other (Bentovim, 1977). The psychoanalyst observing the mother and infant interacting, or the family therapist experiencing family members interacting are both aware of the emotional interaction and play between the individuals, and of the views of each other that are projected to and fro between the participants. There is constant confirmation for each participant of his view of the other, of shaping and of being shaped in turn by the interacting behaviour, in a spiral of benign or vicious circles.

CONCLUSION

In this attempt to integrate child development research and psychoanalytic theory, it has been my endeavour to show that both psychoanalytic theory and child development research have in recent years been focusing on the experiences of the infant. Both implicitly or explicitly a cognitive-affective model of development is used which results, whether through attachment processes or object relations development, in a number of structures which act as a memory of previous relationships and experiences, as guides for future relationships, and as a self support system for further autonomy.

Recent empirical research shows that the infant is born with an innate series of perceptual and cognitive structures; these enable him to enter vigorously into social interactions, with the development of an entraining, enmeshing, intense interaction between self and other. The parent in turn uses her own experience of social relationships to categorize and label and give meaning to the infant's attempts to reach her, with the beginning of a dialogue and an interaction which has qualities of play, and a rhythm of speech and action which initiates and supports the growing social relationship.

There is then some support for the notion that infants are born with an early competence to perceive objects, both human and non-human. Both mother and infant bring important variables to the resulting interaction and in turn influence the quality of the object relations that develop within the infant himself, and the actual relationships which continue within the family. In a sense what is described is an entrainment process between the different elements of psychoanalytic theory and child development research. If considered together, they form a set of object relationships or attachments which can help to create a set of models; these in turn can help the observer to grapple with the complexity of experience and behaviour that is met whether in clinical or scientific practice.

REFERENCES

Ahrens, R. (1954). 'Beitrag zur Entwicklung der Physiognomie und Nimikerkennes', Z. exp. Psychol., 2, 412–454.

Ainsworth, M. D. S. (1969). 'Object relations, dependency and attachment: A theoretical review of the infant–mother relationship', Child Devel., 40, 969–1025.

Ainsworth, M. D. S., Bell, S. M. and Stayton, D. J. (1974). 'Infant–mother attachment and social development: "Socialization" as a product of reciprocal responsiveness to signals', in Richards, M. P. M. (ed.) The Integration of a Child into a Social World, Cambridge University Press.

Als, H., Tronick, E., Adamson, L. and Brazelton, B. (1976). 'The behaviour of the full-term but underweight newborn infant', Devel. Med. Child Neurol., 18, 590–602.

Anthony, E. J. (1957). 'Thus system makers: Freud and Piaget', Brit. J. Med. Psychol., 30, 3, 255–269.

Anthony, E. J. (1976). 'Emotions and intelligence', in Varma, V. P., and Williams, (ed.) Piaget, Psychology and Education. London, Hodder and Stoughton.

Baldwin, A. L. (1968). 'Cognitive theory and socialization', in Gostin, D. (ed.), Handbook of Socialization, Rand McNally.

Balint, A. (1949). 'Love for the mother and mother-love', Int. J. Psycho-Annal., 30, 251–259.

Balint, M. (1968). The Basic Fault, London, Tavistock.

Beckwith, L., Cohen, S. E., Kopp, C. B., Parmelee, A. H., and Maray, T. G. (1976). 'Caregiver–infant interaction and early cognitive development in pre-term infants', Child Devel., 47, 579–587.

Bell, R. Q. (1968). 'A reinterpretation of the direction of effects in studies of socialization', Psychol. Rev., 75, 81–95.

Bell, R. Q. (1975). 'A congenital contribution to emotional response in early infancy and the pre-school period', in Parent Infant Interaction, Ciba Symposium 33, Holland, Elsevier.

Bentovim, A. (1975). 'The impact of malformation on the emotional development of the child', in Berry, C. L. and Poswillo, D. E. (ed), Teratology, Springer-Verlag.

Bentovim, A. (1977). Towards a social systems view of abuse to childrens (in preparation).

Bentovim, A. (1977). 'Play and therapy', in Tizard, B. and Harvey, D. (ed.) The Biology of Play, London, Heineman.

Bernal, J. (1974). 'Attachment: some problems and possibilities', in Richards, M. P. M. (ed.) The Integration of a Child into a Social World, Cambridge Univ. Press.

Bick. E. (1964). 'Notes on infant observations in psycho-analytic training'., Int.J. Psycho-Anal., 45, 558–566.

Bick, E. (1968). 'The experience of the skin in early object relations', Int. J. Psycho-Anal., 49, 484–486.

Bion, W. R. (1970). Attention and Interpretation, London, Tavistock.

Blanck, G. and Blanck, R. (1972). 'Towards a psycho-analytic developmental psychology', J. Am. Psycho-Anal. Assoc., 20, 668–709.

Boston, M. (1975). 'Recent research in developmental psychology', Journal of Child Psychother., 4, 15–34.

Bower, T. G. R. (1974). Development in Infancy, San Francisco, W. H. Freeman.

Bowlby, J. (1958). 'The nature of the child's tie to his mother', Int. J. Psycho-Anal., 39, 350–373.

Bowlby, J. (1969). Attachment and Loss I: Attachment, London, Hogarth.

Bowlby, J. (1973). Attachment and Loss II: Separation, Anxiety and Anger, London, Hogarth.

Bowlby, J. (1977). 'The making and breaking of affectional bonds I, aetiology and psychopathology in the light of attachment theory', *Brit. Journal Psychiatry.*, **130**, 201–210.

Brazelton, T. B., Koslowski, B. and Main, M. (1974). 'The origins of reciprocity: The early mother–infant interaction', in Lewis. M. and Rosenblum, L. A. (ed.) *The Effect of the Infant on its Caretaker*, New York, Wiley.

Brazelton, T. B., Tronick, E., Adamson, L., Als, H. and Weise, S. (1975). 'Early mother–infant reciprocity', in *Parent–Infant Interaction*, Ciba Foundation Symposium 33, Holland, Elsevier.

Brody, S. and Axelrad, S. (1970). *Anxiety and Ego-formation in Infancy*, New York, International Universities Press.

Brody, J., Axelrad, S. and Moroh, M. (1976). 'Early phases in the development of object relations', *Int. Rev. Psycho–Anal.*, **3**, 1–32.

Bruner, J. S. (1957). 'On perceptual readiness', *Psychol. Rev.*, **64**, 123–152.

Bruner, J. S. and Koslawski, B. (1972). 'Visually preadopted constituents of manipulatory action', *Perception*, **I**, 1–14.

Bryant, P. (1976) 'Piaget: causes and alternatives', in Rutter, M. and Hersov, L. (ed.) *Child Psychiatry, Modern Approaches*, Oxford, Blackwell.

Butterworth, G. (1976). 'Perception and cognition: Where do we stand in the mid-seventies?', In Varma, V. P. and Williams, P. (ed.) *Piaget, Psychology and Education*, London, Hodder and Stoughton.

Caldwell, B. M. (1964). 'The effects of infant care', in Hoffman, M. L. and Hoffman, L. W. (ed.) *Review of Child Development Research, Vol. I*, Russell Stage Foundation.

Carpenter, G. (1974). 'Visual regard of moving and stationary faces in early infancy', *Merill–Palmer Quart. Behaviour and Devel.*, **20**, 180–194.

Dare, C. (1976). 'Psycho-analytic theories', in Rutter, M. and Hersov, L. (ed.) *Child Psychiatry*, Oxford, Blackwell.

Escalona, S. (1969). *The Roots of Individuality*, London, Tavistock.

Eysenck, H. J. and Wilson, G. D. (1973). *The Experimental Study of Freudian Theories*, London, Methuen.

Fairburn, W. R. D. (1952). *Psycho-analytic Studies of the Personality*, London, Tavistock.

Fairburn, W. R. D. (1956). 'A critical evaluation of certain basic psychoanalytical conceptions', *Brit. J. Philosoph. of Science*, **7**, 49–60.

Fisher, S. and Greenberg, R. P. (1977). *The Scientific Credibility of Freud's Theories and Therapy*, New York, Basic Books.

Freud, A. (1965) *Normality & Pathology, Assessment of Development*, New York, Int. Univ. Press.

Freud, S. (1905). *Three Essays on the Theory of Sexuality, Standard Edition 7*, London, Hogarth, 1961.

Goren, C., Sarty, M. and Wu, P. (1975). 'Visual following and pattern discrimination of face-like stimuli by newborn infants', *Pediatrics*, **56**, 544–549.

Gorman, R. A. (1975). 'The phenomenological 'humanization' of social science—a critique', *Brit. J. Sociol.*, **25**, 389–405.

Hinde, R. A. (1976). 'On describing relationships', *J. Child Psychol. and Psychiat.*, **17**, 1–20.

Hoffer, W. (1949). 'Mouth, hand and ego-integration', *The Psycho-Analytic Study of the Child*, (3/4).

Hoffer, W. (1950). 'Development of the body ego', *The Psycho-Analytic Study of the Child*, **5**.

Horner, A. (1975). 'Stages and processes in the development of early object relations and their associated pathologies', *Int. Rev. Psycho-Anal.*, **2**, 95.

James, W. (1890). *Principles of Psychology*, Holt, Rinehart and Winston.

Kelk, N. (1977). 'Is psycho-analysis a science? A reply to Slater', *Brit. Journal Psychiatry*, **130**, 105–111.

Kernberg, O. (1970). 'New developments in psycho-analytic object relations theory', Quoted by Freedman, D. A. (1975). *Int. Rev. Psycho-Anal.*, **2**, 189–197.

Klaus, M. H. and Kennell, J. H. (1976). *Maternal–Infant Bonding*, Saint Louise, C. V. Mosley.

Klein, M. (1952). 'Some theoretical conclusions regarding the emotional life of the infant', in Klein, M., Heimann, P., Isaacs, S. and Riviere, J. (ed.) *Developments in Psycho-Analysis*, London, Hogarth.

Kohlberg, L. (1968). 'Stage and sequence: the developmental approach to socialization', in Goslin, D. A. (ed.) Handbook of Socialization, Rand McNally.

Kuhn, T. S. (1970). *The Structure of Scientific Revolutions*, Chicago and London, University of Chicago Press.

Lacan, J. (1949). 'Le stade du miroir comme formateur de la fonction du Je', in *Ecrits*, Paris, Le Seuil (1966).

Laing, R. D., Phillipson, H. and Lee, A. R. (1966). *Interpersonal Perception*, Berlin, Springer.

Lang, R. (1972). *Birth Book*, California, Genesis.

Lapanche, J. and Pontalis, J. B. (1973). *The Language of Psycho-Analysis*, London, Hogarth

Lewis, M. and Rosenblum, L. A. (1974). *The Effect of the Infant on its Caregiver*, New York, Wiley.

Lynch, M. A. (1975). 'Child abuse and ill health', *Lancet*, **7979**, 317.

Lynch, M. A. and Roberts, J. (1977). 'Predicting Child Abuse: Signs of bonding failure in the maternity hospital', *Brit. Med. J.*, **1**, 624–626.

MacFarlane, J. A. (1975). 'Olfaction in the development of social preferences in the human neonate', in *Parent–Infant Interaction*, Ciba Symposium 33, Holland, Elsevier.

Mahler, M. S. (1968). *On Human Symbiosis and the Vicissitudes of Individuation*, New York, International Universities Press.

Mahler, M. S., Pine, F. and Bergman, A. (1975). *The Psychological Birth of the Infant*, London, Hutchinson.

Meltzer, D., Bremner, J., Hoxter, S., Weddell, D. and Wittengerg, I. (1975). *Explorations in Autism*, Aberdeen, Clunie.

Moore, M. R. and Meltzoff, A. N. (1975). *Neonate imitation: a test of existence and mechanism*, paper presented to Soc. for Research in Child Devel., Denver, Colorado, April, 1975.

Mussen, P. H., Conger, J. J. and Kagan, J. (1969). *Child Development and Personality*, New York, Harper and Rowe.

Newson, J. and Newson, E. (1976). 'On the social origins of symbolic functioning, in Varma, V. V. and Williams, P. (ed.) *Piaget, Psychology and Education*, London, Hodder and Stoughton.

Padel, J. (1976). 'No man's formula. A review of Vol. 2 and 4 of The Writings of Melanie Klein' *Bulletin of the European Psycho-Analytical Federation*, **8**, 10–13.

Papousek, H. and Papousek, M. (1975). 'Cognitive aspects of pre-verbal social interaction between human infants and adults', in *Parent–Infant Interaction*, Ciba Symposium, 33, Amsterdam, Elsevier.

Piaget, J. (1953). *The Origins of Intelligence in the Child*, London, Routledge and Kegan Paul.

Piaget, J. (1955). *The Child's Construction of Reality*, London, Routledge and Kegan Paul.

Popper, K. R. (1972, First published in 1934). *The Logic of Scientific Discovery*, London, Hutchinson.

Robson, K. (1967). 'The role of eye-to-eye contact in maternal–infant attachment', *J. Child Psychol. and Psychiat.*, **8**, 13–25.

Sameroff, A. and Chandler, M. J. (1975). 'Reproductive risk and the continuum of care-taking casuality', in Horowitz, F. D., Hetherington, S., Scarr-Salapatek, S. and Siegal S., *Review of Child Development Research, Vol. 4*, Chicago, University of Chicago Press.

Sandler, A. M. (1975). 'Comments on the significance of Piaget's work for psycho-analysis', *Int. Rev. Psycho-Anal.*, **2**, 365–378.

Sandler, J., Holder, A. and Dare, C. (1976). 'Frames of reference in psycho-analytic psychology, narcissism and object-love in the second phase of psycho-analysis', *Brit. J. Med. Psychol.*, **49**, 267–274.

Scaife, M. and Bruner, J. S. (1975). 'The capacity for joint visual attention in the infant', *Nature*, **253**, 265.

Schaffer, H. R. (1971). *The Growth of Sociability*, Harmondsworth, Penguin.

Segal, H. (1964). *Introduction to the Work of Melanie Klein*, London, Heinemann.

Slater, E. T. O. (1973). 'The psychiatrist in search of a science, **II**. Developments in the logic and sociology of science', *Brit. J. Psychiatry*, **122**, 625–636.

Slater, E. T. O. (1975). 'The psychiatrist in search of a science, **III**. The depth psychologies', *Brit. J. Psychiatry*, **126**, 205–224.

Spitz, R. A. (1950). 'Anxiety in infancy: a study of its manifestations in the first year of life', *Int. J. Psycho-Anal.*, **31**, 138–143.

Spitz, R. A. (1965). *The First Year of Life*, New York, International Universities Press.

Spitz, R. A. and Wolf, K. M. (1946). 'The smiling response: A contribution to the ontogenesis of social relationships', *Genet. Psychol. Monogr.*, **34**, 57–125.

Stern, D. A. (1974). 'Mother and infant at play: The dyadic interaction involving facial, vocal and gaze behaviours', in Lewis, M. and Rosenblum, L. P. (ed.) *The Effect of the Infant on its Caretaker*, New York, Wiley.

Stierlin, H. (1970). 'The function of inner objects', *Int. J. Psycho-Anal.*, **51**, 321–330.

Straus, M. A. (1973). 'A general systems theory approach to a theory of violence between family members', *Soc. Sci. Inf.*, **12**, 105–125.

Thoman, E. (1975). 'How a rejecting baby may affect mother–infant synchrony', in *Parent–Infant Interaction*, Ciba Symposium 33, Holland, Elsevier.

Trevarthen, C. (1977a). 'Conversation with a two month old', *New Scientist* (2.5.74).

Trevarthen, C. (1977b). Descriptive analyses of infant communicative behaviour. In Schaffer, H. R. (ed.) *Studies in Mother–Infant Communication*, London, Academic Press.

Winnicott, D. W. (1953). 'Transitional objects and transitional phenomena', *Int. J. Psycho-Anal.*, **34**, 89–97.

Winnicott, D. W. (1960). 'The theory of the parent–infant relationship', *Int. J. Psycho-Anal.*, **41**, 585–595.

Winnicott, D. W. (1965). 'Ego distortion in terms of true and false', in *The Maturational Processes and the Facilitating Environment*, New York, International Universities Press.

Winnicott, D. W. (1971). 'Mirror-role of mother and family in child development', in *Playing and Reality*, London, Tavistock.

Wisdom, J. O. (1968). 'What sort of ego has an infant? A methodological approach', in Miller, E. (ed.) *Foundations of Child Psychiatry*, Oxford, Pergamon.

Wolff, P. H. (1960). *The Developmental Psychologies of Jean Piaget and Psycho-analysis*, New York, International Universities Press.

Chapter 7

Cross-Cultural Perspectives on the Significance of Social Relationships in Infancy

N. Blurton Jones, R. H. Woodson and J. S. Chisholm

INTRODUCTION

There is a large literature reporting the characteristics of infant care in a wide range of cultures. Indeed, there is a school of anthropology (the culture and personality school) which aims to trace the origin of the characteristics of adults of a culture to their childhood experiences. Most of this cross-cultural literature on infancy dwells on: a) the associated hardware—cradleboards and carrying devices, swings and cribs; b) motor development; c) the ideology of child rearing (attitudes, or more precisely, the aims and theories of parents), with the assumption that parents will always succeed in indoctrinating their children in the way they want to; and d) is anecdotal. Notable contemporary exceptions are Whiting and Whiting (1975), and Leiderman, Tulkin and Rosenfeld (1977).

On the other hand, there is very little literature that deals with the variables that current research shows to be important to child development. An earlier era of anthropological fieldwork on child rearing attended to variables which were then felt to be important for child development in western culture. But there was no evidence whether these variables were important. Now that a solid body of research on 'western' infants is accumulating, perhaps there is some point in beginning again to look at other cultures in order to test the generality of theories of child development, to seek enlightening 'natural experiments', to extend the theories to cover cultural situations in which psychiatrists and educators around the world will find themselves increasingly involved, or to explore the role of child development in the maintenance or change of cultures.

The cross-cultural data on infancy that is available at present cannot confirm or disconfirm current theories of child development; it is simply not up to the task. As in other areas of anthropology that have been concerned with observables it has been found again and again that impressions, guesswork and hearsay can be totally misleading. For example it is not safe to assume that we can judge the effect on mother–child interaction of this or that baby care device (e.g. Chisholm, 1978 and below).

Thus, although one may still hope for evidence from the varied cultures of mankind on the role of early social relationships in the individual's development, there seems to be exceedingly little in the way of useful evidence at present. In this chapter we set forth some of the reasons why this information is so often missing and describe some of the steps that would be necessary to obtain it.

Many separate issues need to be clarified. In any single study several arise in combination and each will influence the others, but for the purposes of communication, we discuss them here under four main headings:
1. The nature of the measures of child behaviour and social development.
2. The measures of culture and environment.
3. Sampling and design.
4. The nature of our models or theories of behaviour development.

THE NATURE OF THE MEASURES OF CHILD BEHAVIOUR AND SOCIAL DEVELOPMENT

In any behavioural research, but most especially in cross-cultural work, a fundamental distinction must be made between the study of observable behaviour and the study of the subject's views of his social and physical world. Both are valid and worthwhile subjects of investigation but they must never be confused (cf. Harris, 1968; Richer, 1974). Techniques such as the PARI (Schaefer and Bell, 1958) exemplify the splendid muddle which arises from such confusion. It combines, as if they were of the same status, information from a hodge-podge of sources: parental aims, parental views about how to achieve these aims, behaviours reported by parents, and a few bits of behaviour observed by the researchers. In current research on the infant's social world, this distinction has gradually come to be made, with the result that almost all work on infancy is now concerned with the observable behaviour between infant and others. It is perhaps unfortunate that nowadays the study of parental aims and theories is relatively neglected while the behaviour of parents is studied so effectively. But in the balance of cross-cultural research, the situations continues to be the reverse, with the assumption that what explains all is the 'native's' view of the world. Collecting, modelling and analysis of observables are too seldom the subject matter of such research. Happily, steps are being taken to remedy this situation (cf. Liederman, Tulkin and Rosenfeld, 1977).

For whatever purpose a researcher wishes to compare cultures, the measures must be applicable to each culture examined. In the area of infant–other interaction, this involves selecting the observational units of behaviour. This selection procedure is influenced by the cultural biases of the researchers. The more florid versions of cultural relativism would hold that this selection itself immediately invalidates the results of such research. (Surely items of behaviour thought important in English samples would be of little use in trying to study Melanesians.) Such a position confuses the reasons for selection (our culturally-influenced intuitions) with the methods used to collect and analyse the resulting information. Given the proclivity of much work in social development to assume that what the researcher believes is important about behaviour *is* in fact important, and therefore need never be directly tested, such a position is understandable. If, on the other hand, the techniques of collection and analysis which a researcher uses allow for the testing of those intuitions, the objection is without foundation. The criteria for such testing is that the units observed reflect something about the role behaviour plays in the individual's development. This issue is discussed in more detail elsewhere (Blurton Jones and Woodson, in press).

An illustration of this selection process is the behavioural 'catalogue' constructed by the authors and M. F. Hall for use in observational studies in five different cultures. The catalogue items were behaviours defined in terms of observable motor patterns. It turned out that all of the items were observed in the five cultures: an underprivileged area of east London, families in a remote and conservative part of the Navajo Indian reservation in Arizona and Utah, and Malay, Chinese and Tamil families in rural Malaysia. A handful of items were added by each observer: for example, Chisholm, working on the Navajo reservation, added 'bug wipe'—mother waving or wiping insects from her child's face, 'face thrust to breast', some manipulations of the cradleboard by mother, and 'point with lips', a polite form of pointing in Navajo culture of rare occurrence and never seen in children under two years. Pointing with a finger, not such good form, is of course seen quite regularly in older children.

Of the many considerations involved in the compilation of the behaviour catalogue, the most important was the need to build in the possibility of testing suppositions about the 'meaning' of behaviour. Meaning in this context is not the native's view of a particular behaviour but rather the events both predicting and predicted by that behaviour. While the data analysis of this set of studies is still underway, all indications are that many comparable sequences of behaviour can be found in quite different cultural settings. Specific examples include the similarities between maternal responses to infant crying reported from Baltimore (Bell and Ainsworth, 1972) and observed in rural Malaysian families and the striking parallels between the Navajo toddler's response to strangers and those of the toddler in Kalahari desert Bushman families (Konner, 1972), and in London or Yellow Springs. In a similar vein, the patterns of individual differences in the behaviour of Malaysian newborns are substantially the same as those found in American samples (Woodson and coworkers, in press). This suggests that although samples from different populations may differ regarding the level of any measure (cf. Freedman, 1974) the ways in which individual newborns differ from one another appears consistent across populations.

For cross-cultural research the need is first to describe patterns of variation and then to relate this variation to subsequent development and the antecedent and concurrent events. Whether the comparisons are of absolute frequencies of behaviour or relations among different measures, the measures themselves must be independent of any particular cultural context. The failure to develop these qualities can have extremely unpleasant ramifications, as, for example, in the whirlwind of debate over cultural/racial differences in intelligence (cf. Jensen, 1969). In the area of child development, and especially mother–infant interaction, the situation is rapidly improving. If the concern is to describe what happens to an infant in its interaction with those around him, and to examine the influence of such experiences on development, then a solid basis for comparison is beginning to emerge (e.g. Blurton Jones, 1972; Leiderman, Tulkin and Rosenfeld, 1977; Schaffer, 1977; Chisholm, 1978; McGrew, 1972; Hall, Pawlby and Wolkind, Chapter 9, this volume).

THE MEASUREMENTS OF THE ENVIRONMENT

If one intends to study systematically the development of individuals in different cultures, it is important to bear in mind the wide range of influences to which these individuals are exposed. Those factors capable of influencing behaviour range from the apparently trivial, such as the amount of furniture in the home, to the more subtle, including nutrition and residence patterns and culturally prescribed child-rearing practices. A realistic appreciation of the complexity of influences on development is especially vital when assigning priority, in the causal sense, to one influence while relegating others to covariate status. In most accounts of child rearing in other cultures it is impossible to tell how far the differences that are emphasized arise from differences in immediate situation or from 'culture' *sensu stricto*. We will give four examples of the importance of a neglected and unexpected variable for understanding parent–child interaction in non-European contexts.

1. Studies of mother–toddler interaction in both rural Ugandan (Ainsworth, 1967) and Kalahari Bushmen families (Konner, 1972, 1977) have commented on the high amount of physical contact observed between mother and child. This is much higher than in western settings with comparably aged children. One of the differences between the typical western home and those reported from Africa concerns the presence of furniture. In the European home, chairs are present and mothers use them. This situation radically influences

both the ease with which the toddler can attain physical contact with the mother and the energy expended by the mother in getting the child off the ground into contact. How quickly, one wonders, would western mothers and their one-year-olds change their behaviour if mother sat mostly on the floor or ground? From most accounts of child-rearing in other cultures, it is impossible to tell how far the immediate physical environment accounts for differences as opposed to the influence of other aspects of 'culture'.

2. A popular topic in cross-cultural studies of child development is the 'hardware' each culture uses in child-rearing. In affluent western societies, the toys which surround the infant, toddler or child receive a good deal of attention. With more traditional cultures, the devices used to carry, confine or cache the child seem very appealing as objects of research. But the magnitude of the effect which these materials exert on social development needs to be considered along side other less obvious but perhaps more influential aspects of the environment. For example, a great deal has been made of the fact of Navajo shyness and its possible association with their practice of tightly binding infants onto rigid cradleboards (Gorer, 1949; cf. Mead, 1954). In an attempt to investigate this relationship, Chisholm (1978) conducted an observational study of the Navajo child's social development, working in a particularly conservative area where cradleboard use was extensive. Cradleboards had a consistent effect on the level of arousal of the child, which reflected their use as a means of short-term control of the infant state. Their developmental significance, however, was minimal when contrasted with the type of household group in which the infant lived. Probably the major axis differentiating Navajo children from one another, as well as from non-Navajos, was whether they lived in a neo-local, nuclear family camp or an extended matri- or patri-local family group. Thus, while the use of the cradleboard was shown to alter child behaviour in the short-term, the effects of the number and type of people seen regularly by the child were more profound.

The preceding examples dealt with the material concomitants of cultures. Such influences are often misjudged, because of their trivial obviousness or because they are embedded in a more pervasive yet not so obvious set of influences. There exists another, different set of factors which can be shown to influence aspects of behaviour and development but are often ignored. These are the individual biological aspects of the environment of the culture — the physiology of the people themselves. It will be shown that events apparent on the physiological level are reflected in events on the behavioural level.

3. A recent study (Chisholm and coworkers, in press) concerned predictors of behaviour in Malay, Malaysian Chinese, Malaysian Tamil, and Navajo newborn babies (aged 24, 24, 24 hours and three days respectively). Maternal blood pressure during or at the end of pregnancy was in each sample the best predictor of newborn arousal levels. High blood pressure predicts

high arousal ('irritable babies'). Richards and Dunn found a similar relationship in a sample of home-delivered babies in Cambridge, England (Barnes, 1975). This was a continuous relationship and few, if any of the women were hypertensive. Page and Christianson (1976) and MacGillivary, Rose and Rowe (1969) also show that a continuous relationship holds for blood pressure and perinatal mortality. In Chisholm's analysis of his Navajo and white American data, as well as in Richards and Bernal's data, newborn state had a major effect on mother–infant interaction early in the first year of life. What could easily have been taken for a 'cultural' difference (i.e. the result of different ideas or training in mothering), turns out to result from baby differences (which could be taken for a genetic difference) which may in fact stem from blood pressure differences, a physiological measure. The story does not end there, as Chisholm (1978) points out. Population differences in blood pressure are well documented, and so are the observations that people who move from country to town undergo an increase in blood pressure. So the physiological measures turn out to be dependent on some cultural–ecological measures. Thus the difference between Navajo and Anglo mother–infant interaction early in the first year is indeed 'cultural'. But each culture may have its particular effect on mother–infant interaction through the way that each influences decisions about where and with whom one should live—factors that mediate 'stress'. The causal chain of effects may operate via maternal and foetal physiology as much as or even more than through 'superorganic' and cultural-specific notions of appropriate maternal and child behaviour. Chisholm would have no explanation of the differences in maternal behaviour that he observed if he did not have data on newborn characteristics, maternal blood pressure *as well as* residence patterns.

4. Chavez, Martinez and Yaschine (1974) have reported changes in parent–child interaction and child rearing practices that followed a nutrition program. One might like to see more data in his study to rule out any influence from the ideas and propaganda of his nutrition team, but even so, his evidence is sufficient to show the need to measure many aspects of the environment if we hope to understand what brings about cultural change. He observed parent–child interaction before and after a program in which pregnant women and their subsequent newborns were given extra food. The food-supplemented families showed more play and face-to-face interaction between parent and child, less adherence to a post partum lying-in rule, men began to carry toddlers more, and people began to cover their wells. Chavez argues that all of these result from the nutritional effects on mother (mothers said they felt too well to stay in after the birth), or child (the children were more active than before and did more crawling about; they had more accidents, and parents began covering their wells!). The toddlers were much heavier than before, and seemed too heavy for their

small, once undernourished mothers. Their fathers began to carry them despite traditional pressures for male uninvolvement with small children. It would have been valuable to see a study of attitudes before and after the program. New attitudes to child rearing would be expected to follow behind the material changes quite rapidly.

With these examples we have tried to show that many interesting variables differ between cultures (populations would be a less constricting term but for its use implying genetically isolated populations), in addition to each cultures' ideology of child rearing. Ideology is undoubtedly important (and worthy of study whether or not it is a cause or an outcome) but it is extremely important to note that different informants give different versions of what is right and proper in their society. We think that this gives the anthropologist an enormously valuable tool, even if it requires some departure from earlier theoretical viewpoints. Individual variation in ideology within a culture can be correlated with variation in other meausres. Thus the variation could be used to work out the relationship between ideology and other measures. For example, do parents who profess a belief in rigid punishment actually behave differently with their children, or does the belief seem tailored for a visiting scientific audience, or related to the parents' situation? It is clear that it is absolutely wrong to exclude informants or subjects on the grounds that their ideology is 'not typical'. If ideology is treated as one of the many variables within and between cultures the 'problem' of between-informant variation ceases to be a problem and becomes an advantage, permitting the application of the ordinary methods of science to the study of culture (cf. Goodenough, 1971).

Our example concerning newborn differences is also relevant to a quite different problem in cross-cultural (or cross-population) comparisons: the attribution of cultural differences to genetic differences. In cross-cultural behaviour research the habit of placing residual variation between groups into a category of 'constitutional or genetic differences' is giving genetic factors the status of the null hypothesis, confusing the weak claim of 'not yet disproved' with the untested genetic 'explanation'. Absence of other explanations of differences is not evidence for a genetic 'explanation'. Evidence about genetic influences (genes act through long complicated pathways and therefore their influence does not exclude other influences) comes from the right kind of family studies, not from the exclusion of a few environmental variables. Discussion of genetics in the context of cultural differences has never had much to do with either genetics or epigenetics and the study of development. These discussions have always been full of non sequiturs: one example for instance is the hidden assumption that genetic differences can be called good and bad and that other differences are forgivable. Surely it is enough to point out that this simply does not follow. Secondly, 'genetic differences' cannot be changed as easily as 'environmentally induced differences'—note the treatment of PKU and contemplate the speed at which an I.Q. boosting pill (perhaps interrupting biochemical epigenetic pathways) would come into wide use, and contrast it with the negligible pace at which the known environmental influences on I.Q. have been modified.

A minimum requirement for any study which aims to analyse cultural differences in parent–child relationships (or to use cross-cultural data to test theories of child development) is the measurement of the following variables:

perinatal and infant mortality;
nutritional levels and their variation within the culture;
amount of observation indoors and outdoors;
people present with mother and child, who and how often;
nature of floor and furniture, the physical situation;
baby care devices (cots, swings, slides etc; with systematic observation of when and how they are used);
temperature and precipitation outdoors related to amount mother and child are outdoors;
physiological and behavioural characteristics of newborns;
obstetric services or practices and some indication of the history of the sample of live newborns;
nature and quality of mother's helpers: siblings, relatives, neighbours;
child's social contacts; residence patterns and opportunity for interaction with others of various age/sex/kinship categories;
disease history of children observed;
individual parent's aims and theories of child rearing;
mother's social contacts, quality of marital relationship;
subject's responses to observers;

SAMPLING AND DESIGN

The single most important fact about childhood in the traditional cultures often used in cross-cultural research is that their mortality rates during the early years are high. Many infants, toddlers and children die and so cannot be observed or followed up. This fact has important ramifications for the design of studies which attempt to encompass a range of ages, especially in a cross-sectional design. At least one very influential study (Kagan, 1972) used cross-sectional data from a culture in a poor rural area to argue a longitudinal point and, for this reason, must be taken with caution. The degree of recovery of intellectual ablity reported across a wide age range in this high mortality setting must have been to some extent the result of ultimately non-surviving children contributing disproportionately to the first age point results. One wonders if the same results would emerge from a sample comprised solely of survivors.

Similar considerations would apply, for instance, in those settings in which breast feeding forms a crucial and non-elective part of the infant's nutritional intake. The age of weaning has dramatic effects on infant and toddler mortality in the third world (Morley, 1973). Using samples at ages between which many infants are weaned from the breast could result in quite distorted results, expecially if the differences under scrutiny correlate with early or late weaning. In general, the use of cross-sectional techniques should be viewed with extereme caution in cross-cultural work. Unless the investigator has fairly precise information on the mortality rates for the age range to be studied, cross-sectional designs would seem of dubious utility.

Longitudinal designs also involve certain problems. The impact on mortality and morbidity of alterations in basic technology (e.g. the introduction of piped water, satisfactory toilet facilities, improved medical care and food supply) can be dramatic and sudden. This provides a vital opportunity to examine the influences of the material world upon culture but unless a researcher is sensitive to such secular trends in the population under study, the risk of monumental misinterpretation quickly arises. Consider the nutritional supplement programme undertaken by Chavez discussed above. A group of pregnant mothers in a rural Mexican village received dietary supplements which were continued and extended to the child after birth. In doing this, the researcher placed stresses on this group's child rearing practices and beliefs. The mothers felt too well for the traditional lying-in period following the birth. Infants were too active to be kept in the rebozo inside the house and so had to be put in an outside yard, which meant erecting fences and covering wells. The mothers found the toddlers too heavy to transport; fathers began to carry. Had an uninformed cross-cultural researcher entered the village at this point, he might have noticed that those families with the healthiest most active children were the ones who least fit that culture's norm for child-rearing patterns. From this, it might be concluded that cultural norms and beliefs on child rearing were adhered to by those more marginal families and that such beliefs and practices result in impaired growth.

The above, of course, is a hypothetical situation but it illustrates the danger of ignoring the impact of secular trends on a culture. Traditional, 'primitive' cultures are not fossilized remains, they are integrated systems capable of responding to environmental changes. With the pace of development throughout the world, the environments in which such cultures can be found are in potentially important ways different from those for which the cultures are 'designed'. This fact should be kept in mind when comparing the development of children in more settled environments, especially when significant lengths of time are involved.

THE 'CULTURAL CONTEXT'

We have outlined a wide range of factors that may influence observed differences in behaviour of parents and children. All are important, and are facts of life, even if we find ourselves tempted to regard some as 'sampling errors' and others as 'real differences'. We now wish to discuss ways in which different patterns of correlations among our variables may arise. This discussion is central to two topics that generate a lot of words, printed and spoken, but so far, very little research: 'the cultural context', and 'transactional' theories of development. Transactional theories seek to explain the differing results from different samples. Evidence for the power of 'the cultural context' is drawn from these same differing results from differing samples (whether cultures or subcultures).

For example, it was shown that the effects of separation described by Bowlby (1969) were not evident in response to separations between children and their parents in Nigeria (Goody, 1970). The usual conclusion from such a finding is that separation does not have a universal influence—that its influence depends on 'the cultural context' (or even on whether separation is regarded as normal in that society). The concept of 'cultural context' is dangerously vague. It promises explanation but in fact asserts virtually nothing. It is likely to reduce the chance that anyone tries to decide which cultural variables make a difference and why. It seems to imply that separation will only be an influence under some circumstances, that it will be completely unimportant in other circumstances and that no general theory or fact of child development is possible. We will present an argument that variation in findings from different cultures or samples cannot be taken as evidence against the existence of a set of cause–effect relationships that apply to all children. Variation between samples does not necessarily mean that the same variables are not in action nor that the same causal links are not present. A single causal system can give very different 'results' at different settings of some of its variables.

Transactional theories of development have an extremely important core: the proposition that the characteristics of a child can influence its environment in different ways in different situations (e.g. the child's behaviour interacts with the environment in determining the behaviour of adults to the child). Transactional theory as proposed by Sameroff and Chandler (1975) uses this proposition for the important task of accounting for the inconsistent outcome of perinatal problems. The theory they outline also carries some unnecessary embellishments which distract attention from the commendable verifiability of its core proposition. Again, it would be a pity of the distractions of fine words like 'organismic', 'dynamic', 'a perpetual state of active reorganization', 'restructuring', will delay the application of the core proposition of transactional theory to the study of development. These propositions, first, the interaction of child and environment in influencing what happens to the child, second, the possibility of control systems in development that tend to enable the child to return to a 'normal' developmental trajectory, can be tested with standard methods.

This is best illustrated by presenting a simple, purely hypothetical causal model which has three interesting properties.

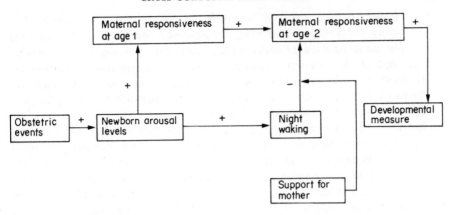

1. It can give opposite correlations between perinatal factors and later outcome in different samples, resulting from exactly the same set of causal relationships.
2. It includes a homeostatic link between mother and child which, in many circumstances, will tend to abolish later consequences of early events.
3. Most unusually, there are ways of showing it to be wrong.

The model is illustrated in Figure 7.1. Boxes in the top row contain maternal measures. Boxes in the second row contain child measures. The box in the third row contains an environmental variable. The contents of the boxes could be any measure; we chose some variables near to our interests, and which were related to the work by Dunn and Richards and Barnes that largely inspired the model. The main interest in the model is in what it can do and how it can be tested, rather than whether this particular model is true. The arrows are causal links, marked with a plus when the variable at one end is claimed to increase the variable at the other end, and a minus when a decrease is proposed. The influence of 'support' is upon the strength of the arrow from 'night waking' to 'mother responsiveness'.

1. *Property One.* Sample One might be a sample where support for mother is high, e.g. a matrilocal extended family or an economically well-off stable middle class sample with few children, in a culture where fathers usually help with the children while at home. In this sample, according to the model, an increase in obstetric problems will lead to a lively newborn that gets its mother into the habit of a high level of responsiveness. It will also be a nightwaker but this will reduce her responsiveness relatively little, because of the support she gets. The net effect will be an increase in her responsiveness and this increases her childs 'D.Q.'. (it must be remembered that all the links and measures are imaginary.) This sample will give us a positive correlation between obstetric events and 'D.Q.'.

Sample Two, on the other hand, may be a culture where the father never helps with babies, or does not even live with the mother, and where the mother has many problems and adverse circumstances weighing on her. In this sample the newborn's influence on his mother may be more than counter-balanced by the negative influence of his later nightwaking upon her responsiveness. This sample will give us a negative correlation between obstetric events and 'D.Q.'. The important point is that these opposite findings have arisen from the same causal system.

2. *Property Two.* At levels of 'support for mother' that are intermediate to the above samples there is a homeostatic effect in which the baby at age 1 increases its mother's responsiveness only to reduce it at age 2. The outcome would be a zero correlation between obstetric factors or newborn behaviour and maternal behaviour at age 2. Such a correlation would probably be interpreted as meaning that the early events were unimportant. But they were only unimportant by virtue of the feedback loop of which they are a part. Bateson (1976) and Dunn (1976) proposed a more functionally biological view of development, suggesting that there may be behavioural parallels to catch-up growth (Prader, Tanner and Von Harnack, 1963). Our model includes a feedback loop that is between mother and child rather than within child. But, subject to the constraints implied by parent–offspring conflict theory (Trivers, 1974), one might expect *behavioural* feedback in development to be between the infant and the more modifiable parts of its environment (such as its parents). It would be interesting to look for compensatory mechanisms in the behaviour of foster child and foster parent that might lead to the catch-up in intellectual development of children removed from residential institutions to foster homes described by Tizard and Rees (1975).

3. *Property Three.* Once one makes explicit propositions about the links between measures then the full range of model-testing statistical analysis is available. In this instance one could use path analysis, or analyse the situation bit by bit with multiple regression. This will be more complicated if one proposes that some of the relationships are non-linear. Predictions could also be made about the pattern of correlations to be found in a new sample, perhaps selected to test the model at extreme levels of one variable; these would differ from the usual replication in that we would predict results that *differ* from the findings in the samples upon which the model was built.

Whether this model represents an interactive developmental theory or a transactional developmental theory is a trivial issue. Its interest lies in its outcomes, its testability and its explicitness. Many other such models can be produced and tested. This one happens in several respects to be wrong. That it is possible to say that it is wrong is to its credit. It is unfortunate that the sociology of research discourages people who say things that can be proved to be wrong, and thus encourages researchers towards untestable generalities. This model is not a theory, it is an example. Real theories, with the predictive power of, for example, current evolutionary theory, are few and far between in any science. Since most theories in psychology have been substitutes for data explicitness is surely worthwhile.

CONCLUSIONS

If the distinction between the scientific observer's point of view and that of the people he or she studies is kept absolutely clear, the way towards gathering usable data on the cross-cultural evidence about the importance of infancy is fairly clear. Any researcher can employ both points of view in the study of a culture, but he must be absolutely clear about when he is using one and when he is using the other.

However, there are at least as many 'independent variables' in a cross-cultural study as in one done at home. We have tried to point out some of the neglected ones: infant mortality, undernutrition, the immediate physical situation in the home. Ideas, norms, prescriptions are only some of the ways in which cultures vary. Little is gained by assuming that parental ideals are automatically fulfilled, or by correlating ideas and outcomes, unless other variables are also measured and the correlations are examined. We cannot merely assume that ideas cause behaviour. How do we tell when an idea is a cause of behaviour and how do we tell when it is a rationalization or simple description?

'The cultural context' is important but not un-analysable. Variation between cultures can arise from a common developmental mechanism. The analysis of this hypothetical mechanism requires the measurements of many more variables than are ordinarily considered. This is an important task because it will show whether to expect western theories of child development and psychiatry to be of any use for the developing world.

ACKNOWLEDGEMENTS

The fieldwork experience and research by Chisholm and Woodson that underlies this paper was supported by a grant from the H. F. Guggenheim Foundation to N. Blurton Jones. Blurton Jones' own earlier field experience was supported by grants from the Wenner–Gren Foundation and The Royal Society. Our current research on children in London which benefits and contributes no less to thinking out the patterns of similarity and differences in child development in other cultures is supported by a Social Science Research Council Program Grant.

REFERENCES

Ainsworth, M. D. S. (1967). *Infancy in Uganda: Infant Care and the Growth of Love*, Baltimore, Johns Hopkins University Press.

Barnes, F. (1975). 'Accidents in the first three years of life', *Child: care, health and development*, **1**, 421–433.

Bateson, P. P. G. (1976). 'Rules and reciprocity in behavioural development', in Bateson and Hinde (eds.), *Growing Points in Ethology*, London, Cambridge University Press.

Bell, S. M. and Ainsworth, M. D. S. (1972). 'Infant crying and maternal responsiveness', *Child Development*, **43**, 1171–1190.

Blurton Jones, N. G. (ed) (1972). *Ethological Studies of Child Behaviour*, London, Cambridge University Press.

Blurton Jones, N. G. and Woodson, R. H. (in press). 'Describing behaviour: the ethologist's perspective', in Lamb, Suomi and Stephenson (eds.), *Social Interaction Analysis: Methological Issues*.

Bowlby, J. (1969). *Attachment and Loss, Vol 1, Attachment.*, London, Hogarth Press.

Chavez, A., Martinez, C., and Yaschine, T. (1974). 'The importance of nutrition and stimuli on child mental development', in Cravioto, Hambraeus and Vahlquist (eds.), *Early Malnutrition and Mental Development*, Uppsala, Almquist and Wiksell.

Chisholm, J. S. (1978). *Developmental Ethology of the Navajo*, unpublished Doctoral Dissertation, Department of Anthropology, Rutgers University.

Chisholm, J. S., Woodson, R. H., and da Costa Woodson, E. (in press). 'Maternal blood pressure during pregnancy and newborn irritability, *Early Human Development*, in press.

Dunn, J. (1976). 'How far do early differences in mother–child relations affect later development?', in Bateson and Hinde (eds.), *Growing Points in Ethology*, London, Cambridge University Press.

Freedman, D. G. (1974). *Human Infancy: An Evolutionary Perspective*, Hillsdale, Lawrence Erlbaum Associates.

Goodenough, W. (1971). 'Culture, language and society', *Addison-Wesley Module in Anthropology*, **7**.

Goody, E. (1970). 'Kinship fostering in the Gonja: Deprivation or advantage', in Mayer (ed.), *Socialisation: The Approach from Social Anthropology*, London, Tavistock.

Gorer, G. (1949). 'Some aspects of the psychology of the people of Great Russia', *American Slavic and East European Review*, **8**, 155–160.

Harris, M. (1968). *The Rise of Anthropological Theory: A history of theories of culture*, New York, Crowell.

Jensen, A. R. (1969). 'How much can we boast IQ and scholastic achievement?', *Harvard Education Review*, **39**, 1–123.

Kagan, J. (1972). *Cross-culture perspectives on early development*, paper read at Annual Meeting of the American Association for the Advancement of Science, Washington, D.C.

Konner, M. J. (1972). 'Aspects of the developmental ethology of a foraging people', in Blurton Jones, N. (ed.), *Ethological Studies of Child Behaviour*, London, Cambridge University Press.

Konner, M. J. (1977). 'Infancy among the Kalahari Desert San', in Leiderman, Tulkin and Rosenfeld (eds.), *Culture and Infancy: Variations in the Human Experience*, New York, Academic Press.

Leiderman, P. M., Tulkin, S. R., and Rosenfeld, A. (1977). *Culture and Infancy: Variations in the Human Experience*, New York, Academic Press.

MacGillivray, I., Rose, G. A., and Rowe, B. (1969). 'Blood pressure survey in pregnancy', *Clinical Science*, **37**, 395–407.

Mead, M. (1954). 'The swaddling hypothesis: its reception', *American Anthropologist*, **56**, 395–409.

McGrew, W. C. (1972). *An Ethological Study of Children's Behavior*, New York, Academic Press.

Morley, D. (1973). *Paediatric Priorities in the Developing World*, London: Butterworth.

Page, E. W. and Christianson, R. (1976). 'Influence of blood pressure changes with and without proteinuria upon outcome of pregnancy', *American Journal of Obstetrics and Gynecology*, **126**, 821–833.

Prader, A., Tanner, J. M., and Von Harnack, G. A. (1963). 'Catch-up growth following illness or starvation', *Journal of Pediatrics*, **62**, 646–659.

Richer, J. (1974). 'Direct observation: A reply to Cooper et al.', *Bulletin of the British Psychological Society*, **27**, 500–502.

Sameroff, A. and Chandler, M. (1975). 'Reproductive risk and the continuum of caretaking casualty', in Horowitz, Hetherington, Scarr-Salapatek and Seigel (eds.), *Review of Child Development Research, Volume 4*, Chicago, University of Chicago Press.

Schaefer, E. S. and Bell, R. Q. (1958). 'Development of a parental attitude research instrument', *Child Development*, **29**, 339–361.

Schaffer, H. R. (ed) (1977). *Studies in Mother–Infant Interaction*, London, Academic Press.

Tizard, B. and Rees, J. (1975). 'The effect of early institutional rearing on the behaviour problems and affectional relationships of 4 year old children', *Journal of Child Psychology and Psychiatry*, **16**, 61–73.

Trivers, R. (1974). 'Parent–offspring conflict', *American Zoologist*, **14**, 249–264.

Whiting, J. W. M. and Whiting, B. B. (1975). *Children of Six Cultures–A Psycho-cultural Analysis*, Cambridge, Harvard University Press.

Infancy and Later Development: Studies of Exceptional Groups

Chapter 8

Early Experience: its Limited Effect upon Later Development

Ann M. Clarke and A. D. B. Clarke

All societies appear to possess, in some sense, a model of man and of his development. In Western culture there is a pervasive belief that the early years are crucially formative, a view which is of great antiquity: 'And the first step, as you know, is always what matters most, particularly when we are dealing with those who are young and tender. That is the time when they are taking shape and when any impression we choose to make leaves a permanent mark' (Plato, 428–348 BC). Freud (1910) was, of course, responsible for the revival of these ideas this century: 'the very impressions we have forgotten have nevertheless left the deepest traces in our psychic life, and acted as determinants for our whole future development'. A more exact statement is to be found in his 1949 book, published posthumously: 'neuroses are only acquired during early childhood (up to the age of six), even though their symptoms may not make their appearance until much later ... the events of the first years are of paramount importance for ... (a child's) whole subsequent life ...'.

Another common view is that development is largely genetically controlled. This is of much more recent origin, dating from the work of Francis Galton, carried forward to the present day in an apostolic succession by Pearson, Spearman, Burt, Cattell, Eysenck and Jensen. It is a model for which increasingly widespread claims are made (e.g. that inconsistency in responding to paper and pencil neuroticism questionnaires, given on two occasions may be under genetic control (Eaves and Eysenck, 1976)).

The early experience and genetic models of man may appear antithetical. their adherents are usually well insulated form each other, taking little account of the opposing view. But in a sense the consequences of the two are similar: a predeterminism which fixes the future of the individual, more or less, either at conception or in the first few years of life or with an interaction of both. The writings of Spearman, Burt and even J. B. Watson among others, are explicit on this point.

From the midnineteen-fifties and onwards, initially because of our own findings on severely deprived, backward and unstable adolescents and young adults, we began to believe that there might be much more resilience and change in human development than either model predicted. By 1960 we had started—but abandoned for lack of sufficient widespread and good evidence—a book on this topic. Instead we wrote papers (1959 and 1960) presenting an analysis of the complex nature of deprivation and some evidence on late recovery.

In 1967, one of us was invited to give the 42nd Maudsley lecture, and we attempted an overall critique of the early experience model, indicating the dubious relevance to man of much animal research, and the increasing number of studies which ultimately implied that there is no set of adverse early experiences from which children have not recovered, partly or wholly, granted some change in their circumstances. Early experiences did not necessarily set for the child an invariant path; it seemed that both the unfolding of genetic programmes and the effects of later experiences were responsible for later changes (Clarke, 1968).

It is, of course, necessary to distinguish the effects of the physical environment from the psychosocial. Obviously, an insult to the growing brain may have profound long term consequences. Even here, however, other factors related to social class may amplify, minimize or overcome these effects (Sameroff and Chandler, 1975).

In the early 1960s, both Kagan and Moss (1962) and Bloom (1964) outlined or reviewed longitudinal studies of particular groups, the results of which were interpreted as showing some moderate, long term stability of developmental characteristics and the importance of early experience. These were, to a considerable extent, misinterpretations of the data, as Kagan (1976) himself now courageously indicates. Yet these books had—and still have—immense influence. In 1972, we reviewed similar data, concluding that variability during the course of normal development was common, particularly in the context of environmental discontinuity.

Our general statement that during development continuities do not seem very marked, like all such statements requires cautionary qualifications. Severe subnormality shows a very complete continuity over the life span; even here, however, one at least raises a hypothesis or two about, for example, unusual Down's syndrome children. We know a few exceptional cases, always drawn from exceptional homes where every attempt has been made to combat the handicap. Then, autism shows very considerable continuity. Even here, however, a minority achieve some sort of adult adjustment (Rutter, Greenfield and Lockyer, 1967). Some cases of mild retardation show very marked changes. Most childhood emotional or neurotic disorders appear not to show continuity with adult disorders but late childhood sociopathy shows high (though not perfect) continuity (Robins, 1966). These examples should suffice to qualify our generalization. However, many studies on continuities in abnormal or deviant behaviour represent a 'natural history' approach, and where the continuities prove strong it is as yet unclear whether these are intrinsic to the disorder or reflect in some measure, ineffective or inadequate rehabilitation.

Our recent book (1976) attempts to enlarge the assessment, and draws upon the work of many authors. As we wrote: 'We have assembled a body of information which suggests a reformulation; this should not be interpreted literally as a counter-balance, which might be an equal and opposite extreme, but rather an attempt to achieve a balanced view' (Clarke and Clarke, 1976, p. 269).

There is as yet no proper model of human development, but a preliminary view which the evidence, accumulating over twenty years, has suggested to us is as follows: development is an ongoing process of interaction or transaction between genetic/constitutional factors on the one hand, and macro and micro social factors, on the other. The biological programme itself causes changes, and even in the most limiting environment (e.g. poor institutions) children alter, absolutely and differentially, because of maturation. No child is reared in a social vacuum, and the social context of each changes at different levels of development. Normally the micro-social environment of the developing child is not static, so there is both an unfolding of biological programmes, as well as of social environments, with complex interactions and feedback between both. Moreover, the child plays an active part in determining the social transactions which influence him. It seems from this view that no particular chronological period in development should be prepotent in the long run. Hence to some extent, development is potentially open-ended; early experience *by itself* will not have any long term effect. Its importance lies only in its function as a link in the developmental chain.

It is not proposed to go over the same ground covered by our book, except very skeletally. In it we reviewed some sixty important studies, the main ones upon which we relied mostly involving some substantial environmental discontinuity, which allowed the persistence or otherwise of early experience to be assessed. Where such a discontinuity does not occur it is usually impossible to disentangle the effects of later from earlier experience. The study by Rutter (1971) is perhaps an exception, although even here some discontinuities are apparent.

It is not proposed to consider animal studies here. One notes, however, that the idea of critical periods is shifting and broadening even in this field, and that Harlow, another scientist of courage, has now denied that there need be a critical period for social and sexual development in monkeys isolated for the first year of life (Novak and Harlow, 1975).

The studies of human development to which attention may be directed are briefly discussed below.

PROLONGED SOCIAL ISOLATION

The study of Isabelle by Davis (1974) is well known. Rescued from permanent isolation with a deaf–mute mother at age 6, under skilled treatment she recovered to normality. One could wish for greater detail, but the case history was independently corroborated (Mason, 1942).

The Koluchová (1972, 1976) reports on twin boys, isolated, neglected and cruelly treated from 18 months to 7 years are much more detailed. These were severely subnormal, rachitic and virtually without speech upon discovery. Now in a most unusual adoptive home, they are cognitively and emotionally normal and have caught up scholastically. Nor can it be said that their first eighteen months of life were ideal. Shortly after birth, they were taken into care for a year following the mother's death. Transferred to a maternal aunt for the period 12–18 months, they were then handed over to the sadistic stepmother.

STUDIES OF THE EFFECTS OF LESS EXTREME DEPRIVATION AFTER CHANGE

There are a lot of these studies, all of which show an average personal change in the direction of environmental shift, with an array of individual differences around such averages. They suggest that the amount and duration of such change is important.

It may be helpful to offer a very abbreviated account of some of these studies:

1. *Lewis (1954)*. Five hundred children with poor backgrounds, the worst in Kent, majority aged over five years, admitted to reception centre. Wide range of presenting disorders (delinquency 32 per cent; severely neurotic 18 per cent; psychopathic 3 per cent; normal behaviour but with slight neurotic symptoms 21 per cent; normal behaviour 25 per cent). One sample of a hundred followed up two years later by means of personal interviews with staff, foster parents, teachers and systematic recording of school data. Another sample of a hundred and twenty followed up by post. Wide variety of placements; no one type of placement had a monopoly of success. Essentially similar results from both follow-ups. Whereas on admission only 15 per cent of the samples had been in 'good' condition, two years later this had increased to 39 per cent. The 25 per cent in 'fair' condition increased to 36 per cent. Thus 75 per cent of the most deprived were in 'good' or 'fair' condition after only two years of better experiences.

2. *Clarke and Clarke (1954, 1959); Clarke, Clarke and Reiman (1958)*. Two total samples of certified 'feeble-minded' adolescents and young adults drawn from early bad or very bad homes (independently assessed from case histories) followed by, on average, several moves through residential schools or institutions, followed by certification. All exhibited mild subnormality, poor scholastic attainments, poor social competence and work capacity. I.Q.s and measures of work and social adjustment taken $2\frac{1}{4}$, $4\frac{1}{2}$ and 6 years after initial assessment. Greater (and substantial) I.Q. and

social improvement in those from the worst homes. All groups had average ages in the mid-twenties at follow-up, but such changes could occur at any time between age fifteen and about thirty, and perhaps slowly and steadily throughout the period. Estimates for change were very conservative owing to selective sample wastage from the loss of the more successful individuals. All data collected independently before being brought together.

3. *Bowlby and coworkers (1956)*. Sixty children who before age four had spent a period (range less than six months–more than two years) in a T.B. sanatorium matched with three controls per child, adjacent in age in some school class in follow-up. Latter took place within age range six years ten months to thirteen years seven months. Average I.Q. 107, S.D. 22. 8, controls 110, S.D. 16.8. Capacity for friendship normal. Maladjustment 63 per cent compared with 42 per cent regarded as usual expectancy. This excess 21 per cent might have arisen from social class and family contexts rather than separation and hospitalization. Indeed, authors carefully point out that such children tend to 'come from families where other members . . . have tuberculosis, so that illness and death are common with their attendant disturbed family relations and depressed economy' (1956, p. 213). Thus 10 per cent of the mothers were dead at the time of follow-up. The authors indicate that 'part of the emotional disturbance . . . is to be attributed to factors other then separation' (see Rutter, 1971).

4. *Rutter (1971)*. Part of a total sample of nine- to twelve-year-old children on the Isle of Wight, plus a representative group of London families in which one or both parents had been in psychiatric care. Antisocial behaviour in boys was associated with ratings of parents' marriage, not separation experiences. Where separation had occurred, the cause was relevant: holiday or illness, no effect; family discord or deviance, larger effect. On the whole separation due to parental death had little effect. It is also suggested that the longer the family disharmony lasts, the greater the risk to the children.

5. *Rathbun et al (1958, 1965)*. Refugee children (thirty-eight), age range five months to ten years, brought to United States from Korea and Greece, hence change of language and culture. Considerable personal disturbance on arrival; adopted by thirty-three families, five children unavailable for six-year follow-up. On average these had above average health, I.Q. and general competence; twenty-one had adequate or superior adjustment, ten problematic and two were clinically disturbed. Authors believe problematic adjustment arose in response to present rather than past problems. The picture is one of 'almost incredible resiliency'. No background details exist; almost certainly a group specially selected by overseas welfare workers in refugee camps.

6. *Kagan (1976)* studied Guatemalan, rural and city children of different ages. From a position of considerable retardation during early life, related to environmental conditions and modes of child care, the rural children

advanced in several cognitive areas by pre-adolescence, attaining Guatemala City and American norms. The report emphasizes placticity of development and its potential discontinuity in relation to changing environmental demands, and that early retardation has no important implication for ultimate normality.

7. *Kadushin (1970)*. Large sample of eighty-plus I.Q., healthy children, typically coming from large families in substandard circumstances, often below poverty level, and suffering physical neglect. Natural parents showed a picture of considerable personal pathology compounded of promiscuity, mental deficiency, alcoholism, imprisonment and psychosis. At average age three and a half, the children had been removed from their homes by court order, and after an average of 2.3 changes of foster home, were placed for adoption just over average age seven, and followed up at an average of almost fourteen years. Adoptive parents older than natural parents and of a considerably higher socioeconomic level. Data obtained from agency records and detailed statements by adoptive parents. The children in general were a source of satisfaction to the adoptive parents and showed a greater degree of psychic health and stability than might have been expected from their background. It is not precisely known how many were excluded from adoption by virtue of low I.Q.s. Population background very smiliar to those in the Clarke and Clarke, and Hilda Lewis studies. Outcome also similar in so far as it is better than would have been predicted (a) from social history; (b) after several foster changes; and (c) following very late adoption.

8. *Dennis (1973)*. Foundlings from very bad institution either adopted at different ages by Lebanese or American adopters, or, if female, transferred about six years to another very bad institution, if male to a very good one. Outcome related to direction of environmental shift or non-shift. Only about half of those adopted were available for study. Evidence of selective adoption policies relating to age at adoption. Average I.Q. outcome for those adopted before age two, subaverage outcome for those adopted later. Very poor status of older institutionalized girls, subaverage for boys. Did differing 'age of adoption' policies or adoption preferences impinge on constitutionally different children? Were children adopted at very different ages taken on by different types of home? Why are results somewhat discrepant with those of Skeels, when the experimental children were all adopted after age two?

9. *Tizard and Rees (1974)*. Sixty-five children reared from infancy in three residential nurseries. High staff–child ratio, material provision good; multiple caretaking, constant staff changes, official disapproval of close personal relationships. Between ages two and four and a half, twenty-four were adopted and fifteen restored to their mothers. At age four and a half I.Q.s were at least average, the adopted children had higher I.Q.s and appeared more stable than those restored or remaining in institution. At eight and a half there was inevitable sample attrition. Children still average or above; earlier

adopted higher than a small group adopted after four and a half, or children restored to parents. Children remaining in institution had declined slightly in I.Q. ($n = 7$). Reading ages reported; little difference among the groups. Affectional relationships with adoptive parents said to be good and home behaviour acceptable. A number of the children were, however, rated by their teachers as troublesome at school.

The American Head Start Programme, which had its roots in the idea of the potency of early experience, is said to have cost 2,000 million dollars between 1965 and 1970. On the basis of our model we were able in 1967, before any results were available to us, to predict that the programme would 'stand or fall not on what it achieves in the pre-school years, but on whether or not these diversions in development are subsequently reinforced' (Clarke, 1968). In the event, the nationwide program was a failure, and induced changes in the children 'washed out' in the early years of primary school, as we had expected. This led to a backlash against trying to help the disadvantaged, and to a recrudescence of the nature–nurture issue, with the publication of Jensen's (1969) paper which attempted to explain this disaster. Since then extremists on both sides have been locked in sterile but politically explosive combat.

Bronfenbrenner's (1974) careful review of 21 of the better studies, selected from hundreds of outstandingly inadequate ones, offers conclusions which exactly fit our thesis. Planned prospective intervention in the early years, if brief, and if not followed by similar environmental changes, has effects which fade. For the most disadvantaged, only long term ecological change has any chance of inducing long term effects.

In this whole connection it is interesting to note that so pervasive is the model concerning the long term role of early experience that Skeels (1966) himself apparently misunderstood his own data, and so have nearly all those who have quoted the study. It will be recalled that initially two young children in a very austere orphanage were found to be severely subnormal with I.Q.s of 46 and 35, respectively, and were removed to a mental subnormality hospital; the prognosis was regarded as poor.

Six months later by chance they were revisited by Skeels and in view of the obvious and surprising improvement, they were reassessed. By this time, I.Q.s had become 77 and 87, respectively. At age $3\frac{1}{2}$ they were adopted. Skeels attributed these results to the attention and stimulation the children, the youngest in the hospital, received from retarded women and ward attendants.

This study was replicated, and with similar results, using 13 children, all operating at a well below average or severely retarded level when transferred. An initially rather brighter contrast group remained in the terrible orphanage; they showed a relative decline in ability over time. Eleven of the 13 experimental group children showed great improvement and were adopted into only rather average homes, since Skeels feared that outcome might be a disappointment to really bright adoptive parents (Skeels and Dye, 1939).

Skeels offers fascinating data on follow-up twenty-five years later. Those children who had experienced a discontinuity (i.e. one *contrast* group child and most members of the experimental group) were normal citizens, spread far and wide over the United States. The one exception in the contrast group was a child who, found to be slightly deaf, was transferred at age 6 into a special school where he, too, enjoyed a compensatory programme. He was at follow-up a compositor for a newspaper, earning more than the rest of the contrast put together. The other members of this sample were easy to locate, many were institutionalized or employed in low level work. The study can be summarized by stating that most of the experimental group started life in the terrible orphanage, and were transferred at about 19 months to an institution for the mentally retarded. This proved to be a compensatory programme, but their roots were once again torn up at an average age of $3\frac{1}{2}$ when they were adopted. As Bowlby (1951) has put it concerning another study, they were 'passed like parcels from one mother to another'. Furthermore, individual case histories from the contrast group and experimental group give evidence that later life experiences were most important.

Now Skeels entitled his monograph 'Adult status of children with contrasting *early* life experiences' (our italics). Yet early life experiences of both groups in the orphanage had been similar, followed in the experimental group by a different form of institutionalization. By his title Skeels appeared to think that what happened in the mental retardation hospital was in some important way relevant to the normal adult outcome. But from the evidence it appears that the differing experiences following early childhood were more relevant. Perhaps the mental retardation hospital's only role in its immediate effect upon the children, was to give Skeels sufficient confidence to take the risk of adoption.

COMMENTARY UPON APPARENTLY RELATED EVIDENCE

We have examined several areas of evidence, some apparently contradictory to our thesis. They may be summarized under several headings.

Animal studies

During the 1950s and 1960s a large amount of experimental research with various species of animal was undertaken with results which apparently showed the importance of early experience for later behaviour. Apart from the vexed question of the implications of these studies for human development, new work is indicating that (a) in some cases there is reversibility and (b) in others the mechanism is as yet not well understood. We have already alluded to the change in Harlow's views (Novak and Harlow, 1975). The stream of work on handling of young rats initiated by Levine, Chevalier and Korchin (1956) is also showing a shift in interpretation. Certainly the view originally suggested that these were solely single experience effects, is now giving way to suggestions that the matter is much more complicated than was formerly believed.

Modern research on infancy

The last decade has witnessed a dramatic burgeoning of research on infancy. A large number of researchers have described the elaborate interactions between mother and baby, and there have been interesting discussions of the stages at which one, the other, or both are responsible for the choreography. In a wide-ranging review, Lipsitt (1977) concludes that 'one import of the data is that newborns and other young infants are unquestionably more highly developed ... than traditionally they have been appreciated to be'. In some infancy data, however, one notes some possibility of confounded variables; e.g. maternal anxiety in pregnancy relates to childbirth abnormalities and to the infant's adjustment at eight months.

All this is fascinating, but no-one has yet suggested that the infant is a more efficient learner than at later stages, nor has it been shown that induced changes are more resistant to extinction than later. Furthermore, as Judy Dunn (1976) has commented succinctly: 'Because psychologists demonstrate that something happens between a mother and baby it does not necessarily follow that it is important in the long run'. Indeed, the implication that it may have long term consequences involves an essentially static concept of both mother and child.

Critical incidents

There is an obvious possibility that severely traumatic incidents may have effects of a different order and persistence than in normal learning. We have suggested that these do not appear to be age specific (e.g. Campbell, Sanderson and Laverry, 1964) and hence not relevant to the question at issue, the effects of early experience *per se*. It is possible that the recent work of Douglas (1975) on the effects of repeated hospitalization, may be seen in this light, although an alternative possibility is that early and repeated hospitalization is merely a symptom of persistent and ongoing adversity. (See also Quinton and Rutter (1976).)

Sensitive period for maternal bonding?

The suggestion that there may be a sensitive period, shortly after birth, for the bonding of the mother to the child has attracted widespread interest (Kennell, Trause and, Klaus, 1975). The process in the mother is not to be regarded as imprinting 'in that there is not a point beyond which the formation of an attachment is precluded ... The process can occur at a later time, although it will be more difficult and take longer to achieve' (Kennell, Trause and Klaus, 1975, p. 88). This research area, while interesting, is only of very tangential relevance to our theme. It is mentioned here for the sake of completeness in outling areas of investigation which have a bearing upon early life, and may be pertinent to the section below.

Transactional effects

It is increasingly recognized that the child does not merely represent the point of intersection between genetic and psychosocial variables, but plays some part in causing his own development in his transactions with the environment. This is one way in which early experiences *may* be perpetuated, albeit indirectly rather than directly. So there is indeed the possibility that early experience may produce particular effects which, acting upon later environments, result in reinforcing feedback, thus may unwittingly via circular arguments be seen as reinforcing early adversity. Even so, the passage of time seems to attenuate such continuities in many cases.

Increased vulnerability

Such writers as Ainsworth and coworkers (1962) argue that overt adjustment following early adversity may well mask an underlying disturbance which may manifest itself later. One would be wrong to write off such a view as being of the 'have-your-cake-and-eat-it' variety, for it would certainly accord with the facts of extinction of learned responses, with subsequent revival when conditions reinforce. We need to know more about this possibility.

Head start pays off in the long run?

Attempts are now being made to 'rehabilitate' the long term usefulness of Head Start Programmes. For our thesis it is necessary to differentiate between those which focused on the child alone outside the family context and those which had as their target a change in the parent–child interaction. The evidence suggests (e.g. Bronfenbrenner, 1974) that, as noted earlier, the effects of child-centred programmes will 'wash out' during the first year or two of school but, like Bronfenbrenner we would expect that *successful* intervention into the parent–child interactive process might initiate an enduring change. However, while accepting the 'wash out' as common, there is now the suggestion of 'sleeper effects' for the reappearance of social, attainment and intellectual differences in late childhood. Indeed there are said to be 96 prospective studies now complete 'all showing some degree of long-term positive effect of early intervention' (Lewin, 1977). But in evaluating these claims, we must remain alert to the methodological problems of separating sample characteristics from programme effects.

Guinagh and Gordon (1976) used a parent education programme when children were aged 3 months until age three. Results three years after the programme's termination, at age six, show a 7–8 I.Q. points difference between experimental and control children. By the early school years at age $8\frac{1}{2}$, there had been considerable sample attrition (88 out of an original 192). There were, however, significant differences, favouring the experimental groups, in achievement, and in assignment to special classes. However, there is no indication of what happened to the families in the interim between programme termination and the school years, nor any evaluation of the drop outs, other than that they were not significantly different in I.Q. at earlier ages from those retained. We know that in general, sample attrition usually involves the most disadvantaged cases, and Bronfenbrenner (1974) has indicated that only the 'upper crust' of the disadvantaged can benefit from parent education. Hence, if these results do not merely reflect the large loss of the worst cases, they are to be attributed to long-term changes in parental behaviour, perhaps initiated by Head Start.

Palmer (1977) reviews his own and other similar findings, presenting a very balanced viewpoint: 'As attrition occurred in the experimental and control groups between the beginning of a study and the latest age of evaluation, is there bias in who remained available? Were the experimental and control groups matched for intellective level in the first place? Did those who did the assessing know which children had received the intervention and which had not, and if they did, was there bias in the administration of the tests or in the collection of school data?' Nevertheless, Palmer concludes that compensatory education has not failed but 'is a healthy child which needs continued support to reach maturity'.

It does not seem that data such as these challenge our thesis. If the results are not an artefact of sample loss nor experimenter bias, then they suggest that long term familial and school influences are responsible. These may or may not have been triggered by a Head Start Programme. As Bronfenbrenner (1974) has indicated, the volunteer parent who allows an educator into her home is different from one who does not, and the most disadvantaged appear not to gain much from such intervention.

Later versus earlier adoption

As we have pointed out (1976), there is evidence from a number of studies that those adopted late fare less well than those adopted early. But in this context 'late' describes a number of very widely different chronological ages. Two additional studies not mentioned in our book add to this picture (Bohman, 1971; and Scarr and Weinberg, 1976). The latter authors studied 176 children adopted into white middle class families, of whom 130 were socially classified as black, 25 as white and 21 Asian or American Indian. There was a large difference in I.Q. at an average age of about 7 years between early and late adopted children. The majority (111) had been placed during the first year of life; the average age of placement, however, was 22 months and the median 6 months, indicating a wide range of placement ages. As the authors show, however, both age and number of placements were correlated, and were, moreover, correlated with lower natural parent education and quality of ultimate placement. Obviously, later placed children had spent less time in adoptive homes than earlier placed. This study, therefore, demonstrates a complex of reasons why one might expect early adopted children to have done better when followed up at a failry early age.

As Tizard (1977) indicates in relation to her study, 'eight years old is still very young and it is encouraging to note that in Bohman's Swedish study of adopted children, *fewer* problems were found at the age of fifteen than at the age of eleven'. Moreover, it seems that Bohman himself believes that selective placement was related to later outcome. It should be noted additionally that the transactional model (see Transactional effects above) suggests that the damaged child may make his new environment less adequate because of disturbed behaviour. This may evoke adverse responses which may feed back upon him, reinforcing his problems. Such perpetuation of difficulties is, however, indirect rather than a direct effect of early experience.

These points are well illustrated in the reports of Tizard (1974; 1977). The children had experienced a very large number of caretakers in their otherwise excellent institutions. On follow-up at age $8\frac{1}{2}$, these late adopted children were more often said by their parents to be 'over-friendly' and attention seeking towards adults than were working class or middle class controls. Moreover, although the majority had formed strong affectional bonds with their parents and were a source of pleasure to them, about half of them showed problems with both adults and peers at school. The remainder of the group were apparently well adjusted both at home and at school. Tizard suggests, by way of explanation, a combination of constitutional sensitivity and also a critical period during the first two years of life for shaping later social behaviour. However, while the latest report (1977) provides evidence for concentrated efforts on the part of the adoptive parents to foster affectional ties and academic achievement, no commensurate attempt was made to help their children get on well with teachers and peers. It is perhaps not surprising, therefore, that in social relationships these difficulties remained. Tizard (personal communication) writes that 'you may well be right. *Most* of the parents did not seem aware of the *extent* of their children's difficulties with their peers and with their teachers, though some certainly did, and some of them definitely dismissed the peer-group difficulties as unimportant'.

Since studies of late adoption are among the more important sources of data on the effect upon development of environmental change, it may be appropriate to summarize certain methodological issues: (1) evidence suggests that there may well be selective factors operating in early versus late adoption which are not as yet properly understood and require further study; (2) the majority of researchers following the fortunes of adoptive children have tended to assess their sample at a particular chronological age. Inevitably this means that there may be wide variations between children in the length of both pre-adoptive and post-adoptive experience. For comparative purposes it would clearly be desirable to hold constant the period within the adoptive home; (3) it is important that longitudinal measures should be taken following adoption, and preferably into adolescence.

SOME IMPLICATIONS

In the preceding section, we have deliberately sought to outline evidence from several areas of research which, on the face of it, appears to threaten the validity of our theme. As indicated earlier, in attempting to reformulate the more traditional view of early development we have not produced a counter-balance which might prove equally extreme, but rather have tried to achieve a balanced view. It would indeed be a matter of surprise to us if future research did not impose a need to sharpen or extend our thesis. It seems clear, however, that the findings reviewed in our (1976) book and in this presentation, pose few difficulties. Our perspective appears to accommodate the data far better than the early experience model.

The revival of interest in early experience which resulted from Bowlby's (1951) monograph has had many excellent effects, sensitizing the public to the needs of children. Our thesis in no way criticizes this humane result, nor does it suggest that 'it does not matter what happens to a young child early in life'. Nor does our position do anything to condone bad institutions, or 'problem' families or refugee camps, simply because their unfortunate effects can in many cases be reversed. Nor would we wish to see nursery schools closed, or indeed opened, simply because of this debate. That such schools fail to show long term effects is no argument against their existence, both for the present benefit of the child and also for the mother. There is absolutely no implication that infancy and early childhood are unimportant, only that their long term role *by itself* is very limited.

Turning to more positive implications, the evidence seems to us to indicate that human development is potentially and to some extent openended, with of course limits set by genetic and constitutional factors. This view fits quite well the research findings of Mischel (1968) who has argued that future behaviour seems to be determined considerably by future learning conditions rather than by generalized internal dispositions. It follows that no early intervention programme seeking to alleviate the effects of social disadvantage has any real chance of success unless it includes as a major focus the social circumstances of middle and later childhood. And even for those living in normal conditions, we perhaps need to place less emphasis upon the notion of necessarily stable attributes such as, for example, intelligence, personality or minimal brain damage. As Kadushin (1970) puts it ' . . . we may need a re-orientation in emphasis, with a greater respect being paid to the present and more recent, proximate experience . . . the present is a countervailing force which exerts a constant pressure, demanding that we live by it'.

We have already referred to the self-fulfilling prophecies which may reinforce early experience effects. For example, a disturbed child removed from parents at age five may not be considered for adoption because he is disturbed and because anyway late adoption is perceived as risky. So he remains in care, in conditions which strengthen his behaviour disturbance. This in turn is seen as justifying the earlier decision.

The belief that early experiences are formative naturally affects the caring professions, as well as the general public. This can lead, on the one hand, to a belief that if all has gone well in the first years of life, all will continue to go well. The later years, when for example, parental interest and affection are no less important, may not receive the same care and attention. On the other hand, a history of early adversity may lead to an underestimation of what might be done, and hence a tendency to inaction. It can also lead to the unfortunate view that almost at all costs, adverse homes must be propped up to preserve an early mother–child relationship.

Vernon (1964) pointed out that for psychiatric patients to focus upon their problems in the early years may be a welcome relief from dwelling upon present problems. One might add that clinician and patient may serve as mutual reinforcers in discovering early anomalies. Increasingly, those concerned with severe problems may find it less profitable to look into early experience, since these may be irrelevant to the solution of present difficulties.

We believe that, in the present stage of knowledge, the only safe assumption to make is that at least the first fifteen or sixteen years of life are critical. By that time, major developments of psychological characteristics have taken place, and achieved some autonomy. But even this view may err on the side of conservatism, for some studies have shown radical personal changes after this age range. Within the time scale suggested there may well be some periods that are more important than others, and these may differ for different processes. They are certainly not uniformly to be found in the early years.

Some have regarded our thesis as an optimistic one. We by no means agree, for we do not think that the identification of psychosocial causes necessarily brings any easy solution. To induce desirable changes in social interactions and social contexts can be very difficult. For example, few deprived children are likely to attain the sort of ideal placement which the Koluchová twins have enjoyed. So merely to indicate that late intervention, for example, is potentially fruitful, is not to say that it can be easily achieved unless considerable resources become available, as in Israel (Feuerstein and Krasilowsky, 1972).

Considerable advances have been made in our understanding of the complexity of development, and new questions are being asked by scientists concerning the nature of the processes, including the interplay of biological and social factors. At the same time, new and increasingly sophisticated research methods, designed for use outside the confines of a laboratory, are becoming available (e.g. Struening and Guttentag, 1975) which, coupled with an analysis of the appropriate questions to ask, should lead to a solid body of knowledge on which to base social and educational policies, and give guidance to the caring professions, as well as parents. It is in our view a matter of some urgency that such research should be carried out with different groups of children, at various stages of development and in different social contexts.

To return to the theme of this volume, the significance of the first year of life for later social development is that it marks the beginning of a life-long path, the direction of which may be maintained or altered by subsequent experiences and unfolding genetic programmes.

REFERENCES

Ainsworth, M. D., Andry, R. G., Harlow, R. G., Lebovici, S., Mead, M., Prugh, D. G. and Wootton, B. (1962). *Deprivation of Maternal Care: Reassessment of its Effects*, World Health Organization, Geneva.

Bloom, B. S. (1961). *Stability and Change in Human Characteristics*, John Wiley, London.

Bowlby, J. (1951). *Maternal Care and Mental Health*, World Health Organization, Geneva.

Bowlby, J., Ainsworth, M. D., Boston, M. and Rosenbluth, D. (1956). 'The effects of mother–child separation: a follow-up study, *Br. J. Med. Psychol.* **29**, 211–247.

Bohman, M. (1971). 'A comparative study of adopted children, foster children, and children in their biological environment born after undesired pregnancies', *Acta Pediatrica Scandinavica, Suppl.* 221.

Bronfenbrenner, U. (1974). *A Report on Longitudinal Evaluations of Pre-School Programs, Vol. 2: Is Early Intervention Effective?*, D. H. E. W. Publ. No. (OHD) 74–25, Washington, D.C.

Campbell, D., Sanderson, R. E. and Laverty, S. G. (1964). 'Characteristics of a conditioned response in human subjects during extinction trials following a single traumatic conditioning trial', *J. abn. soc. Psychol.*, **68**, 627–639.

Clarke, A. D. B. (1968). 'Learning and human development—the 42nd Maudsley Lecture', *Br. J. Psychiat.*, **114**, 161–177.

Clarke, A. D. B. and Clarke, A. M. (1954). 'Cognitive changes in the feebleminded', *Br. J. Psychol.*, **45**, 173–179.

Clarke, A. D. B. and Clarke, A. M. (1959). 'Recovery from the effects of deprivation', *Acta Psychol.*, **16**, 137–144.

Clarke, A. D. B. and Clarke, A. M. (1960). 'Recent advances in the study of deprivation', *J. Child Psychol Psychiat.*, **1**, 26–36.

Clarke, A. D. B. and Clarke, A. M. (1972). 'Consistency and variability in the growth of human characteristics', in Wall, W. D. and Varma, V. P. (eds.), *Advances in Educational Psychology I*, 32–52, University of London Press, London.

Clarke, A. D. B., Clarke, A. M. and Reiman, S. (1958). 'Cognitive and social changes in the feebleminded—three further studies', *Br. J. Psychol.*, **49**, 144–157.

Clarke, A. M. and Clarke, A. D. B. (1976). *Early Experience: Myth and Evidence*, Open Books, London, Free Press, New York.

Davis, K. (1947). 'Final note on a case of extreme isolation', *Am. J. Sociol.*, **52**, 432–437.

Dennis, W. (1973). *Children of the Creche*, Appleton-Century-Crofts, New York.

Douglas, J. W. B. (1975). 'Early hospital admissions and later disturbances of behaviour and learning', *Develop. Med. Child Neurol.*, **17**, 456–480.

Dunn, J. (1976). 'How far do early differences in mother–child relations affect later development?', Chapter 16 in Bateson, P. P. G. and Hinde, R. A. (eds.) *Growing Points in Ethology*, Cambridge University Press, London.

Eaves, L. and Eysenck, H. J. (1976) 'Genetic and environmental components of inconsistency and unpredictability in twins' responses to a neuroticism questionnaire', *Behav. Genet.*, **6**, 145–160.

Feuerstein, R. and Krasilowsky, D. (1972). 'Interventional strategies for the significant modification of cognitive functioning in the disadvantaged adolescent', *J. Amer. Acad. Child Psychiat.*, **11**, 572–582.

Freud, S. (1910). 'Infantile sexuality. Three contributions to the sexual theory', transl. Brill, A. A. *Nervous and Mental Disease Monographs*, No. 7.

Freud, S. (1949) *An Outline of Psycho-analysis*, transl. Strachey, J., Hogarth Press, London.

Guinagh, B. J. and Hordon, I. J. (1976). *School performance as a function of early stimulation*, Final Report to Office of Child Development, Grant No. NIH–HEW–OCD–09–C–638, Gainesville, Florida, College of Education University of Florida.

Jensen, A. R. (1969). 'How much can we boost IQ and scholastic achievement? *Harvard educ. Rev.*, **39**, 1–123.

Kadushin, A. (1970). *Adopting Older Children*, Columbia University Press, New York.

Kagan, J. (1976). 'Resilience and continuity in psychological development', Chapter 7 in Clarke, A. W. and Clarke, A. D.B. (eds.) *Early Experience: Myth and Evidence*, Open Books, London; Free Press, New York.

Kagan, J. and Moss, H. A. (1962). *Birth to Maturity*, John Wiley, New York.

Kennell, J. H., Trause, M. A., Klaus, M. H. (1975). 'Evidence for a sensitive period in the human mother', in Ciba Foundation *Parent–Infant Interaction*, (Symposium 33, New Series) 87–101, Elsevier, Amsterdam.

Koluchová, J. (1972). 'Severe deprivation in twins: a case study', *J. Child Psychol. Psychiat.*, **13**, 107–144.

Koluchová, J. (1976). 'A report on the further development of twins after severe and prolonged deprivation', Chapter 5 in Clarke, A. M. and Clarke, A. D. B. (eds.) *Early Experience: Myth and Evidence*, Open Books, London; Free Press, New York.

Levine, S., Chevalier, J. A. and Korchin, S. J. (1956). 'The effects of shock and handling in infancy on later avoidance learning', *J. Pers.*, **24**, 475–493.

Lewin, R. (1977). '"Head-start" pays off', *New Scientist*, 508–509 (March 3rd).

Lewis, H. (1954), *Deprived Children*, Oxford University Press, London.

Lipsitt, L. P. (1977). 'The study of sensory and learning processes of the newborn', *Clinics in Perinatology*, **4**, in press.

Mason, M. K. (1942). 'Learning to speak after six and a half years of silence', *J. Speech Dis.*, **7**, 295–304.

Mischel, W. (1968). *Personality and Assessment*, John Wiley, New York.

Novak, M. A. and Harlow, H. F. (1975). 'Social recovery of monkeys isolated for the first year of life: I. Rehabilitation and therapy', *Develop. Psychol.*, **11**, 453–465.

Palmer, F. H. (1977). *The effects of early childhood intervention*, paper presented to the American Association for the Advancement of Science, Denver, Colorado, 1977.

Plato (428–348 B. C.) (1955). *The Reupblic*, transl. Lee, H. D. P., Penguin, Harmondsworth.

Quinton, D. and Rutter, M. (1976). 'Early hospital admissions and later disturbances of behaviour: an attempted replication of Douglas' findings', *Develop. Med. Child Neurol.*, **18**, 447–459.

Rathbun, C., Di Virgilio, L. and Waldfogel, S. (1958). 'The restitutive process in children following radical separation from family and culture', *Am. J. Orthopsychiat.*, **28**, 408–415.

Rathbun, C., McLaughlin, H., Bennett, O. and Garland, J. A. (1965). 'Later adjustment of children following radical separation from family and culture', *Am. J. Orthopsychiat.*, **35**, 604–609.

Robins, L. N. (1966). *Deviant Children Grown Up*, Williams and Wilkins, Baltimore.

Rutter, M. (1971). 'Parent–child separation: psychological effects on the children', *J. Child Psychol. Psychiat.*, **12**, 233–260.

Rutter, M., Greenfield, D. and Lockyer, L. (1967). 'A five to fifteen year follow-up study of infantile psychosis: II. Social and behavioural outcome', *Br. J. Psychiat.*, **113**, 1183–1199.

Sameroff, A. J. and Chandler, M. J. (1975). 'Reproductive risk and the continuum of caretaking casualty', in Horowitz, F. D., Hetherington, M., Scarr-Salapatek, S. and Siegel, G. (eds.) *Review of Child Development Research*, Vol. 4, University of Chicago Press, Chicago.

Scarr, S. and Weinberg, R. A. (1976). 'IQ test performance of black children adopted by white families', *American Psychologist*, **31**, 726–739.

Skeels, H. M. (1966). 'Adult status of children with contrasting early life experiences: a follow-up study', *Monogr. Soc. Res. Child Develop.*, **31**, No. 3, Serial No. 105.

Skeels, H. M. and Dye, H. B. (1939). 'A study of the effects of differential stimulation on mentally retarded children', *Proc. Amer. Assoc. Ment. Defic.*, **44**, 114–136.

Struening, E. L. and Guttentag, M. (1975). *Handbook of Evaluation Research.*, Sage Publications, Beverly Hills, Calif.

Tizard, B. (1977). *Adoption: a Second Chance*, Open Books, London.

Tizard, B. and Rees, J. (1974). 'A comparison of the effects of adoption, restoration to the natural mother, and continued institutionalization on the cognitive development of four-year-old children', *Child Develop.* **45**, 92–99.

Vernon, P. E. (1964). *Personality Assessment: a Critical Survey*, Methuen, London.

Chapter 9

Early Life Experiences and Later Mothering Behaviour: a Study of Mothers and Their 20-Week Old Babies

Fae Hall, Susan J. Pawlby and Stephen Wolkind

SUMMARY

In a combined epidemiological and ethological study of 233 primiparous British-born working-class women and their babies, 68 women were observed in interaction with their 20-week-old infants in the home. Women who had come from a disrupted family of origin, where the parents had divorced or separated or either or both had died, interacted very significantly less with their 20-week old babies, than women who had not undergone such an experience. On the other hand, a history in the mother of being cared for away from home for a period of one month or more before the age of 16 appeared to have only a minimal effect on our mothering measures. The finding that children of women from a disrupted family of origin received significantly less physical and social stimulation at the hands of their mothers in their early months is discussed in relation to results from a follow-up study showing that at 27 months, children of mothers from a disrupted family of origin were less advanced than other children in their language development.

INTRODUCTION

Although our society is clearly entering a period of change, it remains for the time being very largely true, in western cultures at least, that the infant's most frequent caretaker in his earliest months is his own mother, and it is his mother who, whether directly through her behaviour towards him or indirectly through other aspects of the environment she provides for him, plays a large part in determining the nature and extent of his experience during his first year.

Studies over the past decade amply demonstrate, of course, that even the very young infant is far from a mere passive recipient of his mother's attentions, but is on the contrary constantly engaged in an active behavioural dialogue with her (e.g. Schaffer, 1971; Richards, 1971) and may within certain limits determine her behaviour towards him (Pawlby, 1977; Trevarthen, 1977). It is difficult, however, to conceive that the extraordinarly wide range of maternal attitudes and resulting practices revealed, for example, by the Newsons' survey of mothers of one-year-olds (Newson and Newson, 1963) could be accounted for solely as a response to the individuality of the child. As current research emphasizes (e.g. Lewis and Lee-Painter, 1974; Stern, 1974), *both* the infant *and* his mother bring with them their own individual contribution to the developing relationship. However, though there is a good deal of recent work looking into possible pre- and perinatal influences on the infant's contribution to the mother–infant interaction (Sameroff and Chandler, 1975; Als, Tronick, Lester and Brazelton, 1977; Packer and Rosenblatt, chapter 1, this volume), and how that affects the mother's handling (Whiten, 1977; Dunn and Richards, 1977), apart from work relating to the very extreme case of child abuse (Helfer and Kempe, 1976), relatively little attention has been given to other possible sources of individual differences in mothering behaviour. In this paper, a woman's behaviour towards her child in his first months is examined in relation to two particular aspects of her own early experience.

In electing to examine individual differences in mothering behaviour in relation to experience in childhood, we are well aware that there must be many other factors which influence the kind of mothering a woman provides. Cross-cultural studies, for example, reveal consistent cultural differences in mothering practices, both between major cultures and among different subcultures (Caudill and Weinstein, 1969; LeVine, 1970; Newson and Newson, 1963). Within single cultures, everyday experience suggests, in addition, that a woman's handling of her child may be affected by her current environmental situation and more particularly, perhaps, by environmental stresses and accompanying emotional factors. There is however some evidence to suggest that the extent to which a woman experiences particular forms of environmental stress and her ability to cope with stress when it arises may be a function of her general coping ability as an adult, and that a woman's adult behaviour in this and in many other respects, may relate to her early history (Blake Cohen, 1966).

The proposition that aspects of adult behaviour are strongly determined by childhood experience has long been current in psychoanalytic thinking, but specific psychoanalytic tenets regarding, for example, the importance of methods of feeding and weaning, or the approach to toilet training have received only doubtful or inconsistent empirical support (Caldwell, 1964). However, two long term longitudinal studies which used dimensions of mothering more general than her management of particular caretaking situations have produced results which are open to a more positive interpretation. In a follow-up of the Fels study (reviewed by Crandall, 1972), where subjects were observed at intervals from birth to 18 years, Kagan and Moss (1962) found that ratings of mother's behaviour on dimensions such as affection–rejection, autonomy–control, protectiveness etc. made in the first three years were better predictors of the child's later behaviour in adulthood than were maternal ratings made at later ages. Similarly, in the Berkeley Growth Study (reviewed by Hunt and Eichorn, 1972), aspects of a child's later behaviour (including I.Q. performance) were found to relate more closely to the mother's *early* behaviour towards her child than to her later behaviour, although in this case positive findings were obtained only for boys. Neither study provides evidence that the kind of mothering a woman herself received influences her own mothering behaviour, but both studies do relate dimensions of mothering to other aspects of the child's behaviour as an adult.

Another line of evidence relating childhood experience to later behaviour concerns children with a history of separation from the mother. Evidence for and against the proposition that separation from the mother may have adverse effects on children has been several times reviewed (Bowlby, 1951, 1975; Ainsworth, 1962; Yarrow, 1961; Rutter, 1972) but two recent findings provide positive evidence of an adverse effect. Thus, Douglas (1975) has shown that in both boys and girls, poor reading ability at age 15, a teacher's rating of troublesome behaviour out of class, delinquency (boys only) and an unstable job history after leaving school were all significantly associated with prolonged or repeated hospital admissions before the age of 5 years. Similarly, Quinton and Rutter (1976) found that repeated hospital admissions starting in the pre-school period were associated with emotional and conduct disorder at age 10 years, but that the association was stronger in children where hospital admissions occurred against a background of high psychosocial disadvantage than for children admitted from homes where the level of psychosocial disadvantage was low. However, despite the statistical significance of the association between multiple hospital admissions and emotional and behavioural disturbance later, Quinton and Rutter point out that for a substantial proportion of children with multiple hospital admissions there appear to have been no adverse consequences. In this connection, Hinde's work with Rhesus monkeys (Hinde and Spencer-Booth, 1970) raises the possibility that the quality of the mother–child relationship before admission to hospital may be an important factor in determining the outcome.

While Douglas, and Quinton and Rutter, have no evidence of the adult outcome for the children in their surveys, they did find evidence of emotional and conduct disorder among separated children in middle and late childhood, and Robins (1970) reviews evidence from 23 studies which very clearly indicates an association between a diagnosis of antiscocial disorder in middle childhood and a variety of adverse outcomes in adult life. In particular, in Robins' own follow-up study of children referred to a child guidance clinic (Robins, 1966), considerable evidence was found of continuity between childhood antisocial disorder and adult sociopathic personality. Robins' evidence relating specifically to the girls in the study, however, shows in addition that though it was the antisocial girls who were least likely to make a good adjustment as adults, the neurotic girls also fared very much less well as adults than did control subjects with no childhood psychiatric history. As an example, among the women, the mean number of symptoms compatible with psychiatric disease in middle adult life was 11.7 for the childhood antisocial group, 9.6 for the childhood neurotic group and only 6.0 for the controls; the proportion of separations and divorces, similarly, was 26% for the previously antisocial girls, 18% for the previously neurotic girls and only 7% for the controls, and the proportion of women with children placed outside the home was 36%, 22% and 11% respectively.

Douglas, and Quinton and Rutter, provide evidence of emotional and behavioural disorder among children with an experience of multiple early separations from the mother, and Robins' evidence suggests that such disorders very often persist into adult life, bringing a variety of personal and material difficulties. There are in addition, a number of epidemiological studies which directly relate a history of separation from the mother to later adult difficulties. From interviews with women having their first baby, Wolkind, Kruk and Chaves (1976) found that women who had been separated from one or both parents before the age of 16 years were significantly less likely to be legally married and more likely to be single and not cohabiting while having their first baby than women who reported no separation in childhood, and they were also significantly more likely than the non-separated women to have become pregnant while in their teens, to have had psychiatric treatment, to have a higher score on a Malaise Inventory based on the Cornell Medical Index and to have current housing problems. Thus in early adult life, women who had suffered a separation of upwards of 1 month while under five, or three months at age 5–16, were more likely than non-separated women to be experiencing serious real-life problems and to be troubled with minor physical complaints and 'their nerves'. To a very large extent, these findings replicate those of Illsley and Thompson (1961) for a sample of 2930 women having their first baby in Aberdeen in 1952–1954. Compared with women coming from intact homes, the 17% of women in the Scottish sample who had for part of their childhood been brought up apart from one or both natural parents were more likely to have left school at the minimum age and taken a manual job, and were also more likely to have conceived while unmarried and while still a teenager. The highest rates of premarital conception and teenage birth were amongst girls who came from homes where the parents were separated or divorced, and in girls who had been brought up by unrelated foster parents or in institutions. Wolkind (1977) also has found significant associations between an 'in-care' experience in childhood and a woman's psychological and social status during pregnancy.

On the psychological side, Brown, Harris and Copeland (1977) in another epidemiological study, have examined the relationship between early experience and adult depression in women. They found that depressed women were more likely than non-depressed women to have lost their mother by death or by separation before the age of eleven. Compared with the loss of the mother, the loss of the father or of a sibling in childhood, or of a husband or child in adult life appeared from the study to play only a minor role in the etiology of adult depression among women in the general population.

In summary, therefore, while there exists only indirect evidence of a relationship between the actual mothering a woman received as a child and her own adult behaviour, there is ample reason to suspect that many girls subjected to one or a series of separations in childhood, especially where these occurred in the context of psychosocial disadvantage, will be likely to experience difficulties in important areas of their lives as adults.

The first indication that these difficulties might extend into a woman's relationship with her own children was obtained by Frommer and O'Shea (1973a) in the course of clinical work at a day centre for disturbed pre-school children. Among women whose children were disturbed or who reported difficulties of mothering, an unduly high proportion also reported a history of separation from one or both of their own parents in childhood. From this it appeared that women with a history of early separation might be especially vulnerable to difficulties of mothering. In interviews with a different sample of women carried out at intervals during the first year after the babies' birth, it was found that 'separated' women were significantly more likely than the 'non-separated' to give a propped bottle and to complain of feeding problems and major sleep problems with the baby at 6–7 months, and were also significantly more likely to report more than one temper tantrum a day in the child at 13 months. Dividing the women into those who did report problems either with their baby or in their marriage during the baby's first year of life and those who did not (Frommer and O'Shea, 1973b), the 'problem' group were, as before, significantly more likely than the 'no-problem' group to have experienced a separation before the age of eleven, but in addition, the 'problem' group were significantly more likely to report a history of a poor relationship with their own father and/or parental quarrelling and divorce or separation of their parents.

These findings of Frommer and O'Shea are of particular interest for two reasons. First, theirs is the only human study of which we are aware in which statistical relationships have been established between certain types of adverse experience in childhood and a woman's later experience and behaviour as a mother. Second, Frommer and O'Shea's findings support the view for which Quinton and Rutter provide firm evidence, namely that an important factor in determining the later outcome for any history of separation in childhood is the psychosocial background against which the separation occurred, and in particular, the harmoniousness of relationships within the child's family of origin. In what follows, we take these two findings as our starting point, and examine individual differences in the mothering received by 20-week-old infants in relation to their mothers' own early life experiences.

METHOD

The sample

As part of an on-going, larger longitudinal epidemiological study of British-born mothers and their first-born babies in an Inner London Borough (details of which can be found in Wolkind, Hall and Pawlby, 1977), a subsample of 68 mothers and their babies were observed together when the babies were 20 weeks old. Of the 68 mothers, 56 were married or cohabiting when they first booked at the antenatal clinic, and 12 were single. As in the larger epidemiological sample, the observational sample is almost exclusively Caucasian and working class in composition. Judged by their husbands' (or in the case of the single girls, their fathers') occupations, 61 of the 68 women fell into social Class III manual or below on the Registrar General's scales, and only 7 into Class III non-manual or above. The mean age of the women was 22.7 years. Of the babies, 35 were boys and 33 girls.

Because our ultimate interest is in tracing factors associated with later behaviour disturbance in the child, the subjects for the observational study were selected from the larger sample with an unduly high proportion of women whom it was thought, on the basis of information obtained when they first booked at the antenatal clinic, might be vulnerable to later difficulties in child-rearing. Each woman was assigned a vulnerability score at the time of antenatal booking on the basis of whether or not she or the father had ever received any in-patient psychiatric treatment, whether or not she had experienced a major separation from one or both parents, and whether or not she had any ongoing major illness or permanent handicap. Other secondary criteria included perception by the woman of poor health in either herself or the baby's father, perception of change in health in pregnancy, evidence of psychosomatic 'malaise' in the woman herself, actual physical ill-health in herself or the father, outpatient psychiatric treatment of herself or the father, poor housing (real or subjective), chronic unemployment of the father, contact with a social worker, and minor separation from one or both parents. Women who were neither married nor cohabiting at the time of the antenatal booking were automatically assigned a high vulnerability score.

Of the 68 women in the observation sample, 34 were randomly selected from the group of 61 married or cohabiting women in the epidemiological sample whose vulnerability score was high, 22 were randomly selected from the group of 91 married or cohabiting women whose vulnerability score was low; and the remaining 12 women were randomly selected from the group of 81 women who were single (i.e. not married or cohabiting). From this description, it will be obvious that the observational sample is in no way a random sample of women from the borough in which we work, but is, on the contrary, a group deliberately selected to include a high level of psychosocial morbidity.

Although interview data is available for all women in the total epidemiological sample, in this paper, the interview data as well as the observational findings relate only to the 68 women in the observational subsample.

The interviews

The interview data presented here are derived from three separate interviews. The first of these, the original screening interview, was very brief and was designed merely to obtain information about the woman's past history and current psychosocial state. This screening interview was conducted in the antenatal booking clinic, usually during the first months of pregnancy. For the women selected for inclusion in the study proper, longer structured interviews were conducted in the home during the 3rd trimester of pregnancy and again after the birth, when the baby was about 18 weeks old. Both of the structured interviews were tape-recorded and answers were rated from the tape. All interview items were tested for inter-rater reliability and only items showing at least 85% agreement between raters were included in the final interview. Areas covered in the pregnancy interview included the woman's health, scholastic and work record and her attitudes to her pregnancy and to motherhood. During the post-natal interview information was obtained on her child-rearing practices and her infant's temperamental characteristics. At both interviews she was questioned about her relationship with her husband and her wider family and friendship circle, about the details and her level of satisfaction with her daily life and on areas relating to her current state of mental health. This latter part of the interview was based on the standardized instrument developed by Rutter and his colleagues at the Institute of Psychiatry, and a disorder was rated as being present only after discussion with the psychiatrist on the team. The women who on this basis were rated as suffering some form of mental disorder were, however, still living in the community, and although many were receiving treatment from their family doctor, only one or two had been seen by a psychistrist and none was suffering any form of major psychosis.

'Disrupted family of orgin' and 'care away from home'—definitions

As in Frommer and O'Shea's studies, at the screening interview in the antenatal clinic, the women were asked the following question: 'When you were a child, were you ever brought up away from your own home for any length of time?' When the answer was positive, the women were asked to provide details of the reasons and duration of the care away from home.

For the purposes of the analysis in this paper, two aspects of the women's early experience were considered. The first of these was 'disrupted family of origin'. A woman was defined as having come from a disrupted family of origin if, before the age of 16, her parents had divorced or separated, or one or both of her parents had died. (Death of a parent was added to the definition after examination of the screening data which indicated that, in our sample, parental death had been associated with considerable social difficulties.) Three women who had experienced total family break-up at an early age and spent most of their childhood in residential care were also included in the disrupted group. The second was 'care away from home'. A woman was defined as having received care away from home, if before the age of 16, she had been cared for away from *both* her parents for a period of one month or more. This included care by relatives, by foster parents, in local authority children's homes, in hospital or at boarding school, and one case where the woman had run away from home at age 15.

Table 9.1 gives a summary of the histories of the women in the observational group who, according to these definitions, had experienced either family disruption or care away from home, or both.

The observations

Two observers, working separately, made observations in the home when the baby reached the age of 20 weeks. The main focus of interest in these observations was the general behaviour of the baby and the mother–infant interaction. The observers had no knowledge of the women's histories when they made their observations.

Our method of observing and recording was one shared with other ethologists such as Leach (1972) and Blurton Jones and Leach (1972), namely that of continuous event-recording. Using a 15-second time interval, behaviour was recorded directly, as it occurred, in an unbroken stream, until a certain time period had elapsed. To facilitate the very rapid recording that this technique requires, we used a shorthand code. We have preferred continuous recording to time-sampling as our main method of data-collection because with continuous recording it is possible to achieve at least some impression of the sequencing of events in time. Continuous recording also allows one to record the total number of occurrences of any behaviour item within one 15-second time interval, rather than just its occurrence or non-occurrence. Thus, a decoded record of events during one 15-second interval might read as follows:

'Baby lying on back, facing mother and within touching distance. Baby vocalizes. Mother looks at baby's face and speaks to it, picks it up, holds it on her lap facing towards her but with no trunk contact, smiles and speaks to it and kisses it.'

Interobserver agreement was calculated as the overall level of concordance between the two observers, using the formula:

$$\frac{\text{Total number agreements between observers in each 15-second time interval}}{\text{Mean number events recorded by the two observers in the same time interval}}$$

Table 9.1 A summary of the histories of those women who had experienced either family disruption or care away from home or both

		Reason for family breakup				Care away from home				
		Parents divorced/separated	Father died	Mother died	Other	Relatives	Foster parents	Local authority care or childrens home	Hospital (1 + month)	Other
Care away from home within context of stable family background	9210								+	
	5010								+	
	1210								+	
	4110								+	+
	2620								+	
	2500								+	
	9700					+				
	4701								+	+
	8030					+				
	9630						+			
	4210								+	
	2030								+	
	5030					+				
	4011								+	
	3701								+	
	(N = 15)									
Disrupted family of origin without care away from home	5220	+								
	6430	+								
	0230	+								
	7130				+					
	3210		+							
	1910		+							
	6810		+							
	(N = 7)									

Table 9.1 contd.

Disrupted family of origin and care away from home	Reason for family breakup				Care away from home				
	Parents divorced/separated	Father died	Mother died	Other	Relatives	Foster parents	Local authority care or childrens home	Hospital (1 + month)	Other
8020	+						+		
6520	+						+		
4901	+						+		
1130	+					+			
4801	+							+	
2020		+			+				
5310		+					+		
3510			+				+		
7320			+		+			+	
0430			+					+	
1020				+			+		
2920				+			+		
9901				+					+
(N = 13)									

According to this rather stringent test, our overall level of interobserver agreement was 0.77.

After a few pilot observations, it became clear that to avoid unconscious selection by the observer about when to observe, it was necessary to work to a predetermined schedule. Our object was to obtain continuous observations covering 100 15-second intervals (25 minutes) of the time when the baby was: (a) awake; and (b) not feeding (feeds were recorded separately.) However, in order to spread the observation time over a longer period of the baby's day than just the 25 minutes required to obtain the continuous observation, we alternated twenty 15-second intervals of continuous observation with 20 intervals in which we merely recorded the distance of the mother from the baby and whether or not the baby was fretting or crying. This was followed by a further 20 intervals of detailed continuous recording and so on until we had completed 25 minutes of each type of observation. If, during the course of the observations, the baby went to sleep, the recording schedule was suspended and then resumed as soon as he woke up. Similarly, the normal schedule of observations was halted as soon as the baby began to take in food, and re-started the moment the feed came to an end. The only allowable adjustments to this basic observation procedure were very minor ones enabling us to ensure that each set of continuous observations included at least one caretaking activity by the mother (usually a nappy change or a bath). Because most of the babies went to sleep while we were in the home and all were fed at least once, the amount of the baby's day spanned by our 25 minutes of continuous observation normally ranged from two to four hours.

The catalogue of behaviour items recorded during the periods of continuous observation was an expanded version of lists included in various papers in Blurton Jones (1972). Our catalogue included over 100 items of mother and baby behaviour and each item was rigorously defined. In this paper, we are concerned only with the behaviour of the mother and Table 9.2 lists, on the right, the most frequency of the mother items, and, on the left, our grouping of them for our purpose in this paper. At this age, we have included as maternal measures the distance between the mother and her baby and also whether or not there was trunk contact when the baby was on the mother's lap. This is because, at 20 weeks of age, the infants were still immobile and any distance change was taken to be determined by the mother. In what follows, the figures given for the mothers' vocal behaviour, touching, looking, smiling or laughing and interaction involving objects represent the total frequency of occurrence in 100 15-second intervals of continuous recording, bearing in mind that in this type of observation, each behaviour item may occur more than once in each time interval. Distance and trunk contact are measured according to the number of 15-second intervals of continuous recording at each distance.

RESULTS

Initial analysis of the observational data revealed striking individual differences in the frequency, during 25 minutes continuous observation, with which each of the mothers engaged in the behaviour items listed in Table 9.2. For example, mothers ranged in the frequency with which they spoke to their 20-week old babies from 6 times to 167 times. Similarly, the frequency with which mothers touched their babies during the 25 minutes of observation ranged from not at all to 76 times. Similar differences were found in the frequency with which individual mothers looked at, smiled at, or presented

Table 9.2 Key to categories of behaviour used in comparing the behaviour of mothers from disrupted and non-disrupted family backgrounds towards their 20 week-old infants

I BEHAVIOUR	
Vocal behaviour	All verbalization directed towards the baby.
	All non-verbal utterances (exclamations, singing, humming and imitations of the baby's noises) directed towards the baby.
Non-caretaking touching	Caressing with a gentle rubbing or patting motion.
	Kissing or nuzzling with the face or chin.
	Manipulating the baby's limbs in bicycling movements.
Look	Mother direct her gaze towards the infant's face.
Interaction involving objects	Offering or giving objects to the baby.
	Showing objects to the baby by holding or placing them in such a way as to catch his attention.
Smiling or laughing	Smiling or laughing performed while gazing at the baby.
II DISTANCE	
Either	Baby on mother's lap or being carried by her
or	Baby not on mother's lap but within reach
or	Baby not on mother's lap or within reach, but within sight.
or	Baby out of sight (in another room).
III TRUNK CONTACT	
Either	Baby's trunk in contact with mother's trunk while on lap or being carried
or	Baby's trunk not in contact with mother's trunk while on lap or being carried.
IV ORIENTATION	
Either	Mother and baby's whole bodies parallel and facing, regardless of direction of gaze
or	One partner's whole body oriented laterally to the other, regardless of direction of gaze
or	One or both partners' whole bodies facing away from one another regardless of direction of gaze.

Table 9.3   The number of intervals or number of occurrences, showing range and median, with which mothers engaged in each of the behaviour items during 25 minutes of continuous observation

Behaviour category	No. of intervals or occurrences	
	Range	Median
Out of sight	0 to 70	13
Baby held	0 to 74	28
Vocal acts	6 to 167	66
Touch	0 to 76	23
Look	10 to 180	67
Smile	0 to 61	18
Presentation of objects	0 to 42	7

objects to their babies, held them or were within sight or out of sight of them. Table 9.3 shows the range in the frequency with which the mothers were observed to engage in each behaviour item with their 20-week old babies.

In an attempt to account for this wide variation in the behaviour of the mothers, we examined the frequency with which each mother engaged in each of the behaviour items in relation to her own early childhood experience. In particular we examined the effects of having come from a disrupted family of origin and the effects of having experienced care away from home upon the woman's later mothering behaviour.

Disrupted family of origin

For each of the items, mothers who came from a disrupted family of origin were compared with those who did not (see also Wolkind, Hall and Pawlby, 1977). On the basis of the findings of Frommer and O'Shea, we predicted that the 'disrupted' mothers would engage in less interactive behaviour with their babies than the non-disrupted mothers and, as Table 9.4 shows, this proved to be the case. Using the Mann–Whitney U test, highly significant differences were found between the disrupted and the non-disrupted groups in the frequency with which they talked to their babies ($p > 0.01$, one-tailed test), in how often they engaged in non-caretaking touching acts ($p > 0.001$), and in the frequency with which they looked at their babies ($p > 0.001$). A trend in the same direction was found for the amount the mothers presented objects to their babies and the frequency with which they smiled at them (in both cases, $p = 0.06$, one-tailed test). In each case the disrupted mothers engaged less frequently in the behaviour. In summary, it appears from these findings that mothers from a disrupted family of origin provide their babies with significantly less interactive and stimulating activity than mothers from a non-disrupted family background.

Differences were also found in the amount of time the disrupted mothers

Table 9.4   Mean frequencies and standard deviations with which each behaviour category was observed to occur during the observation period

Behaviour category	Non-disrupted group($N = 48$)		Disrupted group($N = 20$)		Mann-Whitney U Test (one-tailed)
	Mean	S.D.	Mean	S.D.	
Mothers vocal acts	75.3	$\pm$ 31.3	49.1	$\pm$ 29.6	$z = 2.88$ $p = 0.002$
Mothers non-caretaking touching acts	30.6	$\pm$ 15.9	14.4	$\pm$ 12.9	$z = 4.55$ $p < 0.001$
Mothers looking	77.3	$\pm$ 27.9	50.7	$\pm$ 25.5	$z = 3.49$ $p < 0.001$
Mothers presentation of objects	9.7	$\pm$ 9.0	6.5	$\pm$ 7.3	$z = 1.52$ $p = 0.06$
Mothers smiling	19.7	$\pm$ 11.5	16.5	$\pm$ 13.1	$z = 1.52$ $p = 0.06$

spent in a position which enable them to interact with their babies. Mothers from a disrupted family of origin spent a significantly greater amount of time in a different room from the baby, out of sight of him and also sometimes out of hearing ($p>0.001$, one-tailed test). They also spent significantly less time holding the baby ($p = 0.03$, one-tailed test) and less time at distances where they were either holding the baby or within reach of him ($p > 0.001$, one-tailed test). These findings suggested that while we had already shown that from the baby's point of view, babies of mothers from a disrupted family background received significantly less social stimulation from their mothers than other babies, we should also examine the mother's rate of interaction during the periods when she was sufficiently close to the baby for interaction to be possible. We predicted that even when close to the baby, the disrupted mothers would show a lower level of interaction, and this was found to be the case for vocalizing to the baby ($p = 0.03$, one-tailed test), non-caretaking touch ($p = 0.001$, one-tailed test) and looking at the baby ($p > 0.01$, one-tailed test). Further details of these analyses are given in Wolkind, Hall and Pawlby (1977).

Care away from home

We now turn to a consideration of the possible effects on mothering of early care away from home. Although in principle, coming from a disrupted family of origin and a history of care away from home need not be associated, in practice, family break-up through the death, divorce or separation of parents often results in the child going into the care of persons other than the parents, and statistically, the two types of experience are closely associated ($\chi^2 = 6.64$, $p = 0.01$). Thus, to assess independently the possible effects on later mothering behaviour of care away from home and family disruption, we needed to use a statistical test which would allow for the possibility that the two factors might have independent effects and might also interact. A preliminary test for homogeneity of variance showed that our data were not suited to analysis by parametric means and a standard two-way analysis of variance was thus excluded. Instead, a non-parametric form of analysis was used.

According to their early experience, the women were classed into four groups, and these groups were then arranged according to a model of possible severity of effects based on our knowledge of the literature. In order of presumed severity, the composition of the four groups was as follows:

I. No family disruption and no care away from home ($N = 33$);
II. Experience of care away from home only ($N = 15$);
III. Experience of family disruption only ($N = 7$);
IV. Experience of both family disruption and care away from home ($N = 13$).

The scores of the four groups on two of the behaviour measures used are shown in Figure 9.1.

Using Kendall's rank correlation coefficient (tau), highly significant correlations were found (see Table 9.5) between a woman's rank on the severity

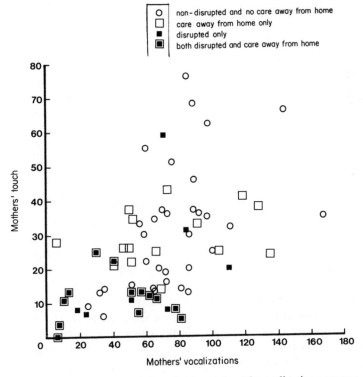

Figure 9.1 The frequency of mother's touch and vocalizations among women with varying childhood experience

Table 9.5   Kendall's rank correlations of severity
of early experience with mothering behaviour at
4 months ($N = 68$)

Mother's behaviour at 4 months	Kendall's tau
Baby on lap	0.13[a]
Baby within reach	0.18*
Baby out of sight	− 0.31***
Mother facing baby	0.26***
In trunk contact	0.26***
Vocal acts	0.28***
Non-caretaking touch	0.36***
Look	0.31***
Smile	0.14*
Presentation of objects	0.17*

[a]$p < 0.10$ *$p < 0.05$ **$p < 0.01$ ***$p < 0.001$
(one-tailed tests)

scale and the frequency with which she engaged in each of the behaviour items listed in Table 9.2.

The results are consistent with the model we adopted, namely that those women who had experienced care away from home in the context of a disrupted family life are the group who interact least with their four-month-old babies; the group who come from a disrupted family of origin but have never experienced care away from both parents show a somewhat higher level of interaction, but do not interact as much as the group who have experienced care away from home within the context of a stable family background; and the highest level of interaction is among women who have suffered neither care away from home nor family disruption.

Further analysis of the data, however, reveals that the effect of early care away from home is very small. Using the Mann-Whitney U test to compare the frequency with which the mothers engaged in each of the interactive behaviours listed in Table 9.2, no significant difference was found between the group of women who had experienced neither care away from home nor a disrupted family background, and those who had experienced care away from home only. Similarly, there was no significant difference between the group who had experienced a disrupted family background only and those who had experienced both family disruption and care away from home.

From these results we conclude that the effect on our mothering measures of early care away from home is negligible, compared with the effect of coming from a disrupted family of origin, and our initial finding stands, namely that women who come from a disrupted family of origin, irrespective of whether they have also experienced early care away from home, interact significantly less with their 20-week-old babies than women who have not experienced such disruption, even though they may have had care away from home.

Analysis of the interview data enabled us to determine whether there are any other factors distinguishing the disrupted from the non-disrupted mothers which could have accounted for the differences in their behaviour. The factors examined included the mother's age, marital status, social class, malaise score, whether or not she was depressed either prenatally or at four months, whether or not she had wanted the baby, the state of her marriage and whether or not she felt she had the support of her husband, whether or not she had frequent social contacts during the week, and whether or not she had any previous experience with children. No significant difference was found in the observational sample between the disrupted and the non-disrupted group on any of these measures; nor did the babies' behaviour as assessed at six days and at four months distinguish the two groups.

One factor, however, on which the mothers from a disrupted family of origin did differ significantly from the group who did not come from such a background was whether or not at 20 weeks the mothers saw their baby as a person. In answer to the question 'It takes a bit of time to begin to see a baby as a person—do you feel this yet?', only 35% of the disrupted group replied that they did positively see their baby as a person compared with 75% of the non-disrupted group ($\chi^2 = 8.07$, $p > 0.01$). This finding suggests that women who have come from a disrupted family of origin perceive their babies in a rather different way from women who have experienced a stable family background.

In summary, our results indicate that certain of a woman's early experiences are related to her own mothering behaviour, one of the most important factors being whether or not she had come from a disrupted family of origin. The effect on a woman's mothering behaviour of having experienced care away from both parents as a child for a period of one month or more appears to be minimal.

DISCUSSION

One of the most striking findings which has resulted from our observations of mothers and their 20-week-old infants is the extent of the variation within a group of mothers in the amount of physical contact they have with their babies and in the amount of social stimulation they direct towards them.

Just as Frommer and O'Shea (1973a) found that simple questions put to a woman at the antenatal clinic about her own early life experiences were effective clinically in picking out a group of women likely to experience difficulties with their baby during the first year of life, so we have found that the same questions will pick out antenatally a group of women who, when their baby is 20 weeks old, interact very little with him.

The questions we asked in the antenatal clinic about the woman's background related to two aspects of her early experience, namely care away from both parents for a period of one month or more, and a history of family disruption resulting from parental divorce, separation or death. Our findings is that of these two types of early experience, each potentially adverse according to the literature, it is an experience of parental death or parental disharmony resulting in divorce or separation which in adult life is most significantly associated with a reduction in the amount of interaction the mother directs towards her first-born baby.

A somewhat similar conclusion was reached by Frommer and O'Shea (1973b) in their study of women who experienced difficulties in the first year of the baby's life, either with the baby himself or in their marriage, and in their study of problem behaviour among 10-year-old children, Quinton and Rutter also found a significant effect of 'psychosocial disadvantage' in which parental death, divorce or separation were inluded.

In Quinton and Rutter's study, however, care away from home in the form of early multiple admissions to hospital had a significant adverse effect even after psychosocial disadvantage had been allowed for, and Douglas also found adverse effects of multiple hospital admissions among children in their teens. Although in our analysis the data will support a hypothesis that care away from home for one month or more in childhood can be ranked with family disruption on a severity scale with respect to their effect on our mothering measures, with care away from home having a less severe effect than family disruption, the actual effect of care away from home seems to be very small. We must, however, qualify this finding in at least two ways. Firstly, our data are not strictly comparable with those of either Douglas or Quinton and Rutter because our category of care away from home includes not only children who have been in hospital, but also girls who have been taken into the care of a children's home. Secondly, in our relatively small observational subsample, we have not been able to make a separation between periods of care away from home before and after the age of 5 years, or between single and multiple periods of care away from home. Since Douglas' and Quinton and Rutter's findings relate specifically to multiple admissions starting under the age of five, this may account for the difference in our findings. It must also be borne in mind that so far in the analysis of our data we have looked only at the total frequencies of the behaviour a mother directs towards her 20-week-old child, and it may well be that we will obtain other results from a different type of analysis of the data or from an analysis of data obtained at later ages of the child.

On our present findings, however, we must conclude that it is an early history of parental death, divorce or separation rather than early care away from home which shows a significant relationship with the amount of interaction a woman directs towards her first-born baby at 20 weeks of age. Although it might be argued that it is not early experience of a disrupted family life *per se* which is responsible for the reduced level of interaction with the baby but rather other associated problems in the present, we have not been able to find any factor in the mother's current life which could in principle affect her behaviour to her baby and which at the same time significantly distinguishes the disrupted and the non-disrupted groups.

The single exception to this statement concerns the apparent failure of the disrupted mothers to perceive their 20-week-old baby as a person. The most obvious possible explanation of this finding would be that the babies of the disrupted mothers were actually different in some way from the babies of the non-disrupted mothers, but on the behaviour measures we used, we could find no difference between the two groups of babies either at 6 days, or at 20 weeks. It does seem very possible, therefore, that the difference between the two groups is in the mother's perception of the baby rather than in any difference in the behaviour of the babies themselves. We do not know, of course, to what extent the disrupted mothers' low level of interaction with their infants is directly attributable to their failure to perceive the baby as a person, but Newson (1974) has already suggested that failure of the mother to see the baby as a person could have important consequences for the development of the child.

In our own study, there are already indications that this may indeed be the case, for in follow-up observations made when the children reached 27 months of age, the children of mothers from a disrupted family of origin showed significantly poorer language development than other children, both as regards expressive language and comprehension (Pawlby and Hall, in press). However, while it is tempting to interpret this 27-month finding as a direct consequence of the disrupted mothers' earlier low level of interaction with their 20-week-old babies, the frequency of mothers' interaction measures and the child's language development at 27 months are significantly related only in girls. Both in principle and in practice, therefore, it is unlikely that the simple *frequency* with which a mother interacts with her 20-week-old baby is the sole determinant of language development at age 27 months.

Nevertheless, our present findings stand. Within a single socioeconomic group, our observations reveal striking variation among 20-week-old babies in the amount of social and physical contact and stimulation they receive at the hands of the principle caregiver, the mother, with evidence in addition of some link between experience provided by the mother at 20 weeks and language development at 27 months. As a group, children of women who as children themselves experienced parental death, divorce or separation are very significantly more likely than their peers to experience very low levels of social and physical contact with the mother, and at 27 months, children of these same mothers are in general less advanced than other children in their language development. These findings rather strongly suggest not only that a woman's experience before the age of 16 may affect her mothering behaviour, but that indirectly *via* the experience she provides for her own child, her early experience may also affect him. Ours is not the type of study which would allow us to explore the subjective feelings which might perhaps provide the link between the woman's childhood experience and her feelings and behaviour towards her child when she herself becomes a mother, but the fact that women from a disrupted family of origin often do not positively perceive their baby as a person perhaps provides one clue to the underlying dynamics of the experience she provides for her child.

ACKNOWLEDGEMENTS

We would like to thank Professor D. A. Pond for his continued interest and encouragement throughout our study. We are also grateful to Liana Reichstul, who carried out some of the observations during this stage of the study, and to Dr. N. Blurton Jones and his associates, with whom we collaborated while compiling our catalogue of behaviour items. Special thanks must also go to the mothers and babies in the study for allowing us to go and watch them. The research was generously supported by a grant from the Medical Research Council and a contract from the DHSS/SSRC project on transmitted deprivation.

REFERENCES

Ainsworth, M. D. (1962). 'The effects of maternal deprivation: a review of findings and controversy in the context of research strategy', in *Deprivation of maternal care: a reassessment of its effects*, World Health Organization, Geneva.

Als, H., Tronick, E., Lester, B. M., and Brazelton, T. B. (1977). 'The Brazelton Neonatal Behavioral Assessment Scale (BNBAS)', *Journal of Abnormal Child Psychology*, **5**, No. 3, 215–231.

Blake Cohen, M. (1966). 'Personal identity and sexual identity', *Psychiatry*, **29**, 1–14.

Blurton Jones, N. (1972). *Ethological Studies in Child Behaviour*, Cambridge University Press, Cambridge.

Blurton Jones, N. and Leach, G. M. (1972). 'Behaviour of children and their mothers at separation and greeting', in Blurton Jones, N. (ed.), *Ethological Studies in Child Behaviour*, Cambridge University Press.

Bowlby, J. (1951). *Maternal care and mental health*, World Health Organisation, Geneva.

Bowlby, J. (1975). *Attachment and Loss, Volume II. Separation: anxiety and anger*, Penguin Books.

Brown, G. W., Harris, T., and Copeland, J. R. (1977). 'Depression and Loss', *British Journal of Psychiatry*, **130**, 1–18.

Caldwell, B. M. (1964). 'The effects of infant care', in Hoffman, M. and Hoffman, L. (eds.), *Review of Child Development Research, Vol. I.*, Russell Sage Foundation, N. Y.

Crandall, V. C. (1972). 'The Fels Study: some contributions to personality development and achievement in childhood and adulthood', *Seminars in Psychiatry*, **4**, 383–397.

Caudill, W. and Weinstein, H. (1969). 'Maternal care and infant behaviour in Japan and America', *Psychiatry*, **32**, (1), 12–43.

Douglas, J. W. B. (1975). 'Early hospital admissions and later disturbances of behaviour and learning', *Developmental Medicine and Child Neurology*, **17**, 456–480.

Dunn, J. B. and Richards, M. P. M. (1977). 'Observations on the developing relationship between mother and baby in the neonatal period', In Schaffer, H. R. (ed.), *Studies in Mother–Infant Interaction*, Academic Press, London.

Frommer, E. and O'Shea, G. (1973a). 'Antenatal identification of women liable to have problems managing their children', *British Journal of Psychiatry*, **123**, 149–156.

Frommer, E. and O'Shea, G. (1973b). 'The importance of childhood experience in relation to problems of marriage and family building', *British Journal of Psychiatry*, **123**, 157–160.

Helfer, R. E., and Kempe, C. H. (1976). *Child abuse and neglect: the family and the community*, Ballinger.

Hinde, R. A. and Spencer-booth, Y. (1970). 'Individual differences in the responses of Rhesus monkeys to a period of separation from their mothers', *J. Child Psychol. Psychiat.*, **11**, 159–176.

Hunt, J. V. and Eichorn, D. H. (1972). 'Maternal and child behaviours: a review of data from the Berkeley Growth Study', *Seminars in Psychiatry*, **4**, 367–381.

Illsley, R. and Thompson, B. (1961). 'Women from broken homes', *The Sociological Review*, **9**, 27–54.

Kagan, J. and Moss, H. A. (1962). *From birth to maturity*, John Wiley and Sons Inc.

Leach, G. M. (1972). 'A comparison of the social behaviour of some normal and problem children', in Blurton Jones, N. (ed.), *Ethological Studies in Child Behaviour*, Cambridge University Press.

LeVine, R. A. (1970). 'Cross-cultural study in child psychology', in Mussen, P. H. (ed.), *Carmichael's Manual of Child Psychology, Vol. 2*, (3rd edition) Wiley, New York.

Lewis, M. and Lee-Painter, S. (1974). 'An interactional approach to the mother–infant dyad', in Lewis M. and Rosenblum, L. A. (ed.) *The Effect of the Infant on its Caregiver*, J. Wiley, U.S.A.

Newson, J. and Newson, E. (1963) *Patterns of infant care in an urban community*, Pelican Books.

Newson, J. (1974). 'Towards a theory of infant understanding', *Bulletin of the British Psychological Society*, **27**, 251–257.

Pawlby, S. J. (1977). 'Imitative interaction', in Schaffer, H. R. (ed.), *Studies in Mother–Infant Interaction*, Academic Press.

Pawlby, S. J. and Hall, F. (in press). 'Evidence from an observational study of transmitted deprivation among the children of women from broken homes', to appear in *Journal of Child Abuse and Neglect*, 1978.

Quinton, D. and Rutter, M. (1976). 'Early hospital admissions and later disturbances of behaviour: an attempted replication of Douglas's findings', *Developmental Medicine and Child Neurology*, **18**, 447–459.

Richards, M. P. M. (1971). 'Social interaction in the first weeks of human life, *Psychiat. Neurol. Neurochir.*, **74**, 35–42.

Robins, L. N. (1966). *Deviant children grown up*, Williams and Wilkins, Baltimore.

Robins, L. N. (1970). 'The adult development of the antisocial child', *Seminars in Psychiatry*, **2**, 420–434.

Rutter, M. (1972). *Maternal deprivation reassessed*, Penguin Books.

Sameroff, A. J. and Chandler, M. J. (1975). 'Reproductive risk and the continuum of caretaking casualty', in Horowitz, F. D. Hetherington, M. Scarr-Salapatek, S. and Siegel G. (eds.), *Review of Child Development Research, Vol. 4*, University of Chicago Press, Chicago.

Schaffer, H. R. (1971), *The Growth of Sociability*, Penguin, Science of Behaviour.

Stern, D. N. (1974). 'Mother and infant at play: the dyadic interaction involving facial, vocal and gaze behaviours', in Lewis M. and Rosenblum L. A. (ed.), *The Effect of the Infant on its caregiver*, J. Wiley, U.S.A.

Trevarthen, C. (1977). 'Descriptive analyses', in Schaffer, H. R. (ed.), *Studies in Mother–Infant Interaction*, Academic Press.

Whiten, A. (1977). 'Assessing the effects of perinatal events on the success of the mother–infant relationship', in Schaffer, H.R. (ed.), *Studies in Mother–Infant Interaction*, Academic Press.

Wolkind, S. N. (1977). 'Women who have been "in care"–psychological and social status during pregnancy', *Journal of Child Psychology and Psychiatry*, **18**, 179–182.

Wolkind, S. N., Kruk, S. and Chaves, L. P. (1976) 'Childhood separation experiences and psycho-social status in primiparious women: preliminary findings', *British Journal of Psychiatry*, **128**, 391–396.

Wolkind, S. N., Hall, F., and Pawlby, S. J. (1977). 'Individual differences in mothering behaviour: a combined epidemiological and observational approach', in Graham P. (ed.), *Epidemiological Approaches in Child Psychiatry*, Academic Press.

Yarrow, L. J. (1961). 'Maternal deprivation: toward an empirical and conceptual re-evaluation', *Psychol. Bull.*, **58**, 459–490.

Chapter 10

A Comparative Study of Mother–Child Communication with Down's Syndrome and Normal Infants

Olwen H. M. Jones

INTRODUCTION

Over the past decade we have been made increasingly aware of the sophisticated communication network that develops between a mother and her baby. In the field of mother–infant interaction research, Bower, Bruner, Newson, Schaffer, Trevarthen and their colleagues have, among many others, provided us with an enormous amount of information on how the normal infant develops the means of social interaction within the intensely supportive and encouraging atmosphere provided by his mother or other regular caregiver. (For some recent reviews of this literature see Jones, 1978; Pawlby, 1977a; Schaffer, Collis and Parsons, 1977; Shotter, 1975.) Between mother and child we witness the development of social dialogue long before the first 'word' as such is recognizable. The infant's activities are assigned meanings by the mother. The child comes to recognize the interpretation and begins to demonstrate degrees of intention in his signals (Newson and Shotter, 1974). Through their specialist and intimate knowledge of each other a pre-linguistic form of communication evolves. Dialogue-type patterns of interaction can be recognized as mother and infant take 'turns' in their play. Such turn-taking activities have been described in patterns of imitation between mothers and their 4-month-old infants (Pawlby, 1977b), and in feeding and looking activities in even younger babies (Kaye, 1977; Jaffe, Stern and Peery, 1973).

What might be the relevance of this preverbal communication between mother and child for the process of language aquisition? Could the findings have implications for children who have difficulties acquiring language? Bruner (1977) stated that he has no doubt that language skills as we know them have their roots firmly fixed in early pre-linguistic interactive events. The 'shared understandings' (Newson, 1974) that the mother and child develop at this stage seem to provide a basis for interpersonal communication of which language is an all important branch.

It was within this research framework that the present study was designed; we set out to examine the pre-linguistic development of communication skills in children who might predictably have language acquisition difficulties. The clinical group of children chosen was a small number of Down's syndrome ('mongol') children. The enormous advantages of selecting such a group is that Down's syndrome, as a chromosomal disorder, is identifiable at birth. The syndrome is associated with mental handicap, and language remediation is usually a recognized necessity by the time the children go to school. Whereas language problems are not often recognized in children until their language is failing to develop (around 3 years of age), with Down's syndrome children language difficulties of some sort are essentially predictable in infancy. Whether Down's syndrome children have more problems with *language* than in other areas of their development is still a moot point. Ryan (1977) presented a critical review of the relevant literature. She concluded that there was insufficient evidence of a specific language difficulty in children with Down's syndrome, but in general they did show problems with language acquisition. The essential aim of our study therefore was to compare these children's pre-linguistic communication skills with those seen in normal children, and thus to determine whether Down's children demonstrate any difficulties at this particular stage of their communication development.

A comparative technique was employed since at the time we began the research little was known about pre-linguistic communication in normal children. A matched pair design was used, comparing individual Down's children and their mothers with normal children and their mothers. The children were matched for sex, social class and family position (1st born, 2nd born). They were also carefully matched for developmental age. There have been many problems in past research with the interpretations made from studies matching normal and Down's children chronologically. If the children are not at the same stage in their general development then any differences in mother–child communication could easily be attributable to this factor alone.

The experimental details of this study were first described in an earlier publication (Jones, 1977). However, at that time the work was ongoing and only initial trends in the results were available. In the following presentation, the major findings of the completed research will be discussed and their implications considered in the light of current research and clinical practice.

METHODOLOGY

Subjects

The Down's syndrome children were selected from the local branch of the Down's Babies Association and Nottingham University Toy Library for handicapped children. Six pre-linguistic Down's children and their mothers participated in the study. The children were in the age range 13 months to 24 months. Six normal children were carefully selected from local health clinics. Each Down's child was matched with a normal child of the same sex, social class, family position and developmental age (Cattell Infant Intelligence Scale). The developmental age range of the six pairs of children was 8 months to 19 months. The chronological ages of the normal children ranged between 8 months and 18 months.

Procedure

All the children were video-taped whilst playing with their mothers at home with a supplied set of toys. The recordings were made every three weeks for a period of fifteen weeks (six recordings). After this time, the children were no longer evenly matched because of the faster developmental rate of the normal children. The video recordings provided us with a source of 'naturalistic' data. As far as possible, the intrusive effect of the observer was reduced to a minimum. A small, portable, battery operated video equipment was used (Sony 'Video Corder'). No extraneous wires or light were necessary. By not responding to any of the child's initial approaches the observer was soon ignored and it was possible to sit quietly in the corner of the living room and film a playing session between mother and child. Each session lasted approximately 15 minutes, the precise time depending on when the child lost interest in the toys. The mother was instructed to start playing with one of the child's own toys then turn to the provided toys (book, box of cotton reels, drum) as she might normally reach to the toybox for 'something else to play with'. The mothers understood that the purpose was to look at the way mothers and children play and talk with each other. 'Showing off' to the camera was markedly reduced by making the film only one part of a full half-day session during which time the child's developmental progress was monitored and the mother had an opportunity to demonstrate her child's latest achievements.

Methods of analysis

These will be described briefly. For further details, see Jones, 1977 and Jones, 1978.

The methods of analysis employed in this study developed from a basis of observation. We did not restrict ourselves to preselected coding categories at the beginning of the project. As hypotheses developed, appropriately sensitive analysis techniques were employed. The open-endedness of the analysis allowed us to concentrate on areas of special interest as they became apparent.

Initial observation necessarily needed to be very detailed. For this purpose video-tape was used for recording observations so that a record of mother—

child activity was available for examination and re-examination. Transcription of the video-tape was completed under the three headings of direction of looking, non-vocal activity and vocal activity for both mother and child simultaneously. Simultaneous transcription of both the mother's and the child's continuous activity was made possible by repeated viewing of the video-tape recording. Such simultaneous information was considered of vital importance to our understanding of the communication sequences. Too often observation is only made of the action going between the communicating dyad, as one might follow the ball in a tennis match. Such records, however, are an artifact of the nature of observation. In a tennis match or in a communication dialogue, the cues influencing each 'player's' behaviour are to be seen in the recipient's activity. However 'passive' this may appear, such activity must be examined if one is to even attempt to understand something about the context of and processes involved in the communication.

Once a written record was available, general categories of communication could be designated and the transcriptions broken down into patterns of communicative activity. The major importance of using such a method of delaying even the crudest categorisation is that the full context of every identified interchange is preserved for reference.

The main features of the interactive model used in this study were based on the communication exchange. This was defined as an event involving both members of a dyad which invites a response or is itself a response. This operational definition enabled us to identify not only obviously intentional interactive invitations and responses but also those exchanges where either the 'invitation' or the 'response' could only be recognized in retrospect by virtue of the fact that the partner responded. For example, as well as the classic type of 'intentional' interchange:

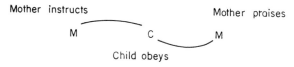

we also have more subtle exchanges:

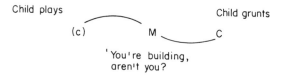

Here the child initiated the interaction but apparently unintentionally.

Another interesting aspect of this particular example is that, in order to 'respond' to the mothers question, the child could have produced almost any type of vocalization for it to be accepted as a response. We will come back to this type of supportive technique used by the mother later. The tremendous importance of such an exchange is that, although it might seem fashioned by the mother, the child *experienced* communication. The experience of such interpretation of his own actions seems to be very important; through such interpretation the child learns to recognize what his own actions mean to others.

Using this classification based on interactions, communication exchanges between the mothers and children were identified and their frequencies, lengths, types, contexts and other qualities compared for each mother–Down's child and mother–normal child pair.

DISCUSSION OF RESULTS

From the initial examination of the video-tapes and subsequent trans- criptions it became evident that the data on communication could be examined in various ways. In order to answer our general query about quantity and quality of mother–child communication, gross data concerning mother– child interaction was needed. However, to understand quality of communica- tion in some depth a more specific study of one aspect of communication might well provide additional information at a more sensitive level. For these purposes vocal interaction was specifically selected for further detailed analysis. The relevance of vocalization to speech and language development made this an appropriate area for special study. Analysis records were therefore made of the vocalizations the children made and the vocally interactive context in which they made them.

Our early observations of the video-tapes had made us particularly aware of something 'unusual' about the form of eye contact used by the Down's children. The precise nature of this observation could not be pin-pointed, though it was repeatedly confirmed by observer colleagues. For these reasons eye contact and its role in communication were also selected for special in- vestigation.

Mother–child interaction

A major question raised in this study concerned the possibility that Down's syndrome children might not be able to participate to the same extent as normal children in communication with their mothers. In view of the micro detail required for this examination, a sample of the taped material was used. The data was based on a total of 1580 interactions in 5760 individually analysed seconds of video-tape. This was taken from eight minutes of play for each mother and child for two seperate play sessions. Figure 10.1 presents a summary of the frequency and length of mother–child communication exchange se- quences. Length is represented in terms of the number of participations in- volved in an interchange. For example, if the mother initiates the sequence

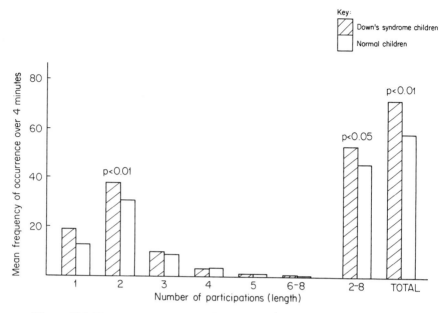

Figure 10.1 Frequency and length of mother–child communication sequences

then the child responds, then the mother responds, the 'exchange' is three participations in length. Length '1' refers to those instances where the mother (or child) invites a response, by for example offering something or asking a question, but the child (or mother) fails to take up this opportunity for response. Our operational definition of an interactional, or communication exchange includes this length 1, since an exchange was defined as any event involving both members of a dyad which invites a response or is itself a response. A diagramatic representation of a length 1 exchange would be:

The mean length of exchange sequences was 2.1. The Down's children produced many more length 2 exchanges than the normal children, and the normal children tended to produce slightly more longer exchanges. From these results it was clearly evident that the Down's children were involved in more interactional exchanges with their mothers than the normal children. The Down's children were by no means inactive and unresponsive in their play activities with their mothers.

Given this initial information about quantity of communicative interaction, we went on to examine the nature of these exchanges. Who for example was usually responsible for initiating and terminating exchanges? What conditions defined the length of an exchange?

Initiation and termination presented a very complex question. They are not easily assigned. Since although we may know who began an interaction sequence, this same participant may not have been responsible for bringing about the exchange. For example, the mother may decide to 'take up' something the child is doing:

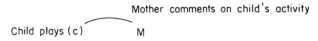

Similarly the one to be last in an interactional exchange may not be responsible for terminating it. For example:

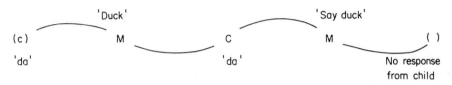

In this example the mother eventually made a specific invitation and appropriately provided the 'space' for her child to respond (indicated by the brackets). In this situation although the last person to speak was the mother, it was the child's lack of response that effectively terminated the sequence.

In recognizing these difficulties of classification we became aware of a feature of the communicative exchange that depended on the mother's skill in providing appropriate *support techniques* which enable the child to participate more easily in communicative dialogue. We have seen above examples where the mother has created a communicative exchange around the child, and provided a 'space', or opportunity pause for him to respond. We then identified further techniques of such supportive interaction. For example, it was possible for the mother to take up something the child was already doing and not only comment on it, but comment in such a way that the child need only continue his play activity in order to respond appropriately, and in so doing complete an exchange of three participations in length:

The mother in this example provided the child with an 'open' opportunity for response, in that whatever the child's next activity, he could be seen to 'participate' in the exchange. The mother's subtle support enabled the child to be included in a communication exchange. Further examples of support techniques included the mother's re-emphasis of her request as the child began to respond (MI +), or the mother's request to the child to do something he was already doing:

'Look!'
M   (c)

Child already attending

Such communications are not really redundant since they serve as a means of ensurance of the child's response. The mothers were often observed to utilise support techniques after a 'failed' invitation. The mother might repeat the request, or make it simpler in some way or even provide the model answer:

'What is it?'   M   ( )
                        I
                        M   ( )
              'It's a DUCK, isn't it?'

In this example of a modified invitation the mother continues to encourage interaction by not only providing the model answer, but by making a more general response from the child acceptable. The child no longer is requested to give the specific response 'Duck' as in the first invitation which failed, but can now quite 'legitimately' provide a more generalized grunt or look which could be interpreted as an acceptable acknowledgment to the tag question 'isn't it?'. The invitation to the child from the mother has in this way been made 'easier' for the child to respond.

Although there were no obvious differences in the frequency with which the mothers employed the techniques of taking up the child's activity and of providing a ready–made response, the mothers of the Down's children did produce significantly more modified invitations and more opportunities for response that were not fulfilled by the child. Overall, as we can see in Figure 10.2, the proportion of successful interaction sequences that were supported by the mother in one way or another, was significantly greater for the Down's children.

Finally, a further aspect of this dialogue guidance provided by the mother was recorded in the form of those interactions essentially directed by the mother as compared with those interactions dependent on the child–whether intentionally or unintentionally on the part of the child. A similar division in styles of mother–child interaction was noted by Bruner (1975). This division can be described as whether the mother insists on directing the interactive exchanges or whether she tends to support the child's initiative. Our distinction was made between exchanges that the mother invited directly (M ....) and exchanges where she could support the child's initiative by, for example, being directed by the child, commenting on his actions, or taking up and expanding his idea (C...., (c) M). Figure 10.3 presents the results on the frequencies and proportions of mother–directed versus child-dependent interactive exchanges. Generally speaking, there were no proportionally significant differences but there was a tendency for the mothers of the Down's children to be more directive than the mothers of the normal children in that there were quantitatively many more interactive sequences where the Down's children's

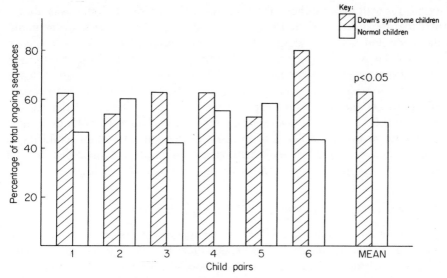

Figure 10.2 Proportion of ongoing sequences which involved support techniques from the mother

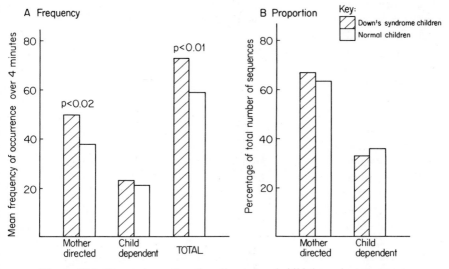

Figure 10.3 Comparison of mother directed and child dependent sequences

mothers directed the activity than those sequences where they followed up their children's initiative.

From these, and related results, we concluded from our investigations that the Down's syndrome children, when matched developmentally with normal children, do not show any significant reduction in the quantity of interactional exchanges with their mothers. However, in *quality* of interaction, it was noticeable that the mothers of the Down's children were working harder to maintain the communication dialogues. It was impossible at this stage to assess whether this was due to some special difficulties on the child's part requiring this extra support, or whether it might have been something to do with the mother's 'awareness' of mental handicap in her child, and her subsequent efforts to got the maximum response from her child. Whatever the reason, these mothers and their Down's syndrome children had apparently developed interactive styles that differed from those of the control mother–child pairs. The result was a more heavily structured communicative environment for the Down's child, with less opportunity to experience control in dialogue.

The communicative quality of the children's vocalizations

In order to examine in particular the quality of communication in the children's vocalizations, every vocalization made by each child within a specified time was recorded in its full context, with special emphasis on its *vocal* context (that is, what the mother may have replied, or not replied, or what the child may have gone on to say). This provided us with a large sample of child vocalizations with full information on the communicative role of each of these vocalizations. The selection of data for this analysis included every vocalization made by the child in the first two minutes of play for each of the four toys in three (every other) video sessions. This provides a total of 1,770 child vocalizations, analysed in their context. These excluded potentially non-verbal sounds such as coughing, fretting, laughing, sneezing etc. The role of these particular sounds in interaction had been taken into consideration in the initial micro analysis, but this specific investigation was restricted to potentially verbal vocalizations and their pre-linguistic role in vocal interaction.

First of all, measures were taken of the frequency, syllable length and syllable variation of each vocalization. Figure 10.4 presents the overall means of these results, but no significant discrepancies were apparent between the developmentally matched pairs of children. Their vocalizations at each developmental level seemed similarly copious and colourful. However there was significant variation in the amount of repetition of any one vocalization within the same play session (see Figure 10.5). The normal children produced a significantly greater proportion of new vocalizations and there was a distinct tendency for the Down's children to use the same vocalization proportionally more often in any one play session. They tended to perseverate on a favourite sound. This was our first indication of contextual differences. Although the Down's children produced sounds in generally similar quantities and variety, they did not vary the pattern of production in the same way as the normal children.

Categorization of the children's vocalizations into classically recognizable developmental stages (babble, jargon, idiosyncratic 'words' and words)

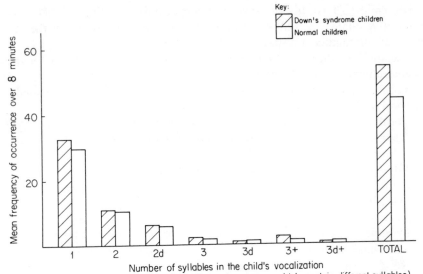

Figure 10.4 Frequency, syllable length and syllable variation of the children's vocalizations

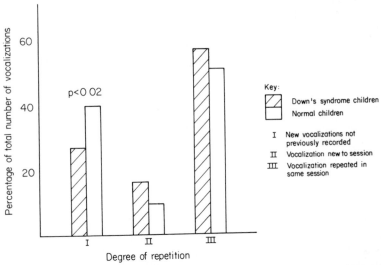

Figure 10.5 Degree of repetition of the vocalizations produced by the children

again did not differentiate between the pairs of children. The developmental matching also appeared to be reflected in their pre-linguistic level of language development. But here again reconsideration of the same vocalizations in their context revealed a very different story.

The children's vocalizations were recategorized according to their communicative quality in context. In order of increasing sophistication the categories of communication were:

1. 'Isolated' vocalizations that are produced by the child apparently for their entertainment value. Context of no vocal response from mother.
2. Vocalizations taken up by mother so that they are in effect enclosed in vocal dialogue ((c͡)M). Dialogue essentially structured by mother.
3. Vocalization that apparently are in response to the mother's vocalization. Their context is such that vocal dialogue is observable, but this time instrumented by the child (M͡ C).
4. Vocalization by the child that seems from its context to be a 'comment' in that it is highly intonated, or it is accompanied by an established gesture (e.g. 'Doo-doo?' or 'Uh' plus point to desired object).
5. Vocalization by the child that is word-like, but is necessarily supported by a clear gesture or environmental context to give it meaning (e.g. 'Ta' with hand held out, or in the case of one child 'ba!' consistently meant 'gone' when something disappeared).
6. A word.

Figure 10.6 presents the proportion of vocalizations falling into these categories. Major differences were recorded in categories 1 and 4 where the Down's children produced proportionally more 'isolated' vocalizations, and fewer 'comment' type vocalizations. Together these results suggest that when vocal context is considered the Down's children were producing relatively fewer vocalizations with communicative potential.

The vocal context in which the children produced their vocalizations was

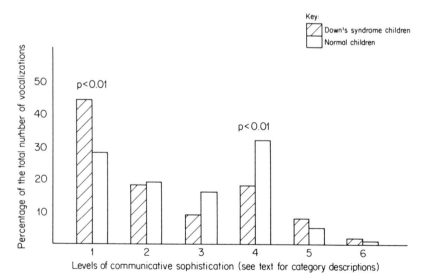

Figure 10.6 Communicative quality of the children's vocalizations

also examined for patterns of 'dialogue'. We discussed earlier how very young infants have been observed to participate in turn-taking activities, including the phasing of their vocalizations in early vocal imitation (Pawlby, 1977b). Observation of such vocal dialogue in our tapes revealed an interesting aspect of this 'turn-taking'. It was noted that although the mothers usually provided 'opportunity spaces' for their children to answer, the children in turn did not always give their mothers a chance to reply to their vocalizations. There was variation in the way the children *phased* their vocalizations. For example, they might sometimes produce vocalizations followed by pauses of one second or more which would be adequate time for the mothers to respond, or they might vocalize at length or in quick succession with no such adequate pauses so that the mother would find it very difficult if not impossible to join in. From our observations, the one-second pause appeared to be a critical period of time for response. Mothers would usually respond within this time and similarly leave approximately one-second pauses for the child to fill. After one second, if there was no response from the child, the mothers would normally continue. Where the invitation and response apparently occurred within the second this gave the impression that the 'response' was probably already forthcoming before the invitation was given, that is, the phasing seemed to be far too short for reception and response. These patterns of dialogue phasing were studied by means of subcategories of the classification outlined above, with this additional time basis. If a vocalization was followed by a subsequent vocalization with at least a one second pause between them, then it was labelled as 'a' type, (e.g. 'Da' . . . 'Da'). If a vocalization by the child was followed by another vocalization *within* one second then it was labelled as 'b' type, (e.g. 'Da', 'Da', 'Da'). This included extended vocalizations (e.g. 'Daaaaaa, aaaaaa') as these would be broken by a breath pause in the same way as the other vocalizations, but still not provide time for the mother to respond. This timing measure was in practice only applied to those vocalizations falling into types 1 to 3 in the classification as these were more appropriate to this particular measure of dialogue phasing. Once the child is producing more sophisticated strings of jargon such 'spacing' becomes more complex to measure.

Figure 10.7 presents the proportions of vocalizations falling into categories 'a' and 'b'. Although most of the children produced both types of vocalization, the large majority of vocalizations were 'a' type. However there was a significant difference across the pairs indicating that the Down's children produced larger proportions of the 'b' type vocalizations. That is, their vocalizations were more frequently closer together than those produced by the normal children.

Schaffer, Collis and Parsons (1977) commented on this dialogue phasing of vocalizations produced by mother and child. They felt that the successful phasing was solely due to the mother's skill at fitting herself in with the child's spontaneously produced sounds. However, the findings in this study show that Down's syndrome children frequently fail to provide these 'natural' pauses.

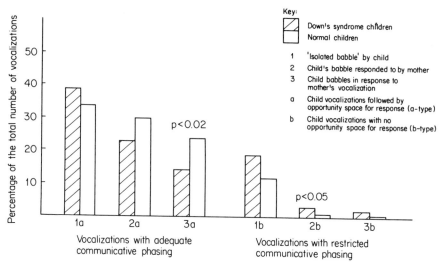

Figure 10.7 Communicative phasing of the children's vocalizations

This suggests that the normal infant is indeed demonstrating a certain level of 'skill', in that he does at least provide plenty of opportunity spaces for his mother. From our results it would seem that the normal children are continuing to demonstrate, for most of the time, this 'consideration' for their mothers' turn, but the Down's children were failing to demonstrate this basic communication skill consistently.

Analysis of the mother's vocal responses to their children's vocalizations indicated that the mothers of the Down's syndrome children responded significantly more often with one word expansions and acknowledgements (e.g. 'Yes', 'mm') rather than expansion to phrase, or comments on the child's activity, which were more frequently produced by the mothers of the normal children. However in the light of the findings on time phasing, this is understandable. The mothers of the Down's children did not often have the time between their children's vocalizations to produce the longer verbal response. Acknowledgements are, after all, more socially acceptable vocalizations if the other fails to stop talking; saying 'mm' whilst someone else is speaking is not seen as being 'rude'. Nevertheless, this pattern of interaction is rather restricted in that for the child's developmental age, it contains less rich, expansive verbal feedback contingent on the child's own vocalization. This is therefore an example of the child effectively limiting the quality of his own verbal context.

Eye to eye contact

Eye contact has a well recognized role in adult non-verbal communication (Argyle and Cook, 1976). Its importance has also been established in infant attachment studies (e.g. Robson, 1967) and it is noted for its absence in autistic children (Hutt and Ounsted, 1966). However, it is not usually associated with language development in Down's children. It was studied in this present research because of the initial impact on the observer of something unusual in the eye contact of the Down's children and their mothers. Its relevance to the development of communication skills in these children was at this stage unknown, but was soon to become a particularly important feature for discussion.

Generally speaking eye contact was relatively infrequent during the sessions of play with toys. All the children tended to concentrate on the toys and eye contact was made on average about once a minute. Eye contact is more frequent in non-toy, face-to-face lap games, but we were interested to see what communicative role eye to eye contact plays in this type of interaction over a 'topic' such as a toy.

To ensure that a reasonably sized sample was selected for analysis, all the tape recordings were examined throughout. All observed eye contacts were recorded and described in their full context. A total of 1,030 eye contacts were identified and analysed from the full 931 minutes of tape recording.

There was a significant difference between the total number of eye contacts made by the Down's and normal children. Eye to eye contacts occurred less frequently between the Down's syndrome children and their mothers. Since the tendency was for the mothers to watch their children continuously during the play session, the onus for making eye contact was on the child for the large majority of the time. This therefore suggests that the Down's syndrome children were less likely than the normal children to initiate eye contact with their mothers. However this finding did not fully explain the unusual quality of eye contact that was observed. In order to examine further the quality of the eye contacts and also their role in communication, eye contact was divided into three categories. These categories were the simplest breakdown that could be made from general observation. They included a 'Personal' category which accounted for eye contacts made in an essentially social context; for example, when the child approaches the mother for a hug, or the couple are just smiling at each other. A second category included eye contacts made during a game in which the eye contact served a specific role in the game such as in 'peek-a-boo'; this eye contact was labelled 'Game' type. The last category of eye contacts included those eye contacts made during interaction when the child appears to be referring to something he is doing. For example the child plays with the toy, then looks up to the mother. Typically the mother would respond to the 'look' and the child would look back to the toy. This type of eye contact was labelled 'Referential' eye contact.

A summary of the mean rates and proportions of these types of eye contact are presented in Figures 10.8 and 10.9. Generally speaking the frequencies of eye contact falling in the categories 'Personal' and 'Game' were not significantly different for the Down's and normal children. However, the normal

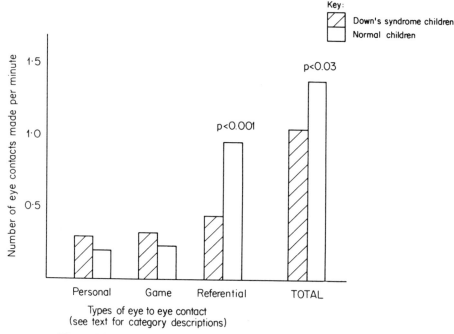

Figure 10.8 Rates of eye-to-eye contact between mothers and children

children did make significantly more 'Referential' eye contacts than the Down's syndrome children. Whereas with the Down's children about a third of their eye contacts fell into each of the three categories, almost three quarters of the eye contacts made by the normal children were of the referential type.

How can we interpret this result? Although they might have done so less frequently, the Down's children were quite able to produce the referential type of eye contact, demonstrating appropriate use of it. This particular difference between the children cannot for this reason easily be explained in terms of developmental delay on the part of the Down's syndrome children; they had apparently reached this 'stage' of development. There was similarly little evidence to suggest that referential eye contact followed any developmental increase over the age range of the children in this study (8 to 22 months). The rate of referential eye contact did not appear to relate to the various developmental ages. We therefore reconsidered the role of referential eye contact in terms of pre-linguistic communication.

Although the definition of referential eye contact given above was essentially operational, it is noteworthy that a key feature of this type of eye contact was the readily recognisable form of 'reference' situation. Examination of the types of response given by the mothers to this particular 'look' from the child revealed that they invariably *answered* the signal. That is, the mothers responded as

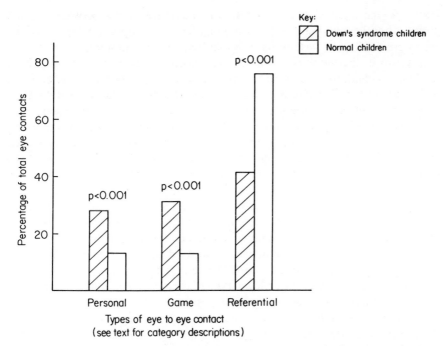

Figure 10.9 Proportion of total number of eye contacts categorized as personal, game, and referential

if the child had asked a question. Adultomorphisms came readily from observers; 'He looked at her as if to say, "Aren't I clever?" or "What happened then?" or "Is that right?" etc'. The mothers seemed drawn to reply; they just *had* to answer this appeal. Given these contextual clues we can see that the eye contact from the child seemed to have the power of an interrogative. At this particular stage of communication development this might be seen to represent a primitive question structure and one of the child's main methods of initiating interaction. In terms of pre-linguistic communication the child would seem to be demonstrating a most powerful form of interactive skill.

In this way the referential eye contact might be associated with early language development. Language itself does after all represent the ultimate form of social reference. The Down's syndrome child's 'reluctance' or limited ability to utilize this powerfully interactive signal appears to be a further example of the child depriving himself of an enormously rich opportunity for verbal feedback contingent on the child's own actions.

CONCLUSIONS AND IMPLICATIONS

It is not possible to generalize about pre-linguistic development in Down's and normal children on the basis of the small numbers of children studied here.

However, the detailed micro-analysis of interactive events between a small group of mothers and children has highlighted some important aspects of the early communication systems used by children and their mothers.

In terms of the quantity of interactive episodes between mother and child, the Down's children were by no means inactive and unresponsive in interaction with their mothers. Despite an enormous range of ability in the Down's children, they were involved in certainly as many and often more interactive sequences with their mothers as the normal children. However, closer examination of the structure of the interactive exchanges between the mothers and children indicated that the Down's children were being considerably 'supported' by their mothers in their communicative role. The Down's children did not take the initiative in interaction as much as the normal children and the mothers of the Down's children tended to be more directive in interactive situations. The reduced use of referential eye contact by the Down's children illustrated one way in which these children failed to use their initiating skills.

Different *patterns* of communication were identified when the interactive context was taken into consideration. The most significant features of this were the differences in the way the children phased their participations in interaction. Although children have normally been seen to demonstrate turn-taking skills within the first six months of life, the Down's syndrome children in this study were repeatedly demonstrating poor timing in their interactions with their mothers, and this created considerable problems for their mothers as partners in the dialogue. We found examples of this in the children's interactive skills, their vocalisations and their use of eye contact. The difficulties the Down's children had with appropriate timing seems to suggest that they were not as skilled as the normal children at turn-taking in communicative dialogue. They seemed to lack sensitivity to the potential for response from their mothers.

Whatever the explanation for this relative difference between the children, the effect was for the Down's children to experience less opportunity for enriched feedback. Through these feedback differences the Down's children seemed to be providing themselves with a less stimulating environment. The mothers of these children appeared to compensate as far as possible but naturally found themselves restricted by the pattern of their children's responses. We observed therefore an interaction pattern between the Down's children and their mothers where the mothers were relatively more likely to be directive and restricted in their approaches to their children.

The Down's syndrome child appears somehow to be failing to recognize the implications of his actions. The relative lack of referential eye contact and inconsistent phasing of vocalizations both seem to indicate lack of expectancy of response. The children did not seem to be fully aware of their mother's role in communicative dialogue.

Newson and Shotter (1974) pointed out that children are provided with plenty of opportunities to develop expectancy and intention. For example the child may at first make some random vocalization or gesture which is interpreted by the mother to have some socially significant meaning. The child comes to recognize its specific effect on the environment from the mother's consistent interpretation of the activity e.g. 'Dada'—mother responds 'Yes, Daddy'; or child reaches out saying 'Da' and mother provides the object. The vocalization may then be produced by the child in order that the usual response should occur. The child now demonstrates intention and expectancy in this action. Shotter (in press) writes: 'And thus the process continues, with the child being "helped" by his mother in this way to retrospectively evaluate his states of feeling and the consequences of his actions. . . . he learns meanings and socially significant uses for a feeling he may have or movement he might make at any time.' Shotter goes on to say: 'In acquiring knowledge of how to order his activities in relation to others the child *himself* learns how to act; he learns, gradually how not to rely upon others to complete and give meaning to his behaviour, but to relate what he does and what he feels to his own know-ledge of his own momentary 'position' in his culture; he relates his own activity to his own self.'

From this particular theoretical viewpoint the process can be described as involving a certain knowledge of 'self'. In terms of our practical findings it could be said that the Down's children, in not demonstrating 'expectancy' to the same extent as the normal children, demonstrate that their understanding of their relationship to others in a social context is less adequate than that observed in normal children at the same stage of development. Recognition of this role in communication situations would seem to be essential to the development of language.

These findings have several implications for clinical practice with respect to types of therapeutic support provided for mothers and children presenting the patterns of difficulty described. We have indicated that the Down's children took relatively little initiative in interaction, which may in turn have influenced the mothers so that they tended to be more directive. However this may well be a 'chicken and egg' situation. Knowing that their children are retarded the mothers may elect to take the initiative. In either case the therapist might be advised to encourage these mothers to reduce the 'pressure' and sit back a little to allow their children to have more opportunity to follow their own play activity. By more support of the children's initiative the mother can encourage the child to practice taking the lead in interaction. In this way the child has more opportunity to learn about the effects of his own behaviour on the environment in which he finds himself. Repeated examples of consistent in-terpretation from an adult within his environment should help the child to come to a better understanding of the meaning of his own actions.

Appropriate phasing of the child's interactive role is a more difficult skill to encourage. However the same principles may be applicable. It is possible that after repeated demonstration of mother responding to child, the child might come to associate 'Mummy's turn' with his turn and begin to demonstrate a degree of expectancy of her response.

Difficulties with 'expectancy' were also evident in the Down's children's lack of use of the referential eye contact. Although these children could, and did, use this type of eye contact, their relative lack of use of it suggested that they did not fully 'appreciate' the powerful role it served in gaining response from the mother. In this instance repeated examples may be helpful if given in an encouraging atmosphere. For example the mother might be able to increase the liklihood of this particular behaviour by placing the child on a chair or settee at home, and then, presenting an open book under her chin, face the child to speak to him. In this *en face* position the child can make eye contact more easily. By using plenty of attractive exaggerated facial gestures (e.g. 'Ooo! Look at the cow!') the mother might well be able to encourage referential eye contact. It could of course be argued that such a method does not involve the child's cognitive intention, and the eye contact is therefore artificial, but even if this is an 'empty' act to begin with, it does at least provide the mother with a stimulus for her response. Without this the children are missing an opportunity for the rich, contingent feedback which we found was associated with this particular pre-linguistic communication gesture. After repeated, exaggerated examples of this type of interaction the child may come to recognize the influence of his referential eye contact and begin to use it more intentionally.

The communication difficulties we have observed with these Down's children might in general terms be interpreted as slow learning of the roles of partners in dialogue. But whatever the reason behind their difficulties it would not be accurate to describe the Down's syndrome children in the study as simply 'delayed' in this development. In comparison with the developmentally matched normal children they were observed to be as active and to produce appropriate types of potentially communicative behaviour. However, in the context of communication with their mothers the patterns of interaction suggested basic difficulties with some of the underlying concepts involved in interpersonal communication. It is noteworthy that these subtle communication difficulties were only brought to light when the mother–child interactive context was taken into consideration. This approach serves to emphasize the need for any communication therapy to be essentially mother–child orientated at this pre-linguistic stage of development. It is only through this sensitivity to the intersubjectivity of communication that we can really begin to understand some of the complexities of what is an essentially socially-based skill.

REFERENCES

Argyle, M. and Cook, M. (1976). *Gaze and mutual gaze*, Camb. Uni. Press, N. Y.
Bruner, J. (1975). 'The ontogenesis of speech acts', *J. Child Lang.*, **2**, 1–19.
Bruner, J. (1977). 'Early social interaction and language acquisition'. in Schaffer, H. R.

(ed.), *Studies in Mother–Infant Interaction*, Academic Press, London, 271–289.

Hutt, C. and Ounsted, C. (1966). 'The biological significance of gaze aversion with particular reference to the syndrome of infantile autism', *Behavioural Science*, **11**, 346–356.

Kaye, K. (1977). 'Toward the origin of dialogue', in Schaffer, H. R. (ed.), *Studies in Mother–Infant Interaction*, Academic Press, London, 89–117.

Jaffe, J., Stern, D. N. and Peery, J. C. (1973). "Conversational" coupling of gaze behaviour in pre-linguistic human development', *J. Psycholinguistic Res.*, **2**, (2), 321–329.

Jones, O. H. M. (1977). 'Mother-child communication with pre-linguistic Down's syndrome and normal infants', in Schaffer, H. R. (ed.), *Studies in Mother–Infant Interaction*, Academic Press, London, 379–401.

Jones, O. H. M. (1978). *Mother–child communication: a comparative study of pre-linguistic Down's syndrome and normal infants*, Ph.D. Thesis, University of Nottingham.

Newson, J. (1974) 'Towards a theory of infant understanding', *Bull. Br. Psychol. Soc.*, **27**, 251–257.

Newson, J. and Shotter, J. (1974). 'How babies communicate', *New Society*, **29**, No. 618, 345–347.

Pawlby, S. J. (1977a) *A study of imitative interaction between mothers and their infants*, Ph.D. Thesis, University of Nottingham.

Pawlby, S. J. (1977b) 'Imitative interaction', in Schaffer, H. R. (ed.), *Studies in Mother–Infant Interaction*, Academic Press, London, 203–224.

Robson, K. S. (1967) 'The role of eye to eye contact in maternal–infant attachment', *J. Ch. Psychology and Psychiatry*, **8**, 13–25.

Ryan, J. (1977). 'Mental subnormality and language development', in Lenneberg, E. (ed.), *Foundations of Language Development*, U.N.E.S.C.O.

Schaffer, H. R., Collis, G. M. and Parsons, G. (1977). 'Vocal interchange and visual regard in verbal and pre-verbal children', in Schaffer, H. R. (ed.), *Studies in Mother–Infant Interaction*, Academic Press, London, 291–324.

Shotter, J. (1975). *Methodological issues in the microanalytic study of mother infant interaction*, Paper Presented to Loch Lomond Symposium, Sept. 1975, University of Strathclyde.

Shotter, J. (in press). 'The cultural context of communication studies: theoretical and methodological issues', in Lock, A. (ed.), *Action, Gesture and Symbol: The Emergence of Language*, Academic Press, London.

Chapter 11

Early Experience and Later Social Behaviour

Barbara Tizard

This chapter describes a study of the effect of an unusual early social environment on children's later development. The children in the study had shared a very similar institutional rearing in their early years. Later, they were moved to families which, although differing in many ways amongst themselves, all provided a marked contrast in social environment to the institution. Because we were able to assess the children at the age of two whilst they were still within the institutions, and at the ages of four and eight after they had left them, we were able to describe both the immediate and the long term effects, if any, of their early experiences.

THE EARLY INSTITUTIONAL EXPERIENCES

At the age of twenty-four months all but two of the children were living in one of twenty-five residential nurseries run by three large British voluntary societies. They had been admitted to the nurseries before the age of four months, and had not been moved since. All but one of the children were illegitimate. About half of the mothers had asked for adoption, but the children had not yet been placed, usually because of their colour, or because of a family history, e.g. of epilepsy, which was at that time considered a bar to adoption in infancy. The rest of the mothers hoped to reclaim their children at some later date. All the children had been healthy full-term babies, and were not considered by their physicians to be suffering from any mental or physical handicap.

The twenty-five residential nurseries were remarkably similar, and were in many respects as good as any in the world. The great majority cared for between fifteen and twenty-five children, in spacious houses set in beautiful grounds, in the country or by the sea. Until the babies were about twelve months old they were looked after in a special unit within the nursery. Considerable efforts were made to stimulate them; they were always fed on the nurse's lap, and the nurses were encouraged to talk and play with them after feeds. Cots and prams were supplied with toys, and from about the age of four months most of the time that they were awake the babies were put in playpens or on the floor with toys. Nevertheless, their handling tended to be impersonal; they were fed, got up and put to bed according to a strict timetable, and the care they received, although kindly, was brisk, and certainly not intimate or personalized. The reasons for this are described in the next section. Once the babies were weaned to a cup, and could partly feed themselves, they were moved from the baby unit. The transition was always a gradual one, the baby paying longer and longer visits to his new 'family group' of about six children, with a mixed age range extending to the upper age limit of the nursery, which in most cases was four and a half years. Each 'family group' had its own suite of bedroom, living-room and bathroom: the living room was furnished in a home-like style, with carpets, sofas and rugs, and with easy access to the garden, and the children played outdoors for part of each day. The gardens always contained a further range of play equipment—swings, climbing frames, tricycles, and so on.

All the nurseries had a nursery school or playgroup for children over two or three years of age. The children were read to every day, and often taken for walks outside the grounds, or on expeditions to shops and parks. In some nurseries the staff were encouraged to take one of the children out with them on their free day, and occasionally when they went home for weekends and holidays.

STAFFING

The staffing, too, was generous. Two or three staff, more in the baby unit, were on duty with each group of six children. The staff had few housekeeping duties and could devote themselves to child care. This generous staffing was made possible by the fact that each nursery was a training centre for nursery nurses.

At the age of seventeen, girls entered the nursery and undertook to remain for three years. For two years they worked part of their time in the nursery, the rest of the time attending college. In the third year they became staff nurses. Each group of children was thus in the care of a 'qualified' nurse, usually aged 19 or 20, assisted by two to four younger students, and sometimes a nursery assistant as well. The nurse in charge of the baby unit was usually the oldest and most experienced of the staff.

Unquestionably, the children in the nurseries appeared to be very well looked after. The physical environment and the play equipment was of a style and lavishness far exceeding anything that their mothers could offer them, and the children appeared to be receiving excellent attention in small groups from professionally qualified staff. What could not be seen by the casual visitor were two characteristics of the nurseries which distinguished them from almost any private family—the large numbers of adults who looked after each child, and the absence of close relationships between adults and children. Both these characteristics were closely tied up with the dual functions of the nurseries as institution and training-school.

This system of staffing, although it ensured a generous supply of staff at low cost (since students and assistants were paid very little), also resulted in very poor continuity of care. This was because the nurse in charge of each family group was only appointed after qualifying, and usually only remained in the nursery for one year thereafter, hence her tenure as 'group mother' tended to be brief. Even during that period, for two days a week and three or four weeks a year she was on leave, and in most of the nurseries for one week in every four to six weeks she was on night duty.

When the 'group mother' was off duty, she was usually replaced by a 'floating nurse', or more typically by the senior student working with the group. Since the students worked only three days a week, a different student was on duty each day.

Stability was further reduced by the practice of moving students from group to group every two, three or four months, to widen their experience. Thus a a student during her two years' training would expect to spend some time in the baby unit, the feed preparation room, the playgroup or nursery school, and in each of several 'family' groups. Usually she would spend about one week in seven on night duty. The lowest echelon in the nursery, the nursery assistants, were typically sent each day to help where they were most needed. In any one week five or six different girls, therefore, worked in each group. We discovered from an analysis of the staff books that by the age of twenty-four months the average child had been looked after for at least a week by twenty-four different people; by the age of four and a half years an average of fifty different nurses had looked after him for a week or more.

Further, no attempt was made in any of the nurseries we visited to reduce the number of adults handling each child by assigning the care of particular children to particular members of staff. Thus a child might be dressed by a different nurse each day, and if four nurses worked on one group during the day a child might be dressed by one, toiletted by a second, taken for a walk by a third and put to bed by a fourth. It was not uncommon, indeed, for tasks to be allocated by seniority—e.g. the most junior nurse on duty would be assigned the task of dressing any child who had wet his bed, or changing children who were subsequently wet or soiled.

Partly in response to this situation, in all the nurseries close personal relationships were discouraged. As one matron put it, 'It isn't fair to them, it isn't fair to us, to get too fond of the children.' It was argued that if a child became closely attached to a nurse he would suffer when she was off duty or left the nursery, and he would find it difficult to relate to his mother or foster mother when his time to leave the nursery came. From the point of view of the staff, close attachment to one nurse made it difficult for other nurses to handle a child, and led to intense rivalry problems with the other children. Treating all the children in a detached way was seen as the best guard against favouritism. Close attachments might also lead to a matron or nurse becoming reluctant to part with a child, and deter them from trying to foster him or return him home.

The emotional climate of the nurseries was in consequence cool. A child who tried to get affection or special attention from a nurse would generally be distracted, and junior staff who joined the nursery would quickly learn that they were expected to tidy up or get on with the nursery routine, and not spend time with an individual child. In practice, of course, the system did not always work, and close attachments between staff and children sometimes developed — two children in our series were adopted by a nurse after she married. Generally, however, as an observer one could confidentally predict that if a child and an adult were paying close and prolonged attention to each other, then either the child or the adult or both were not part of the nursery establishment.

Finally, not only did the nursery child's experiences with adults differ markedly from that of any child in a private family, but their experiences with their peers were also unusual. Few private families contain six babies, or six children between the ages of one and four, and in none does the child population keep changing. Our study children had stayed a longer-than-average time in the nurseries: not only had they to contend with many staff changes, but also with many peer-group changes.

THE CHILDREN AT TWO

At twenty-four months, the children's intellectual development was slightly retarded—their average 'mental age' was only twenty-two months (Tizard and Tizard, 1971). Most of this retardation was in language; some children knew only a handful of single words. Most, but not all, of the children were also rather silent, compared to children living at home.

Confronted with a stranger, the nursery children tended to be shy and cling to their nurse. We tried to make an unbiased assessment of this behaviour by noting their response to a series of standardized 'overtures'. For the first five minutes of the interview the child sat on his favourite nurse's lap, in his own nursery, and the psychologist paid no attention to him, but chatted to the nurse. Then she turned to the child, smiled and said, 'Hullo.' Next she opened a picture book and said, 'Would you like to come here and look at this book?' Finally, she smiled and said, 'Would you like to come over here and sit on my lap and see the book?' At each of these stages she rated the child's response to her overture on a seven-point scale, ranging from 1 (cries or runs away) to 7 (smiles and approaches). A few minutes later she asked the nurse to leave the room briefly, with the door ajar. Again, the child's response was noted on a scale ranging from 1 (child leaves room, looking unhappy) to 4 (child stays in room and shows no distress) (Tizard and Joseph, 1970).

Compared with a contrast group of children living in working-class London families, the nursery children were much less willing to approach the psychologist, and more of them ran away or showed distress when left alone with her. The nurses' account, also, suggested that the nursery children were much more clinging than the home-reared children: many of them cried when the nurses left the room and ran to be picked up when they entered the room, behaviour which most of the home-reared children had long ago outgrown. More unusual was the fact that the nursery children seemed to be attached to a large number of adults. Although most of them had a favourite nurse, they would run to be picked up when almost any one of the staff entered the room, and cry and try to follow her when she left. By contrast, the two-year-old home-reared children would usually only 'go to' their parents and grandparents.

In most other respects, however, the behaviour of the nursery children differed little from that of the home-reared children. None of them appeared to be very unhappy or disturbed, and 'institutional' behaviour, such as head-banging and rocking, was rare. However, despite strenuous and systematic attempts fewer of the institutional children than home-reared children were toilet trained. The majority of the institutional children sucked their thumbs (whereas many home-reared children had 'dummies'), and they tended to cry and whine rather frequently over minor mishaps. They were also described as being less willing to share than home-reared children, and more aggressive.

But tantrums and feeding problems were no more frequent than among home-reared children of the same age. In some ways, indeed, the institutional children were easier to handle than home-reared children—fewer of them woke at night, and more of then had learnt to amuse themselves, and not to expect to be occupied by an adult.

SOCIAL DEVELOPMENT AT THE AGE OF FOUR

By the time the children were four-and-a-half, fifteen had been restored to their natural families, twenty-four had been adopted, and 26 remained in institutions. The adopted children included some whose mothers had originally hoped to reclaim them, whilst the restored children included some whose mothers had wanted them adopted, but for whom an adoptive home had not been found. All the children had left the institution at least six months before the visit, the adopted children at an average age of 3.1 years, the restored children at an average age of 3.5 years.

The adoptive parents differed from the natural parents in a number of respects. On the average they were ten years older, and the majority of fathers had professional or managerial positions. Half were childless, whilst the other half had older children of their own, and were motivated in part by a wish to offer a home to an institutional child. More than half of the natural parents were single parents, some with other children; others were living with a man who was not the child's father, and four children were restored to families where they found a younger child of the union already ensconced. Two children were restored to professional households, but the majority returned to impoverished and hard-pressed families. The restored and institutional groups now had average I.Q.s, whilst the adopted children tended to score well above average (Tizard and Rees, 1974).

The technique of rating the child's response on meeting a strange psychologist, which was used at two was used again at the second assessment (Tizard and Rees, 1975). The shyness and fear of strangers which was noticeable in the institutional children at twenty-four months had by now disappeared, and both the adopted and restored children tended to be unusually friendly for their age. Half of both groups smiled and answered when greeted and two-thirds of them approached, talking, to look at the toys. (In a comparable study with London working-class children we found that only a quarter of the children responded in this way.) Only one adopted and two restored children seemed definitely shy or solemn. During the second half of the session, two-thirds of both these groups of children made spontaneous, friendly conversation. Nearly half of the restored children, but only three adopted children, were not only friendly but excessively attention-seeking. They climbed on the interviewer's lap and demanded attention from her to the extent that the interview was impeded.

This unusual degree of friendliness was also noted during psychological testing, when both adopted and restored children were much more talkative than the London family-reared children. In other ways the behaviour of the adopted and restored children differed during the test. The adopted children were an unduly cooperative group of four-year-olds—half of them seemed definitely to enjoy the test situation, and two-thirds of them concentrated well. Only four of the twenty-four children had to be checked from wandering round the room. Their behaviour compared very favourably with that of the London working-class four-year-olds.

The restored children were much more difficult to test than the adopted children. Two-thirds of them refused to attempt some of the test items, and eleven of the fifteen children had very poor concentration. They seemed not to listen to the psychologist, and they had to be checked from playing with the test materials; some of these children were very silent and reluctant to speak, others talked so much, usually on irrelevent topics, that it was hard to get through the test. Three-quarters of both the adoptive and the natural mothers described the children as attention-seeking, and a third of both groups of mothers described the children as overfriendly to strangers. Overall, however, the children did not present more problems than the London family-reared children, and, the adopted children presented fewer problems. The restored children did, however, more often show certain signs of anxiety than other groups; e.g. a third of them twitched or picked their faces, and three-quarters of them tended to follow their mother about the house.

At two, most of the institutional children, no doubt because of the large numbers of staff who had handled them, had not developed close attachments to one or two adults. Instead they tended to respond affectionately and, indeed, to cling to any adult who took a friendly interest in them. At our second assessment, both groups of parents described the ex-institutional children as exceptionally affectionate. Most of the children responded affectionately not only to their parents, but to anyone they knew well, or in some cases to any friendly stranger. Nevertheless all but four of the twenty-four adoptive mothers thought the child had a particular, deeper, attachment to his new parents. The relationship between the natural parent and her child, on the other hand, was sometimes clouded by guilt, anxiety and resentment. Nine of the fifteen natural mothers thought that the period in the nursery had damaged their relationship with the child. Four mothers expressed an open dislike of the child, and others felt that they did not love the child as they should.

THE EIGHT-YEAR-OLD ASSESSMENT

When the children were eight, we decided to visit them again. Because marked changes had already occurred in their development at four, it seemed reasonable to expect that the 'normalization' process would continue. Further, by the age of eight we would be able to avail ourselves of evidence from their teachers, and discover how the children coped with their peers, other adults, and with the learning demand of the school.

Unfortunately, not all the children could be visited. Of the twenty-four adoptive families, one had left the country, and three refused permission. Of the fifteen natural parents, two had emigrated, two refused permission, one had returned her child to care, and another had sent her child to live abroad with grandparents.

It is impossible to know how these losses biased the results, but the evidence suggested that the effect was to increase the incidence of problem behaviour in the adopted group, and decrease it in the restored group. This was because three of the four 'lost' adopted children had had lower than average behaviour problem scores at 4 years, whilst two of the restored children were 'lost' to us because their mothers would not look after them, and the mothers of three 'lost' restored children had expressed a definite dislike for them at the age of four.

An additional group was, however, available for study: five adopted and four restored children who had been assessed in the institutions at the ages of four, and had left the institutions between the ages of four-and-a-half and seven-and-a-half. The adoptive couples who took these children were comfortably off, and middle-aged, either childless or with grown-up children. The restored children, on the other hand, returned to manual working-class homes; their natural parents had all remarried and had had further children, so that the restored child entered his family as both the oldest child and a step child. These two groups will be referred to as the 'later adopted' and 'later restored' children.

Because 17 of the 25 adoptive families whom we could interview were non-manual workers, we added an additional 'contrast' group of middle-class mothers.

OBSERVED BEHAVIOUR AT EIGHT

By eight it seemed no longer appropriate to assess the children's social behaviour by noting their response to a stranger; eight year olds are not likely to show fear in this situation. Our rating of the children's observed behaviour was therefore confined to their behaviour during testing (Tizard and Hodges, in press). As at four years, the restored children were unusually friendly and attention-seeking during testing, but this was no longer true of the adopted children. At the same time a larger proportion of the restored children than of any other group were anxious during testing, and needed a great deal of encouragement to persevere. However, the poor concentration and uncooperativeness which was a notable feature of the restored children at four, had by eight disappeared.

EVIDENCE OF THE PARENTS

The parents of the restored children more often reported 'nervous' stomach aches, and 'nervous' habits, e.g. picking, scratching, and stammering, and very poor peer relationships, than any other group. Sixty-two per cent of the restored children, but only 12% of the adopted children, had been referred to a doctor because of behaviour problems. As at four years both the restored and the adopted children were more often than other children described as attention-seeking and 'overfriendly', and this was the only 'problem' mentioned by the parents which significantly differentiated the adopted children from the control groups.

At four, both groups of ex-institutional children had been described as unusually affectionate, and at eight the adoptive parents still described their children in this way. The restored children, on the other hand, were now less often described as affectionate than both the adopted and the control groups, a change which may reflect the continued unsatisfactory relationships within many of the natural families. Whilst twenty of the twenty-five adoptive mothers were confident that a deep attachment had developed between themselves and their child, this was true in the case of only half of the natural mothers. If we had been able to interview all the natural mothers the proportion might well have been lower, since two had meanwhile relinquished the care of their child, and we were unable to visit three who had expressed a definite dislike of the child to us earlier. Further, less than half of the restored children who had acquired a step-parent were said to be on good terms with him.

There was no evidence that the attachment of the adoptive child to his parents was 'insecure'–very few children followed their parents around, protested if they went out at night, or were described as clinging. Although a number of the ex-institutional children were considered overfriendly by their parents, very few were indiscriminately affectionate by eight; however, they remained more likely than the control children to allow a stranger to put them to bed.

CHANGES IN AFFECTIONAL RELATIONSHIPS OF CHILDREN WHO LEFT THE INSTITUTION AFTER THE AGE OF $4\frac{1}{2}$

Marked changes had occurred in the affectional behaviour of the children who has left the institution since our last visit. Of the nine children adopted or restored to their natural parents after the age of $4\frac{1}{2}$, three had been described as very affectionate and closely attached to their nurse when they were four-and-a-half. None of these three children were thought by their parents at eight to be either affectionate or attached to them. But of the six children whom the nurses had not considered closely attached to anyone, five were said to be closely attached to their mothers at eight. Two children who had not been considered at all affectionate when in the nursery were now considered to be so: the other children were considered affectionate on both occasions (Tizard, 1977).

EVIDENCE FROM THE TEACHERS

The teachers assessed the children with the Rutter 'B' scale, together with some supplementary questions. The ex-institutional children were compared not only with the London control group, but with a classmate of the same sex and nearest in age to them. The results for these two control groups were very similar. Both the restored and the adopted children had significantly higher scores than the control children on both the Total Problem Score, and and the Antisocial scale. The items which differentiated them from the other children fell into three groups—restless behaviour, poor peer relationships and disciplinary problems. On eight out of twelve items a greater proportion of restored than adopted children received an adverse rating. In addition, many more ex-institutional children than controls were described as attention-seeking. The most common attention-seeking behaviour was not 'naughtiness' but what the teachers saw as an excessive number of social approaches, e.g. 'he tells you unnecessary things just to get attention', 'he tries to help when not asked.'

AGE AT LEAVING THE INSTITUTION IN RELATION TO BEHAVIOUR PROBLEMS AT 8

The adopted childrens' problems at eight did not seem to bear any relation to the age at which they had left the institutions; this was true of the number of problems reported by the teacher, the number of problems reported by the parent, whether or not the child was considered by the adoptive mother to be attached to her, or the mother to the child, or whether or not the child was considered 'overfriendly'. Some of the most difficult adopted children had been placed between the ages of two and three, whilst the oldest child to be placed was the most problem-free. This was less true of the restored children, when there was a marked tendency for the later restored children to be less often attached to their parents than the earlier restored children.

PROBLEMS AT EIGHT IN RELATION TO EARLIER INSTITUTIONAL REPORTS

The children's case notes in the institution contained 6 monthly reports on on their progress. Whilst these were usually couched in neutral or positive terms–e.g. 'A normal healthy child developing satisfactorily'—they sometimes included remarks which suggested that the child was a management problem— e.g. 'very strong-willed, constantly looks for attention'. The eight adopted children whose last report before leaving the nursery included such a comment had a significantly higher mean Teacher Problem Score at age 8 than the other adopted children. They also had a significantly higher parent problem score at 8 than the other adopted children.

After placement in their new homes, the families had been visited by social workers. In nine cases, the social workers reported that the child was a management problem at that time, usually because of frequency tantrums. Seven of these children also had unfavourable nursery reports'. The mean Teacher Problem Score at 8 of these 9 children was significantly higher than that of the other adopted children. The mean Parent Problem Score of the children was also significantly higher.

DISCUSSION

The first conclusion which it seems reasonable to draw is that the later effects of early institutional rearing are greatly modified by the environment in which the child is subsequently reared. The only difference between the kinds of problems reported by the adoptive mothers and their middle-class controls was the greater frequency of attention-seeking and 'overfriendly' behaviour in the adopted children: but the restored children were said by their mothers not only to be attention-seeking and 'overfriendly', but also to have nervous tics and a variety of nervous habits, e.g. nervous stomach aches and stammers.

Moreover, whilst both groups of ex-institutional children were reported to present many more problems at school than the control children, the problems were more severe and more widespread in the restored children.

Whether or not a close attachment developed between the child and his parents was also dependent on the characteristics of the family in which he was placed. Whilst twenty of the twenty-five adoptive parents believed that they had developed a deep mutual attachment with their child, this was true of only half the natural mothers, and few of the rest displayed the unusual warmth and supportiveness towards the child which was common amongst the adoptive families. Contrary to our expectation, the development of attachment seemed to depend on the efforts which the parents put into courting the child and not on his presenting characteristics. For example, one child who had been disliked by the nurses, and had seemed uninterested in them at 2 and $4\frac{1}{2}$ years, was adopted at 7, and at $8\frac{1}{2}$ seemed to have developed a close affectionate relationship with both parents, though holding aloof from other adults and from children. Another child, who had had a close affectionate relationship with the matron of a small home was restored at 5 to a natural parent, step parent and younger step brothers, all of whom were strangers. At eight, she and her parents seemed indifferent or hostile to each other.

Why had the adopted and restored children fared so differently? The adoptive and natural parents differed in a number of respects, quite apart from social class. The adoptive parents, having very much wanted a child, were willing and happy to devote a great deal of time to him. The mothers of the restored children, who had left their child in care for several years, had been ambivalent or definitely reluctant to take him back. Moreover, the restored children tended to have more siblings, especially younger siblings, who occupied the mother's time and for whom she often openly expressed a preference. Further, whilst both adoptive parents were unusually affectionate and welcoming, many restored children returned to a step-father who was indifferent or even hostile to them, or showed an open preference for his own children.

The later the child was restored, the less likely was it that a mutual attachment had developed. This was not true of the adopted children, and it appears to reflect the fact that the longer the mother left the child in care, the less room she had for him in her life. Few natural mothers played with their children, and they expected the child to be very independent, e.g. most of the restored children but only one adopted child regularly put themselves to bed. The adoptive mothers on the other hand spent a great deal of time playing with the children, and seemed ready to accept and even enjoy dependent behaviour patterns more appropriate in younger children. This was probably not only because they had very much wanted a child, but because most had asked for a child younger than the one placed with them.

Nevertheless, both ex-institutional groups did share certain characteristics, notably a tendency to be more attention-seeking than other children and to have greater difficulty with their peers. The major complaints of the teachers were with respect not only to attention-seeking behaviour, but also restlessness, disobedience, and poor peer relations. However, it seemed possible that all the children's problems at school stemmed not from a conduct disorder of the usual kind, but from two basic characteristics, both concerned with their social behaviour—an almost insatiable desire for adult attention, and a difficulty in forming good relationships with their peer group, although often they got on much better with younger and older children. Indeed several of the parents suggested to us that the children's restlessness and disobedience at school, which was very much more marked than at home, were secondary to attention-seeking. As one mother put it, 'I think her teacher doesn't praise her enough—praise is what she's seeking all the time. I know they can't always single her out for attention, but the time when she was in least trouble at school was when she was in a small class'.

It is at first sight surprising that despite their early group rearing the ex-institutional children were more often quarrelsome, unpopular and solitary than family-reared children. This finding appears to conflict, with the evidence of strong peer-group solidarity found in children reared in a kibbutz. There are, however, important differences between a kibbutz and a residential nursery, notably the stability of the child and adult population in the kibbutz, and the presence of the parents, who lavish attention on their children for several hours a day. Both at two and at four years the institutional children were described as aggressive and competitive; many of the adoptive parents noted that far from missing the company of their peers after adoption the children preferred to be with their parents, or with much older or younger children. (A much fuller account of the children and their families is published in Tizard, 1977.)

Up to this point it has been assumed that the unusual characteristics of the children were the product of early institutional rearing. Other explanations of the findings are of course possible. Firstly, there is the possibility that these children were genetically predisposed to emotional instability. In support of this, one could point to the fact that many had been left for at least two years in the institution either because their family psychiatric history was considered suspect (in fact, none had a history of schizophrenia) or because their mothers could not decide either to reclaim them or to offer them for adoption. A genetic hypothesis is very difficult to test in any direct way. The best evidence might come from a comparison with children born to the same parents but reared at home. A finding that such children had a much lower rate of behavioural difficulties would be strong evidence against the genetic hypothesis. However, only two of the children had such a sibling.

Secondly, one could argue that the mothers of all these children must have been under considerable stress during pregnancy, and during and after child-birth, and that this stress in some way led to the children's subsequent difficulties. If it were this factor, rather than early institutional rearing or a particularly unstable genetic inheritance which was responsible for our children's problems, then one could expect to find similar disturbance in other adopted children, who had not been reared in institutions. The most comprehensive study of adopted children in Britain is that of the National Child Development Study, on the children in the 1958 birth cohort who had been adopted (Seglow and coworkers, 1972). Most of these children were placed in the first six months of life, and only 3% after the age of two. Twenty-five per cent of the adopted seven-year-old boys were considered maladjusted by their teachers, using the Bristol Social Adjustment Guide, compared to 17% of boys in the whole birth cohort. However, the difficulties were largely in the sphere of peer rela-tions; attention-seeking behaviour, and restlessness were not significantly greater in the adopted group. A Swedish survey of adopted children, who again were almost all adopted in the first few months of life found that at age eleven 20% of the adopted boys, compared with 10% of their classmates, were considered to have behaviour problems at school. (Bohman, 1971).

It seems likely that the ex-institutional children in our study more often had problems at school, and of a particular kind, than children adopted in infancy, and that an explanation simply in terms of the effects of maternal stress before and after the child's birth is not adequate. Another possible explanation is that some aspect of their present situation could account for their behaviour. The environment of the adopted and restored children was so different, however, that it is difficult to see a common element which could be responsible. A third of the children were black or of mixed race, and it could be argued that this fact may have led to problems at school, but in fact these children had no more nor less problems than the white children. It could be argued that the frequency of attention-seeking behaviour might be related to the children's position as the only or youngest child of middle-aged indulgent parents. However, this behaviour was shown just as frequently by children adopted by younger couples, and similar and even more pronounced behaviour was found in children restored to large and impoverished families where the child was more often neglected than indulged. Finally, the evidence of the children's case notes showed that the most difficult children had generally already been identified as such in the nursery.

Whilst, therefore an explanation for the children's behaviour in terms of their current environment cannot be ruled out, it is difficult to think of one which could account for the data. It seems more likely that the common difficulties of many of the restored and adopted children were due to their early institutional experiences, perhaps in interaction with genetic or biological factors. The multiple and everchanging caretaking which these children had experienced—on an average 50 different caretakers by the age of $4\frac{1}{2}$— must be unique in the history of child-rearing, and it would be surprising if it had not at the time affected the children's social development. It also seems likely that attention-seeking, poor peer relationships, and 'overfriendliness', once established, are difficult behaviours to modify. An 'overfriendly' child tends to produce a friendly response from strangers, and it is virtually impossible for parents to anticipate or prevent all these encounters; attention-seeking is reinforced by both positive and negative responses from adults, and poor peer relationships can only be modified by skilled adult guidance. For the most part the parents were concentrating on developing their own relationships with the child, and helping him to live in a family, and none of them had received expert advice on the child's general behaviour.

It is important to note that only perhaps a half of the adopted children and three-quarters of the restored children had particular problems. Nothing in our data, for example with respect to the number of institutional caretakers or the characteristics of the families the children entered, explains why this should be so, but our measures of the two environments were certainly crude.

These findings do suggest that the nature of the child's early dependency relationships may have an important effect on his later social development. These effects were not those described by Bowlby in his earlier writings—there was little to suggest that the children were likely to become 'affectionless psychopaths', capable at the best of only indiscriminate affectionate relationships. Twenty out of the twenty-five adopted children seemed within six months or a year of leaving the institution to have formed a close mutually affectionate relationship with their new parents. It was rather with other adults who were not their parents, and with other children, that about a half of these children had problems. Whether or not the child became attached to his new parents seemed to depend *not* on his relationship with the nurses in the institution but largely on the willingness of the new parents to accept a dependent relationship and to put a lot of time and effort into developing it.

It does not, of course, follow from our data that the first two years are critical for social development—we did not study children who had entered the institutions at two or three. It is therefore possible that similar experiences for any part of the early period of dependency would have had similar effects on the children. Nor does it follow that these effects were inevitable, and could not have been avoided by skilled preventative treatment.

As to whether the difficulties of the children will be permanent or irreversible, and if so, which aspects of his adult behaviour will be affected, it is much too early to say. Eight years old is still very young, and it is encouraging to note that in Bohman's Swedish study of adopted children *fewer* problems were found at the age of fifteen than at the age of eleven (Bohman, 1971).

Nor is it possible from this study to make inferences about the effect of early institutional care in general. It seems very likely that a different kind of institution—e.g. one where the amount of interaction with the children was much less, but where the children were looked after by fewer adults—would have quite different effects. This pattern was, of course, characteristic of some pre-World War Two institutions, where toys and books were in short supply but staffing was stable. The outlook of the staff was often narrow, their discipline severe, and not all of them were kindly, but they did tend to remain in their posts until marriage or more usually retirement.

The problem in the advanced Western societies today is that while it is relatively easy to provide a child with a rich and stimulating perceptual and verbal environment, it seems impossible to provide continuity of care once a child had left his own parents. With the increasing trend to professionalize residential child care, the staff turnover in institutions continues to increase, rather than decrease. This is not only because staff go off for training, but because in order to advance their career they need to move through successive posts of increasing status and salary. To this is added an increasing and well-meant tendency for young people to work in children's homes for six months or a year, with the aim of widening their experience and giving service to the community. There is no easy solution to the problem of providing continuity of care; this is one of the principle reasons for attempting to contain a child within his own family, or if that is neither possible nor desirable, of placing him in a adoptive home.

REFERENCES

Bohman, M. (1971). *Adopted Children and their Families. A Follow-up Study of Adopted Children. Their Background, Environment and Adjustment*, Stockholm, Proprium, 118.

Seglow, J., Kellmer Pringle, M., and Wedge, P. (1972). *Growing up Adopted*, National Foundation of Educational Research in England and Wales, 16.

Tizard, Barbara (1977). *Adoption: A Second Chance*, Open Books, London.

Tizard, Barbara and Hodges, Jill (in press). 'The Effect of Early Institutional Rearing on the Development of Eight-year-old Children', *Journal of Child Psychology and Psychiatry*.

Tizard, Barbara and Joseph, Ann (1970). 'The Cognitive Development of Young Children in Residential Care', *Journal of Child Psychology and Psychiatry*, **11**, 177–186.

Tizard, Barbara and Rees, Judith (1974). 'A Comparison of the Effects of Adoption, Restoration to the Natural Mother, and Continued Institutionalization on the Cognitive Development of Four-year-old Children', *Child Development*, **45**, 92–99.

Tizard, Barbara and Rees, Judith (1975). 'The Effect of Early Institutional Rearing on the Behaviour Problems and Affectional Relationships of Four-year-old Children', *Journal of Child Psychology and Psychiatry*, **16**, 61–73.

Tizard, Jack and Tizard, Barbara (1971). 'Social Development of Two-year-old Children in Residential Nurseries', in Schaffer, H. R. (ed.). *The Origins of Human Social Relations*, London, Academic Press.

Index

Note Numbers in *italics* refer to figures or tables on those pages.

Psychoanalytic theories (*cont.*)
  integration with child development research, 97–111
    cognition and perception, 102–6
    mother–infant interaction, 99–102
    object permanence, 103–4
    object relations theory, 99–102, 108–9
    post-dictive theories, 101
Psychodynamic theory, 3

Recovery from early adversity, 1–2, 3, 135–51
  after environmental change, 138–42
    adoption, 140–41, 145–7, 201–11 *passim*
    head start programmes, 144–5
    importance of long-term changes, 141, 147
Refugees, 139
Reproductive cycle, continuity of phases of, 46
Rutter Teachers Scale, 205

'Scaffolding' behaviour, 94–5
School performance, 58, 83–4
  relation to pre-school neurology and behaviour, 61–2
Separation from parents
  care away from home, 160, 161–2, 166–7
  and subsequent mothering behaviour, 157, 167–8, 170
  hospital admissions, 42–3, 139, 143, 155, 170
  internalized image during, 102, 103, 104
  neonatal period, 22–3, 37–54, 108
    after 'abnormal' birth, 46–9
    discharge without infant, 47
    effect on parents, 44–9
    effects on social interaction, 42–4
    importance of fathers, 47–8
    in special care baby units, 38–9, 43–4, 46–8, 49, 51
    long-term effects, 42–3, 44
    minimization of, 49–52
    mothers' lack of confidence, 47
    variability of effects, 49
  Nigeria, 126
  relation to later behavioural and emotional disorders, 155–6
Sleep problems, 17–18, 85–6
Smiling, 94, 108

Social behaviour
  continuities in interaction, 79–82
  cross-cultural research, 117–31
    and transactional theories of development, 126–8
    comparable behaviour sequences, 119–20
    environmental factors, 120–23, 124
    measurement, 118–20
    problem of genetic differences, 123–4
    research design problems, 124–5
    selection of observational units, 119
  development of, 99–102
  effect of early institutional care, 197–211
    attachments, 201, 203, 204–5, 207, 210
    attention seeking, 202, 204, 205–6, 207, 208, 210
    clinging, 200–201
    over-friendliness, 202, 204, 207, 210
    peer relations, 208, 210
    response to strangers, 200–201, 202
  imitation, 105
  newborn, 7–8, 99–100
    experimental studies, 15–17
    indirect assessment of, 17–18
    neurobehavioural tests, 14–15
  see also Communication, pre-verbal; mother–infant interaction
Social class
  influence on behaviour, 83–4
Social isolation
  recovery from, 137–8
Special care baby units, 38–9, 46–8, 49
  admission policies, 51
  extra stimulation in, 43–4
State, *see* Behavioural state
Strangers
  response to, 200–201, 202
Subjectivity, 97–8
Subnormality
  continuity in, 136
  recovery from, 138, 141
Sucking, *see* Feeding

Talking
  discontinuities in mothers' response to, 81–2
  see also Language acquisition; Language development
Task orientation, 58
  relation to neonatal neurology, 60, 64